THE NEVADA ADVENTURE

★ ★ ★ ★ ★ A HISTORY

Sixth Edition

Nevada landscape

THE NEVADA ADVENTURE

A HISTORY

★ ★ ★ ★ ★ ★ ★ ★ ★ ★ ★ ★ ★ ★

Sixth Edition

BY JAMES W. HULSE

Illustrations by Don Kerr

UNIVERSITY OF NEVADA PRESS
RENO AND LAS VEGAS

ILLUSTRATION CREDITS (top, *t*; middle, *m*; bottom, *b*; right, *r*; left, *l*)

Nevada Department of Transportation: ii, 3, 11, 51*b*, 143, 195, 213, 217*b*, 233, 259, 287*t*. University of Nevada Press: 18*t*, 51*t*. Nevada State Museum: 18*b*, 26. Nevada Historical Society: 41*t*, 70, 81 (from Dan De Quille's *The Big Bonanza*), 87 (from J. Ross Browne's *A Peep at Washoe*), 97*t*, 100*t*, 100*b*, 111*t*, 111*b*, 113*t*, 119*tl*, 119*tr*, 119*b*, 121*t*, 121*m*, 121*b*, 127, 147, 159*t*, 159*b*, 167*t*, 175*t*, 175*b*, 181*t*, 181*b*, 183*t*, 183*b*, 243*tl*, 243*tr*, 243*bl*, 243*br*, 247*tl*, 247*tr*, 247*ml*, 247*br*, 275*bl*, 275*r*. Nevada State Library: 41*b*. Special Collections, University of Nevada, Reno, Library: 45 (from John C. Frémont's 1845 *Report of the Exploring Expedition . . .*), 117, 161*t*, 167*b* (from the *Nevada State Journal*, Reno, Oct. 25, 1892). National Museum of American Art, Smithsonian Institution: 97*b*. Office of Information, University of Nevada, Reno: 111*m*, 161*b*, 263*t*. Bancroft Library, University of California, Berkeley: 113*b*. Las Vegas News Bureau: 211*t*, 211*b*, 217*t*, 231, 292. Mike O'Callaghan: 247*mr*. Paul Laxalt: 247*bl*. Reno Convention Bureau: 253. University of Nevada, Las Vegas: 263*b*. *Las Vegas Review-Journal*: 275*tl*. Las Vegas Convention Bureau: 287*b*. Echo Bay Mines, 296*b*. Reno News Bureau, 296*t*. Harry Reid, 299*b*. Richard Bryan, 299*t*.

Library of Congress Cataloging-in-Publication Data

Hulse, James W.
    The Nevada adventure : a history / by James W. Hulse :
illustrations by Don Kerr. — 6th ed.
      p.   cm.
    ISBN 0-87417-159-8 (alk. paper)
    1. Nevada—History.   I. Title.
F841.H8   1990
979.3—dc20   90-12160
                                                      CIP

University of Nevada Press
Reno, Nevada 89557 USA

to

Delora C. Hulse

and

Winifred C. Cutler

Preface

THIS BOOK IS AN effort to meet the need for a short, nontechnical history of Nevada. Although the volume of books on Nevada topics has increased sharply in the last quarter-century, no new chronological summary of the state's past has appeared during that time.

The present work is aimed primarily at the schools of Nevada, although I hope adult readers will find it interesting. It seeks to do what no other work has done in this century: to summarize the history of the state in a single volume. It is not designed to meet the specialized needs of professional historians. They will probably have to wait for the forthcoming work by Dr. Russell R. Elliott, chairman of the History Department at the University of Nevada.

Every author of a work of this kind faces the frustration of being unable to thank all who have given him help. This book has benefited from the aid of many persons inside and outside the university community. During my research, I was assisted especially by the staffs of the University of Nevada library and the Nevada Historical Society. Dr. Russell R. Elliott gave me the benefit of his extensive knowledge of Nevada history. Dr. Paul Smith and Winifred Heron made perceptive comments about the text. Henry G. Vermillion, Director of Information at the Nevada Test Site, critically reviewed Chapter XV, and Robert Horton of the Nevada Bureau of Mines made excellent suggestions for Chapter XI. Thomas Buckman, emeritus staff member of the university's extension service, offered valuable information on Nevada agriculture. The staff of the University of Nevada Press, and especially Robert Laxalt and Yolande Sheppard, gave much help beyond the normal requirements of that office. The maps were drawn by Betty Bliss.

My wife, Betty, contributed indispensable services as secretary, critic, and counselor. I assume responsibility for any errors or inadequacies in the work.

Reno, Nevada   J.W.H.
July, 1964

IN THE TWENTY-FOUR YEARS that have passed since this book first appeared, five revisions have been necessary. Nevada has changed so rapidly in that period that some chapters needed substantial changes, and for this sixth edition a new chapter has been added to summarize the events of the 1980s. The friends and colleagues who have criticized and commented on my previous efforts in a helpful manner are far too numerous to be included here; they now number in the hundreds. I am especially grateful to the University of Nevada Press, which made the first edition of *The Nevada Adventure* its pioneering book in 1965 and still wants to keep it alive after all these years, in spite of its obvious faults.

September, 1989   J.W.H.

Contents

1. The Natural Setting

WE WHO LIVE IN NEVADA are likely to forget what a strange and forbidding landscape our state presents when compared with the usual habitats of men. Most of us spend our time in cities and towns, occupied with human affairs, ignoring the fact that for hundreds of miles across Nevada the land is not very hospitable to human activity and civilization.

Most of Nevada is life-threatening desert. We may love its scenery and we may be excited by the feeling of freedom which it gives; we may like to hunt game or to explore the mountains. But we must recognize that we could not well live here without our modern equipment, even for a short time. Most of us could not bear to live away from our cities, towns, or ranches, in the heart of the barren valleys or rugged mountains.

This explains, in part, why Nevada has a relatively short history. Civilized man has found it possible and desirable to inhabit these parts only in recent times, and then only in rather restricted areas.

Men make a habit of thinking of the world and the universe in terms of the use they make of it, and they tend to evaluate portions of the earth in terms of their own projects or objectives. The desert does not supply many crops or provide employment for many people. Therefore one occasionally hears the desert called a waste or a wasteland.

About 85 per cent of the land is in the public domain; that is, it is still controlled by the federal government and not owned by private individuals. It serves the miner, the livestock owner, the sportsman, or the tourist at times, but most of it is of little use for the general public.

Although much of Nevada is a "desert waste," the history of the state is a living example that the unwanted land of one era may be most valuable to a later age. Much of our story will be related to the fact that men have been able to extract valuable minerals from the Nevada mountains, making important contributions to the commerce and technology of modern society. The desert has many important advantages and possibilities as a playground and recreation center in a country where open space is becoming more difficult to find. Besides, our Nevada desert is becoming an important world laboratory in man's quest to reach the stars: it provides the nuclear rocket-testing grounds in the southern part of the state.

Much of Nevada history, then, shows Nevada's desert is not really a "wasteland" but a challenge and opportunity for civilized man.

MOUNTAINS, DESERTS, AND WATER

Nevada's deserts and mountains present a story of great drama. Everywhere in the state there is evidence of nature's turbulence in past ages. Jagged mountain peaks are the products of gigantic earthquakes which occurred a million years or more ago. Blackish volcanic rocks tell of fiery fountains of lava which once roared from the earth. Broad, fanlike masses of dirt and rock, stretching out onto valleys from canyons, testify to thousands of years of storms which have eroded the mountains. High on the sides of mountains we can see the evidence of seas or lakes which disappeared in the distant past.

It seems that nature played a violent game with Nevada and much of the rest of western North America before the white man, less than a century and a half ago, came onto the scene. Nature built and destroyed great mountains several times, made and un-

Earthquake faults east of Fallon

made massive lakes, and for millions of years allowed the prehistoric ichthyosaur to inhabit this part of the world. Remarkable remains of one of these reptiles were discovered in central Nevada a few years ago. The giant mammoth, similar to an elephant, once lived here, probably in a semitropical climate. Huge forests once covered northern Nevada; petrified wood of great size has been found in bleak, barren regions. Prehistoric horses and weird sloths once roamed here.

The features of Nevada's landscape today are the products of the last million years. The Sierra Nevada range which skirts the western border is young, as the geologists reckon things, and this is also true of most other ranges of the state. The evidence of lakes and shorelines in many parts of Nevada may have been placed there only tens of thousands of years ago. In fact, the face of the land is changing even now, although very slowly and slightly by man's standards.

Many residents of Nevada can remember some small but impressive earthquakes which show how drastically nature can alter the land. On July 6 and August 23, 1954, huge forces beneath the ground twisted and shook the surface of the earth near Fallon and Lovelock, damaging walls and roofs, destroying chimneys, and cracking roads. Several dams, canals, bridges, and other facilities were wrecked, and it cost several hundred thousand dollars for repairs. On December 16 of the same year, another jarring earth movement occurred about thirty miles east of Fallon, in the Dixie Valley–Fairview Peak region. This jolt moved the ground upward or downward for several feet in some places and opened frightening cracks. Had this earthquake happened in a city or town, much death or damage could have resulted. Fortunately, nature has confined her major earth movements in Nevada to generally unpopulated areas for the past hundred years.

There had to be hundreds of earthquakes, much more fierce than man has seen, to throw up the Sierra Nevada range of California and the Wasatch range of central Utah, plus the approximately 160 ranges between. And there had to be thousands of years of storms and winds and flooding to wear down the mountains and to build up the wide, long valleys of Nevada. Anyone who has lived in Nevada for a few years is familiar with this process of erosion. Reno has had three damaging floods since the 1940's, with tons of debris being carried down from the Sierra to the lower lands. Las Vegas and other communities have also seen troublesome floods in recent years. By such events, nature gradually tears down the mountains that she so long ago thrust up.

The mountains, particularly the Sierra of California and the Wasatch of Utah, determine much of the character of Nevada. Between these two ranges, which are about 500 miles apart, lies the region which explorer John Frémont called the Great Basin. Frémont determined that the streams in this area do not flow to the sea; they stay within the region and form lakes, or evaporate, or sink into the ground. For this reason, Frémont thought of the area as a great bowl or basin and the name stuck.

Actually, the word "basin" does not describe well the land between the Sierra and the Wasatch; there is no great depression between them. It would be more accurate to compare the Great Basin with a full bowl of mashed potatoes. The sides of the bowl are higher than most of the potatoes inside, but in the center of the bowl, in some places, the potatoes are heaped higher than at the sides. The edges of the Great Basin to the south and north are not nearly as high as the Sierra and Wasatch mountains, or as some of the mountains in the center. Also, the Great Basin is not really basin-shaped. Southeastern Nevada, including Las Vegas, and a small part of northeastern Nevada are outside it, while parts of California, Oregon, Idaho, Utah, and Wyoming are in it.

Even if the Great Basin is not exactly what its name implies, the area may logically be regarded as a single geographic unit, because it is hemmed in between the California and Utah mountains in such a way that the climate is significantly affected. Most of the western moisture-laden winds from the Pacific Ocean strike the Sierra or the mountains farther north and deposit their water there in the form of rain or snow, watering the valleys of California on the western slopes. Few of the storm clouds penetrate through or beyond the Sierra into the Great Basin. Some of these leave their moisture on the mountains or valleys of Nevada, but most of them go all the way to the Wasatch before they deposit their precious liquid.

Since not much rain finds its way to Nevada, and since no great rivers run into the region, the shortage of water is a fundamental fact. For human habitation, moisture must be stored, and here the mountains again have a vital part to play. The Sierra Nevada peaks that receive most of the snow and rain hold their catch like a precious prize for several months and then release it—usually slowly—to the valleys below. The water flows into the valleys to the east, forming some of Nevada's most important rivers. The Truckee River, fed by Lake Tahoe and other mountain sources, winds north and east to Pyramid Lake, whose beautiful blue charm seems out of place in the arid desert.

The Carson River, also cascading northeastward from the Sierra, used to flow aimlessly into the desert to form the Carson Sink (which usually became dry during the summer months). Now man makes use of this water by storing it in reservoirs and diverting it for agriculture in the dry seasons. Likewise, the Walker River rises in the snow-favored Sierra and carries water from two sources into the desert, finally forming Walker Lake. These rivers, although small, were great aids to man in his battle with the desert.

A hundred other mountains in the Great Basin hoard the rain and snow in underground crevices. In some places, this gives life to aspen, pine, spruce, juniper, or other trees, but it can also provide a stream or spring for a valley. Many of Nevada's ranches are situated in valleys near the slopes of high mountains, where springs or creeks pour out of mountain sources.

The most important offspring of the Nevada mountain streams, from the history student's point of view, is the Humboldt River, which flows across northern Nevada approximately from east to west for about three hundred miles. Rising in the northeastern part of Elko County, gathering rivulets from the Ruby Mountains, adding the contributions which the mountains make to the Reese River and the Little Humboldt, this river wanders toward the Sierra, as though it intended to meet the Carson or the Truckee, which come partway to the east to approach it. But the Humboldt disappears into a sink before a union is made. Occasionally, in past years, the waters of the Humboldt Sink joined with those of the Carson Sink, because the two depressions are rather close together.

Usually, however, both rivers had surrendered their water to the hot earth or the dry air before they made a connection. The fact that a barren expanse of desert exists between the end of the Humboldt River and the ends of the Carson and Truckee rivers became a source of great trouble to American pioneers of the last century.

In earlier times, the Humboldt River did have a meeting place with the Truckee, Carson, and Walker rivers; all of these once flowed into a great lake, which we call Lake Lahontan. Much more rainfall came over the Sierra in those days, and the climate was colder; there were glaciers on some Nevada mountains. The lake existed only a few thousand years ago and gave an entirely different character to western Nevada.

Lahontan was a large, oddly shaped body of water, stretching about 200 miles from north to south and about 175 miles from west to east, with many mountainous islands and long, twisted bays. It covered parts of the land stretching from south of Walker Lake to Winnemucca, and as far west as Susanville, California. As the weather became warmer and drier, the vast Lahontan began to evaporate, leaving some of the dry lakes which are seen in western Nevada today. Pyramid Lake and Walker Lake are the only large remnants remaining of Lake Lahontan, and they have been shrinking in recent years. Perhaps some day, in the distant future, the Truckee and Walker rivers will disappear into sinks, like the Humboldt, instead of emptying into large lakes. Nevada's rivers, like her mountains and deserts, can be changed by nature's whims, and the rivers are also subject to man's interference. The waters of the Humboldt, the Carson, and the Truckee have all been dammed and rerouted by men in the past hundred years.

All rivers and bodies of water so far mentioned are in northern and western Nevada. Farther south, another pattern emerges. We find many high mountains and valleys, as in the north and west, but since the climate is hotter, there is less snow and more rapid evaporation. No great rivers flow here, except for the Colorado River, which brushes the southeastern edge of the state, giving little benefit to Nevada until recent times. The Amargosa, southern Nevada's strangest river, is notorious because its water is bitter and because it flows underground during part of its course, before disappearing in Death Valley.

The Colorado River has a few tiny tributaries which collect small amounts of water from the Nevada hills. The Virgin River enters the state from Arizona and irrigates a few miles of land. The Muddy River salvages some of the scant moisture that falls on the Sheep Range and carries it southeasterly. The Meadow Valley Wash—so narrow and so irregular in its flow that it is not called a river—tries to collect and transfer the water from 150 miles or more to the north. Most of it never reaches the Colorado River. It is important that these streams flow southward, away from the Great Basin. Between this family of rivers and the Humboldt-Truckee-Carson-Walker family to the north, there is a wide, parched expanse which frightened most Nevadans during the first part of the state's history. Only in the twentieth century did Nevada discover the value of its hot, arid southern triangle.

Nature's Oddities

Nature, with all her turbulence and her games with wind and water, has created some strange forms in Nevada. The earliest pioneers observed a number of remarkable sights, and later generations have not ceased to marvel at the variety of unusual physical features.

One of the phenomena of the southern Nevada countryside is the colorful Valley of Fire near Overton. When the bright sun hits the sandstone rocks of this region, it has the appearance of brilliant red flames. Eerie, twisted rocks make the land look even more weird. Further north, near Pioche, the rains and winds have shaped majestic rock patterns in a canyon called Cathedral Gorge. Both of these areas have been set aside by Nevada's government as state parks, to be preserved for future generations as scenic wonders. One may also find freak rocks in such places as Jarbidge Canyon in Elko County, at the "pinnacles" at the north end of Pyramid Lake, or in several other places in the state.

Near the peak of Mt. Wheeler in White Pine County there is a crevice which still contains an active glacier—remnant of the ice age. Near the base of the peak on the eastern side are the large underground Lehman Caves, with peculiar stalactites and stalagmites formed by thousands of years of dripping water. The caverns are so unusual that the United States government has made them a National Monument, and the whole region may soon be a National Park.

Within Nevada's borders are many hot springs and warm springs, reminders of the past ages when live volcanoes spilled forth molten matter from deep underground. Some of the most famous are in western Nevada, but they are scattered throughout the state—bubbling from the base of the rocky "pyramid" in Pyramid Lake, forming odd "mud pots" near Beowawe, boiling in the large "Devil's Punch Bowl" (or "Diana's Punch Bowl") southeast of Austin, and in many other places.

In a few places, the winds have created massive sand piles for no apparent reason. Sand Mountain near U.S. Highway 50 east of Fallon is sometimes called the "Singing Mountain" because of the humming sound which the breezes make as they drift over the sand. Large dunes north of Winnemucca, stretched over many square miles, provide a contrast with the surrounding mountains and desert.

Add together these curiosities—and scores of others not mentioned—in their arid setting, and the strangeness of Nevada becomes more apparent. The unusual and the frightening are normal in Nevada. John Frémont wrote in his journal that the strange features of the Great Basin were often disbelieved when described to people who had made their homes in the friendly eastern climate of the United States.

THE CHALLENGE TO LIFE

Although nature once allowed great forests and giant animals to exist in Nevada, she has not been nearly so generous or ambitious in recent centuries. The dry climate makes living conditions trying, and the extremes of temperature further restrict the varieties of life which can exist here. Many plants need long growing seasons, and most of Nevada has a relatively short period each year when frost does not threaten. In some northern regions of the state, there are normally fewer than 80 consecutive frost-free days during the summer.

Toiyabe Range and Smoky Valley

When winter storms do not deposit the normal supply of snow on the mountains, wildlife and human communities are threatened. The drought of the mid-1970's — one of the most severe in the recorded history of the state — forced Nevada communities to curtail the use of water. Many ranchers had only a fraction of their normal flow for irrigation.

In some valleys of western Nevada, where rich soil and water are available, frosts sometimes come during the summer months; there are often hot days and cold nights in rapid sequence, which many plants cannot survive. In southern Nevada, where the growing season is much longer, water and soil are often inadequate. Nature was being playful, even stingy, when she apportioned her life-giving resources to modern Nevada.

Yet, if you walk almost anywhere in the deserts and mountains, you will become aware that much life can flourish in spite of the roughness of the country, the dryness of the air and land, and the extremes of temperature. Many varieties of plants and animals have learned to overcome the obstacles. The sagebrush—that strong-scented, gray-green shrub which blankets so many Nevada valleys—is known as Nevada's state flower because it has learned so well the laws of life with little water. Many other hardy brush plants have also adapted themselves to the severe tests; the small, round-leafed shadscale, the greasewood, and the yellow-flowered rabbit brush are typical examples. About thirty types of cacti can be found in the state, and the picturesque yucca trees which manage to draw liquid and nourishment from the parched flats of southern Nevada.

Or walk into the mountains and observe how the trees can overcome the physical handicaps. Dwarfed pinon pines and juniper trees have made their homes in thousands of improbable places. Their seeds—the pine nuts and juniper berries—have fallen in extremely rocky, almost barren, places and somehow have taken root. On hundreds of mountain slopes, the misshapen mountain mahogany or the stately spruce and fir make their homes in the face of some of earth's most trying conditions. High on several of our mountains—such as Wheeler Peak in White Pine County and Charleston Mountain in Clark County—one finds the lovely bristlecone pine, one of the oldest living plants in the world.

Such hardy brush plants and trees dominate the desert and mountain landscape, but they do not have exclusive sway. Flowers appear from time to time and from place to place as if to give a touch of joy to the land. Though the delicate wild flowers usually do not survive for more than a few weeks in the spring, they return annually. In their own ways, the Indian paint brush, the blue lupine, and the prickly poppy are tough members of the desert community, constantly renewing themselves in bleak surroundings.

Among the animals and birds, also, there is a perpetual fight for survival. The familiar jackrabbit and the cottontail of the broad valleys cover great distances for food, always alert lest they become a meal for the fox or coyote. Likewise, the swift-footed mule deer in our mountains and the elusive pronghorn antelope of our valleys are both hunters and hunted, threatened by a scarcity of food and an abundance of meat-eating enemies. The mountain lion likes rocky slopes and rough terrain, where he can play his role in maintaining the balance of nature.

Not many large animals make their homes in Nevada, but legions of small creatures live in the face of stern hardships. Squirrels, chipmunks, gophers, rats, mice, and other scurrying ground creatures greet the explorer in all parts of the state. Here and there, where special conditions exist, one might find the beaver, the muskrat, the porcupine, the American mink, or the skunk. The rattlesnake commands almost universal respect in his rocky habitat, and he intensifies the fight for survival. Less known but just as evident are the gopher snake, the whip snake, the striped racer, the garter snake, and the varieties of lizard. All are engaged in the gamble for life. Frugal though she has been with her plant life in Nevada, nature has provided enough flora to give sustenance and hiding places to her lesser creatures.

Another group of participants in the struggle of the desert are the birds. Hundreds of varieties find Nevada's terrain marvelous for their activities. The fierce-looking golden eagle, which occasionally sits defiantly by the roadsides of eastern Nevada, and the delicate hummingbird represent the extremes of the winged creatures. In between are the proud and elusive sagehen, the skittering quail, the chukar partridge, the white pelican of Pyramid Lake, the vulture, the raven, the duck and goose, the owl, the mountain bluebird, and hundreds more. The feathered fraternity becomes a testimony to nature's abundance even in one of her less favored lands.

Lastly, as an evidence of how ironical nature can be, we note the relative abundance of fish life in Nevada. While water is scarce, the streams and lakes that are large enough allow remarkable examples to flourish. Lake Tahoe at the western edge of the Basin has had mackinaw trout which have weighed as much as thirty pounds. The strange waters of Pyramid Lake have cutthroat trout which have weighed as much as sixty-five pounds, and they still provide a home for the cui-ui (pronounced kwee-wee) which is extremely rare. Suckers, catfish, trout of various kinds, bass, and even salmon have done well in some waters of Nevada, even before men undertook to stock the streams with fish.

The fish, game, trees, and plants of the Great Basin have sustained human life for centuries, but only in the last few years have men and women been a significant factor in this part of the American continent. In the early 1800's, only a few thousand Indians lived here, and even during the mining boom days, Nevada had only 70,000 or 80,000 people. By 1980, however, more than 800,000 people were making their homes within the state on land recently regarded as useless desert.

In addition, an American civilization with new needs for resources and space was making increasing demands on the deserts and mountains. In the 1950's, huge defense and testing laboratories were opened in Nevada, and in 1979 it was proposed that a massive missile system—the largest construction scheme ever devised—be located in the Great Basin, mostly in eastern and central Nevada. Our story of the state's history must range from the most primitive to the most awesome of man's efforts to survive on this planet.

2. Prehistoric Man in Nevada

MEN LIVED IN NEVADA for thousands of years before Europeans reached the North American continent, and, like the animals and plants, they had a constant struggle for existence. In many parts of the state, scientists have found evidence of what Nevada natives ate and wore and of how they fought and played before the coming of the white man.

The information that modern archeologists are assembling about the earliest Nevadans tells us about special talents which enabled them to make the best of their surroundings. There is much to admire in the accomplishments of the ancient inhabitants of the Great Basin.

Yet most white men who came to Nevada in the pioneer era had only contempt for the Indians they found here. The earliest English-speaking visitors regarded the native Americans as little better than animals and treated them accordingly. To the explorers and emigrants, the Indians appeared to be lazy, untrustworthy, and a threat to life. Some of the Indians were guilty of occasional acts of murder and theft against early white settlers in this region, and the newcomers sometimes engaged in wanton killing of the Indians. These atrocities fortified the hatred between the races.

The attitude of animosity persisted for generations, and only in our times are Indians finally getting an opportunity to share the benefits of American society on an equal basis. The white men treated the Indians with contempt and failed to recognize their remarkable skills.

HOMELAND OF ANCIENT MAN

White men have inhabited Nevada for only slightly more than a hundred years, but other peoples lived here for thousands of years before that, and archeologists have only recently begun to apply scientific techniques to reconstruct the prehistoric period in the state.

In various parts of Nevada rock hunters have found a few "Clovis points" believed to have been made 10,000 years or more ago. Clovis points are stone dart points apparently used as weapons by men long before the invention of the bow and arrow. They were found near the Carson Sink, near Tonopah and Beatty, and in Washoe Valley. Perhaps in the future others will be found in circumstances which will reveal more about the men who made them.

Much of the evidence about Nevada's earliest inhabitants comes from places where they camped or hunted. Early man found large caves and rock shelters suitable for living. A few of these have remained very dry for centuries, and food particles, implements, and bones of prehistoric humans have been preserved well enough to allow the archeologists to tell us something about the way men lived in our state thousands of years ago.

The scientists are not yet certain when man first lived in Nevada, but several discoveries indicate their presence here about 11,000 years ago. In 1952, scientists discovered human bones in a cave near Winnemucca Lake (a dry lake east of Pyramid Lake) which are believed to be some of the oldest yet uncovered in the Western Hemisphere. Some bones of extinct horses and camels were also discovered with the human remains, suggesting that the earliest men in this region may have shared the countryside with large animals which no longer live in the Great Basin.

At another spot farther east, near the Humboldt Sink, scientists have found human remains which appear to be about 11,000 years old, stone dart points about 7,000 years old, and some fragments of hand-woven baskets believed to be 5,700 years old. This site, known as Leonard Rockshelter, is at a spot which was once close to the shoreline of ancient Lake Lahontan.

Southern Nevada has also provided some exciting discoveries about our primitive predecessors. In the Frenchman Mountains near Las Vegas there is an opening in the earth known as Gypsum Cave. About 8,500 to 10,000 years ago men were camping in or near the cave, eating animals they had killed, and losing or throwing away some of their weapons. Here, human remains were found together with more bones of camels and primitive horses, and also with the remains of the giant sloth, a prehistoric creature somewhere between an ape and a bear in appearance. Perhaps men wandered over the Las Vegas Valley and visited Tule Springs (12 miles northwest of Las Vegas) in that era. In recent years scientists of the Nevada State Museum have been attempting to determine exactly how long ago humans first used that site.

A number of other sites in Nevada have offered tantalizing bits of evidence. Etna Cave south of Caliente, explored in 1942, revealed four different levels of human habitation, the earliest of which may have coincided with the most ancient period of the Gypsum Cave. Other caverns—such as the Jarbidge Cave in Elko County, Lehman Cave in White Pine County, Hidden Cave in Churchill County—all seem to have sheltered men or to have served as burial places centuries ago.

Such caves reveal much about man's slow progress toward civilization. As the centuries passed and as dirt and refuse accumulated at the bottom of the caves, implements and tools slowly became buried. The scientists usually find more advanced handiwork in the upper levels of the cave floors than when they dig farther down. Important findings about the caveman's life of 3,000 years ago have been made in caverns of the Humboldt Range in places where Lake Lahontan once splashed ashore near the mouth of the caves. The so-called Lovelock Cave was apparently a favorite dwelling place; it is thought to have been occupied from about 1,000 B.C. until recent centuries. The nearby Humboldt Cave shows signs of

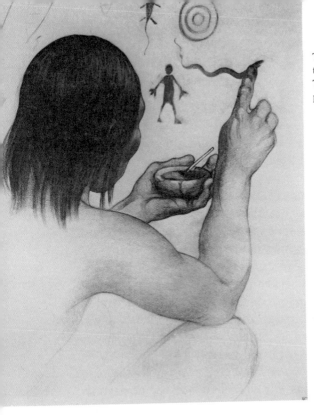

The life of Native Americans was often portrayed by Nevada artist Robert C. Caples. This charcoal sketch shows the creation of a petroglyph

A museum model depiciting ancient life near Lake Lahontan

human occupation from about the beginning of the Christian era until recent generations.·

The men who lived in the Lovelock Cave 3,000 years ago knew nothing about the bow and arrow; they still relied on a dart as their main weapon for hunting. They were, however, talented basket makers and they skillfully created nets for catching rabbits and woven bowls for storing their foods. Because the Lovelock Cave was especially dry for centuries, many tools were well preserved, and scientists found rabbit skins and feathers fashioned into clothing and decorative items.

Some of the most interesting creations of the Lovelock Indians were decoy ducks. They learned to twist tule reeds together, bend them in a special manner to make them look like a swimming duck, and then paint them with appropriate colors. By hiding in the tall grasses at the water's edge and floating their decoys on the water, the Indians would lure flying ducks within range of their darts.

The residents of these caves knew nothing about agriculture, and their lives must have become more difficult as the waters of the great lake receded. Their skills at decoy-making, basket-making, bone-tool making, and hunting were not enough to sustain them as the climate became more and more arid. We do not know whether the people of the Lovelock and Humboldt caves perished or left the area or adapted their lives to new conditions. It is not known whether the modern Paiutes are their descendants, but the latter-day Paiutes did not have the same techniques of basket-making.

Conditions were changing also in southern Nevada twenty or thirty centuries ago. Some men found it possible to build a new way of life along the banks of rivers. One group of people who lived in the Muddy River and Virgin River regions about 300 B.C. are known as Anasazi. From about 300 B.C. until about A.D. 500— or approximately during the same period as the rise and fall of ancient Rome—men were living in pit houses near the southern Nevada rivers. These were only excavations in the ground, probably covered by some brush to keep out the sun and rain. These men also used darts for hunting and fashioned crude knives and scrapers from stone. They apparently did not know how to make pottery or bows and arrows.

In a later period, estimated at about A.D. 500 to A.D. 700, the Anasazi began to use pottery. Perhaps they obtained the first vessels by trading with their distant neighbors in other regions, because they began mining salt in these years and some of the salt was probably transported to other tribes. There were more elaborate pit houses during this era, some of them with masonry walls made of adobe and rocks. A few had bins for storing food. Also, the Anasazi now learned to use and make the bow and arrow, which were much superior to the dart or spear for hunting animals. And they formally buried their dead relatives, leaving pottery with them in their graves.

These sound like rather elementary changes in the life habits of the first Nevadans, but they represent fundamental steps toward civilization. Europe and Asia were, of course, far ahead of America in civilization during these years, but slow and remarkable progress was being made here.

The greatest achievement of the Anasazi in southern Nevada— and perhaps the most important before the coming of the European peoples—occurred in the years between about A.D. 700 and 1100, when these early inhabitants of the Virgin and Muddy valleys began to farm. They raised corn, beans, and squash in these rich valleys which have been so successfully cultivated in recent years, and they developed an irrigation system.

Some Anasazi now constructed their homes above the ground, building them from adobe. The ruins of about a hundred of these adobe "pueblos" have been found, some of them consisting of only one or two rooms but some having more than a hundred chambers. A small city flourished, supported by a more reliable food supply because of agriculture.

The Anasazi did not cease their hunting when they learned to plant and harvest vegetables. They killed deer, mountain sheep, rabbits, and other creatures for meat, and they gathered wild seeds and nuts (including pine nuts), but these only supplemented their diet. They wove rather elaborate baskets and made more attractive pottery than the earlier pit dwellers.

Scientists who dug into the ruins of this community—usually called the Pueblo Grande of Nevada or the Lost City—also found evidence that Anasazi engaged in mining and trade. They extracted salt from underground deposits near the Pueblo community and they mined turquoise nearby. They probably carried or sent these items to the east and west, getting pottery or seashells in exchange. It is believed the Anasazi of Lost City traded with contemporaries in Death Valley, who probably had obtained shells from the California coast. They probably got some of their pottery from tribes living in Utah and northern Arizona.

In the salt mines, scientists found rocks which had been fashioned into pick-like instruments, crude types of rope materials, and gourds which had been used to carry water underground. All these implements testify to the skill of these adobe-house dwellers.

A museum of Lost City relics is maintained at Overton, and we can obtain a good impression of how the Anasazi must have lived a thousand years ago by looking at the reconstructed displays there. The site of the original Lost City is now covered by the waters of Lake Mead.

For some unknown reason, the Anasazi did not continue to progress and flourish in southern Nevada. Sometime about 1150, they abandoned their homes and fields, making way for the southern Paiute Indians. These Indians had probably been moving gradually into southern Nevada for several generations, and there may have been war or conflict between them and the Anasazi. Some time around 1100, the Anasazi built a large house of eighty-four rooms on an elevated site above the valley floor. It was constructed around a central square with limited entrance facilities. This may suggest that the Anasazi felt the need for a fortification; perhaps they feared the Paiutes. But all of this is speculation, and archeologists have not yet found any tangible evidence of a battle between the Anasazi and the Paiutes. Possibly disease or a changing climate drove the dwellers of Lost City away.

Before they disappeared, the Anasazi had learned to domesticate dogs, to cultivate cotton, and to make fancy baskets, sandals, and netting. They had achieved the level of the "neolithic" or new Stone Age people in all major respects.

The southern Paiutes did not learn the arts and skills of the pueblo-dwelling Anasazi. They were primarily a wandering people, spreading out over a vast area instead of confining themselves to the banks of the rivers. They did learn to grow crops—one of the few Nevada tribes to do so—but this was a less important source of food than hunting and gathering seeds. Probably their descendants moved northward along the eastern edge of the Sierra Nevada into western Nevada; these northern Paiutes did not carry with them the tradition of agriculture. The Paiutes made relatively little progress from the time they reached Nevada—perhaps a thousand years ago—until the arrival of the white man.

Mysterious Rock Pictures

Early men who lived in Nevada left one important and baffling reminder of their existence which may someday tell us more about them than we now know. In many places throughout the state, strange designs have been hammered on large rocks or into the sides of cliffs. In some places, there are only odd circles, spirals, or criss-crosses; in other places there are crude but clear representations of men, deer, and mountain sheep.

No one understands the meanings of these symbols today. Modern Indians have been unable to explain why or when they were put there, but scientists have tried in recent years to discover a pattern which will give us a clue to the mystery.

The rock-pictures are scattered throughout the state; they have been found in about a hundred places. Some of the most remarkable are in the Valley of Fire near Overton; perhaps they are related to the people who lived at Lost City. Some of the pictures hammered into the rocks resemble the kinds of large animals which the pueblo people hunted. Other dramatic designs exist in Condor Canyon near Panaca, in the Meadow Valley Wash south of Caliente, near the Truckee River east of Sparks, near Fort Churchill on the Carson River, on some of the steep cliffs near Walker Lake, and in several places in Churchill and Pershing counties.

In 1962, two investigators from the University of California made a careful study of many places where rock pictures are found, and developed some ideas about their meaning. Where pictures can be identified, they often represent large animals like deer, antelope, or mountain sheep. The scientists found they often occurred in places where such game existed. There are very few symbols of rabbits or fish, and none of the rock art seems to suggest seed-gathering, although men for thousands of years must have hunted rabbits and gathered seeds for food.

Putting these facts together, the California scientists decided that the rock pictures of large animals must have some special meaning and may be related to hunting. In certain locations, the pictures seemed to be near hiding places where men could lie in ambush, waiting to surprise a large animal so they could hurl rocks or darts at him. Such practices must have been necessary in the days before the bow and arrow came into use. Different types and patterns of rock art exist in northern and southern Nevada, which may reflect different climates and hunting factors in the two regions. The California scientists concluded that the ancient men believed there was some magical power created when they carved the image of a deer on a rock cliff near the site of their hunt. Much effort was devoted to the rock pictures; it is more logical to believe that the ancient men attached some importance to their designs than to believe that they were merely "doodling."

Man's knowledge of the past is constantly expanding, and new methods are being found to solve the riddles of life and nature. Perhaps someone will find the key to explain the strange rock pictures. Until then, they must remain among Nevada's many mysteries.

Modern Nevada Indians

Although some rock pictures seem to have been made in recent centuries, apparently all were done generations before white men reached Nevada. The Paiute and Shoshone Indians who occupied most of Nevada when the earliest explorers arrived knew nothing about the peoples who had preceded them, and few of them had learned anything about tilling the soil. They were basically food gatherers rather than food growers, and most of their energies were devoted to a persistent search for enough nourishment to keep them alive. The search was not easy in the Nevada desert without the aids and conveniences of civilization.

The Paiute, Washo, and Shoshone Indians of northern Nevada depended heavily on pine nuts in those years when the pinon trees produced a good crop of the tasty brown nuts. The Indians would swarm into the hills and gather the nuts in great quantities, storing them in special pits in the ground for winter use. But when pine nuts were not in season, and when the crop was not good, the Indians had to depend for their diet on other seeds and on small animals and insects. They caught and ate great quantities of grasshoppers during the summer months, and they stored some for winter after roasting masses of them. Other insects and bugs were also caught, crushed, and formed into small cakes.

The Indians in the vicinities of the rivers and lakes managed to catch fish and to kill waterbirds from time to time to supplement their diets. They obtained their fish with nets and spears, or sometimes they drove the fish into small pools for easier capture. The lake and river Indians seem to have fared better than their companions in the desert, because their source of food was more stable. At Pyramid Lake, the cui-ui and the trout were plentiful, but it took skill to catch them with the implements the Paiutes had a century and a quarter ago.

Among the most impressive devices the Indians used to get food was the rabbit net. A group would cooperate in weaving a net or barricade from brush and weeds; it would be about four feet high and perhaps a hundred feet or more long. This obstacle would be constructed in a strategic place, possibly in a canyon, toward which rabbits and other small game could be chased. Then a band of Indians would drive the animals into the barricade and shoot them with arrows or beat them to death with clubs. This sounds crude to modern man, but it was a vital necessity for the Indians; the rabbits were among the main sources of meat and a vital part of the diet. Large animals were much more difficult to chase and kill, although some Indians worked energetically at driving antelope into confined areas where they could be killed with arrows.

The quest for food meant constant wandering in the spring, summer, and fall, but the small bands gathered in groups of fifty to one hundred as the cold weather approached to spend the winter months in larger units. These larger groups conducted rabbit hunts and occasionally antelope drives or deer hunts. There was a need for much cooperation and sharing of responsibility whether the bands were small—one or two families—or large. The women usually gathered seeds, often taking their small babies with them, while the men hunted. The women also prepared meat and seeds in the autumn for winter use.

Although the Nevada Indians wandered widely, there were rather clear divisions between the territories of the different groups. The Washo lived in the vicinity of Lake Tahoe, in the nearby Sierra Nevada, and in the valleys of extreme western Nevada. Their immediate neighbors to the east were the northern Paiutes, who occupied the region from eastern Oregon, south to the vicinity of Pyramid Lake, the Humboldt Sink, Walker Lake, and the drier region between. In northeastern Nevada the controlling branch was the Shoshone, and in southern Nevada, the southern Paiutes and Mojaves predominated. The northern groups seem to have fought each other on occasion over the right to hunt game and gather pine nuts, but the Nevada Indians generally were not a warlike people.

Some of the customs and habits practiced by the northern Paiutes until very recently can be cited as examples of how the Indians adapted to their desert surroundings. Since they moved so frequently in search of food in the warmer months, they had no permanent homes, but crude types of shelter. Often they fashioned these from brush, piling the scrubbly growth against a few upright poles to provide a partial covering. For winter months, they prepared a more stable structure, often consisting of a number of poles erected in a circle and connected at the top, and then covered with layers of brush, weeds, and mud to form a teepee or wicki-up. By leaving a small hole in the top and digging a depression in the ground within the teepee, the occupants could have a small fire to survive the frigid nights; winter, of course, was the season when the weak members of the tribes were most likely to perish.

The desert does not provide much material for clothing. The rabbit drives and antelope or deer hunts were important because they supplied not only food but hides for blankets and clothing. The Paiutes became very skillful in sewing the furs of dozens of

An Indian shelter made of reeds

rabbits into a robe or blanket; such a garment could be a treasured item. Even more skill was required to render the bark of sagebrush into clothing, as the Indian women managed to do. The outer fibers of the brush could be rolled and twined together in such a way that it provided diapers for infants, skirts for the women, and crude string for many purposes. It was slow, difficult work, and it is easy to understand that the Paiutes wore very little during the warm months.

Household implements and tools were found which revealed their ingenuity. They made excellent arrowheads and other stone tools; they also learned to construct a variety of household implements from grass and reeds. All Nevada Indian groups had members who were talented at making baskets and containers. By rolling grasses or reeds together into strong cord or string, they could weave or twine baskets of great utility. Some were shaped in bottle form, covered with pine pitch, and used for carrying water. Others were shaped with an open top, finished with pitch, and used for cooking. Such a basket, of course, could not be placed over a fire, but a skillful Paiute wife could put water in a container, dump hot stones into it, shift the stones quickly to keep the basket from burning, and eventually bring the water to a boil by adding new, hot stones from time to time.

The Indian women wove large, tray-like devices for winnowing their seeds—separating the food particles from the hulls or shells around the seeds. They fashioned cradles for their infants, spoons for stirring, plates for eating, nets for fishing, and a dozen other implements. Many of them developed baskets for ceremonial or artistic purposes.

Some of the basket work of Nevada Indians has aroused the admiration of modern America. The making of a basket with a design on the side—representing an animal or just an abstract pattern—required the careful selection and preparation of fibers. The artist would have to choose his bark or reeds with care and delicately chew or roll or twist them into shape. Then the weaving or twining would begin, sometimes with the worker giving meaning to his or her basket by incorporating a special design. Probably no two designs were ever alike, because each Indian sought to make every decorated basket unique.

The Washo Indians were the most talented of the Nevada basket makers, and the best known member of this group was a woman known as Dat-so-la-lee. She spent most of her life in the Carson Valley and Carson City area, living among the whites for about a half-century; she died in 1925. Some of the baskets from her hands required several months to make, but they were so excellent in their construction and so attractive in design that they were worth thousands of dollars. Her work is admired in a number of modern museums. No other Nevada Indian developed such remarkable skill, but Dat-so-la-lee represented a long, rich tradition in basket-making. In spite of their difficult surroundings and their hard life, the Nevada Indians had a deep sense of beauty.

Their sense of beauty did not always run in the same direction as our own. The Paiute girl of about 125 years ago would tattoo her chin or paint her face with red mud to "improve" her appearance. If she decided to dress up, she might be fortunate enough to make a small garment of deer skin, or she could make a necklace of porcupine quills or bird bones. The toes of deer were prized items for ornaments.

There was time for play and recreation, in spite of the demands and challenges of the landscape. Some groups played a kind of football or soccer, and there were gambling games in which sticks were used. The children knew how to make toys from mud; at a young age some of them made small animals, which they used as targets for their miniature bows and arrows. The boys had to begin early to learn the techniques of hunting.

The religion of the desert Indians included the notion that there was a spirit land where the dead existed, keeping watch over the affairs of the living. Everything was peaceful and pleasant in the spirit land, and no evil could occur there. The Indians also believed that special powers lived in some of the elements of nature; the mountains, the winds, and the fog had special qualities with unusual forces. The wolf was regarded as a symbol of the good and desirable, and the coyote of the evil. There were no priests, but there were medicine men and persons believed to have magical powers.

The habits and thoughts of these primitive Nevadans show how different life was in the state before the white man came. He transformed the Indian cultures with great speed, and in the process many Indian skills and talents were lost. The greed, brutality, and contempt of the white man destroyed much of the beauty of Indian life and prevented the Indians from entering the white man's culture. When Indians were placed on reservations, some aspects of their cultures were preserved, but many of their rights were taken away and much of their choice land confiscated. Old Winnemucca, the leader of the Paiutes in the 1840's and for many years thereafter, originally dreamed of whites and Indians living together in mutual respect and friendship. This did not happen, however, until the twentieth century. First the U.S. government tried to place them on reservations, away from the main communties and travel routes of the whites. Next, under the Dawes Act of 1887, the government tried to break up the reservations and begin the process of absorbing Indians into the cultural patterns of the majority. Then, in the 1930's the Indian New Deal sought to correct injustices of the past and to restore some lands to the original Americans. In 1946, Congress created an Indian Claims Commission, which conducted long investigations about the value of lands that were wrongly taken from the Indians as the frontier moved West. The hearings held on the claims of the Northern and Southern Paiutes, the Shoshones, and the Washos found that many Nevada Indians were entitled to compensations for lands their ancestors lost.

Most Nevada Indians of the last hundred years believed their ancestors to have been happier than they. Sarah Winnemucca Hopkins, a daughter of Old Winnemucca and one of the first of her tribe to accept civilization, wrote that her people were much more content in the days before the coming of the white settlers. She was author of one of the first books to appeal for equal justice for American Indians and a forerunner of a movement to achieve justice for Native Americans. This had become a respected political force by the early 1980's.

3. The First Explorers, 1826-1844

NEVADA CAME LATE onto the stage of history. The primitive Indians apparently had no system of keeping written records. It remained for men of European ancestry to create a written account of this land and its inhabitants.

English settlers and their descendants had lived on the North American continent for more than two hundred years before any of them saw Nevada. The Declaration of Independence was fifty years old before any carrier of Western civilization set foot here. Five presidents had already served their terms of office and the War of 1812 was a decade-old memory before any American of English descent entered these parts. This was the last large portion of the continental United States to be seen and examined by the men who built our country.

Between 1826, when the first Anglo-American explorers entered Nevada, and 1845, most of Nevada's topographical and geographical features were discovered by hardy groups of mountain men, fur trappers, and government agents. The stories of their early adventures are filled with reports of hardship and peril. The first English-speaking men to visit Nevada were no better prepared than the Indians to survive the rigors of the desert; in fact, the earliest explorers were ignorant of the water holes which sustained the Indians.

Considering the dangers and the obstacles which they had to face, it is remarkable that a small number of explorers managed to discover Nevada's main features in only nineteen years. And even before the explorers had completed their initial work, wagon trains of emigrants were venturing through the region. Although Nevada's history started late, it developed rapidly once it had begun.

THE WESTWARD MOVEMENT

Much of the story of America concerns the westward push of a civilization that began on the eastern shores of the continent. As the population of the thirteen original English colonies—and later the United States—grew, men went inland in search of new opportunities and new land. It was to be some time, however, before they thought of extending their society to the Far West. In fact, the generation which fought in the Revolutionary War period had only a dim knowledge of the region beyond the Appalachian Mountains, and they knew almost nothing of the great inland areas.

The Spaniards who conquered and partly colonized Mexico were the first men of European descent to penetrate the vast region between the Rocky Mountains and the Pacific Ocean. They had explored New Mexico in the 1500's, and they established communities there early in the 1600's—at about the same time as the earliest Englishmen landed on the Atlantic Coast, 2,000 miles away. For more than a century and a half, however, Spanish explorations probably did not enter Nevada. In 1769, Spaniards began to establish colonies in California. Within a few years, they had settlements and missions stretching up the coastline to San Francisco Bay.

In 1776, the year of the Declaration of Independence, Spanish explorers made two attempts to find new routes from their older settlements to the California missions. One group was led by a famous Catholic missionary named Father Francisco Garcés. They traveled from Yuma, Arizona, northward along the Colorado River and westward to California. Perhaps Garcés followed the river far enough north to have entered the southern tip of the future Nevada, but his written report about his route is not clear on this point.

In the same year, two Franciscan fathers from Santa Fe decided to search for a northern route. Father Francisco Silvestre Vélez de Escalante and Father Francisco Atanasio Dominguez, together with a few soldiers, traveled northward into Utah. When they reached Utah, they observed a few small rivers running west, and learned much about Indian life in the region. But they became discouraged by bad weather and decided not to go on to California, and therefore did not enter Nevada. When later mapmakers recorded information about the rivers which the fathers had seen, they guessed that the rivers must run westward all the way to the Pacific Ocean. Because of this guess, the cartographers of the early 1800's drew maps showing an imaginary river named the San Buenaventura, and many later explorers searched in vain for a waterway which extended from the Utah mountains into San Francisco Bay.

For the next fifty years, no other European is known to have entered Nevada. Some Spanish and Mexican traders did get into Utah, exchanging goods with the Ute Indians, but the huge region to the west remained largely unknown to these people. As late as the 1820's, when Mexico won its independence from Spain and became theoretical ruler of the region, no formal exploring had been done in Nevada. Mapmakers of both Europe and America accepted the word of the Dominguez-Escalante party regarding the San Buenaventura.

If it seems odd that the Spaniards skirted the edge of Nevada as early as 1776 and then displayed no more interest in the region for nearly fifty years, Americans were not interested either. In fact, most of the Far West was still unknown. In 1804-1806, Meriwether Lewis and William Clark made a famous expedition up the Missouri River to its source and then into the Columbia River Basin. Soon afterward, Zebulon M. Pike explored as far west as Colorado, but these explorations were exceptions to the general American disinterest. The United States government did nothing more to explore the Far West for another twenty years. Many persons felt that the great plains were unfit for cultivation and gave little thought to what might be possible on the western half of the continent.

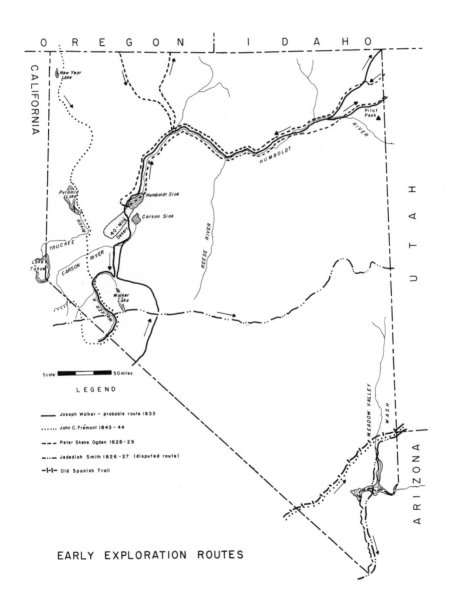

EARLY EXPLORATION ROUTES

THE FUR TRADERS: OGDEN AND SMITH

Yet, some people were showing interest in the Far West; reports of Lewis and Clark told of rich lands and fur-bearing animals. Within two or three years, bands of hardy young men were following the rivers into the western mountains in search of animals whose hides would bring handsome prices. Fur-trading was a risky, difficult business, but it attracted persons equal to the challenge. In 1826, almost fifty years after the American Colonies had proclaimed their independence from Great Britain, the first fur traders penetrated Nevada.

The Americans and British were still having troubles in the 1820's. Both countries had claims in western North America, and the fur trappers of both Canada and the United States were competing for control of the fur resources of the continent. The British-Canadian trappers had a monopoly on trapping beavers and other fur-bearing animals in most of the Columbia Basin—including the future states of Washington, Oregon, and Idaho. By 1825, a new American organization known as the Rocky Mountain Fur Company was penetrating the Far West. The British interests, represented by the famous Hudson's Bay Company, decided to expand their operations southward and eastward from the Columbia River basin to trap as many animals as possible in the inland region. This, they believed, would make trapping poor for the Americans and would discourage them from moving farther west.

The main trapper of the Hudson's Bay Company in 1825 was a 30-year-old adventurer named Peter Skene Ogden. He led a band of men from the company's headquarters near the mouth of the Columbia River deep into the Rocky Mountains and southward to the Great Salt Lake. In 1826, he explored the area now within southwestern Idaho and possibly entered the extreme northern part of Nevada on the Bruneau and Owyhee rivers. Historians are not certain of his exact route. If he did get far enough south to enter Nevada during his explorations of 1826, he did not see much of it. It was not until 1828 that he and some companions discovered the Humboldt River.

Shortly after Ogden had wandered through the hills and valleys along the northern fringes of Nevada in the summer of 1826, a group of fifteen Americans of the Rocky Mountain Fur Company set out to the southwest from the Great Salt Lake. They were destined to pass across the southern tip of Nevada into California. The leader of this band of trappers, Jedediah Strong Smith, knew almost nothing about the lands which he was entering. Across central and southern Utah, he and his small party looked unsuccessfully for fur-bearing animals. In the late summer he reached the Virgin River and pursued its course to the southwest, entering Nevada near the present town of Bunkerville. From there, he went on to the river which the Spaniards had named the Colorado. There he found some Indians who guided him across the torrid deserts westward to the San Gabriel Mission established by the Spaniards near the present site of Los Angeles. He had found no new regions for trapping, and he had wandered into lands controlled by the Mexicans. Technically he was trespassing on foreign soil.

The Mexicans treated his party well enough, but they insisted that Smith and his associates must leave by the same route they had used to enter California. Disregarding the command, Smith took his party northward into the San Joaquin Valley early in 1827. They found it would not be easy to cross the snow-covered Sierra Nevada, so Smith decided to leave most of his party in California and to return to Great Salt Lake with only two companions, hoping to come back and guide the other men eastward at a later date. Smith apparently hoped that once across the mountains, he could find the San Buenaventura River and follow it easily to his destination. Instead, he found the forbidding landscape of central Nevada.

If Smith had been farther north, he would have been able to follow the Humboldt River for several days, but he did not know of its existence. Crossing the mountains at a high pass, the three men experienced one of the most difficult trips ever made across a scorching desert. The trek over the Sierra Nevada had been most difficult, but at least there had been water; once in the Great Basin, they found very little. They ate their horses when they could not find game. In some places they had to fight steep mountains, in others deep sand. One day, they dug holes in the ground to protect themselves from the blistering summer sun. One of the men nearly died of thirst when they failed to find water for several days. By a combination of bravery and desperation, they finally reached the Great Salt Lake and their trapping headquarters early in July. They had crossed the Sierra ranges, the middle of Nevada, and half of Utah in a month and a half.

Smith went back the same year for his companions in California, following the southern route down to the Colorado River and westward again. He did not challenge the deadly obstacles of central Nevada this time. When he returned to the east, he went far northward into Oregon, thus avoiding the perils of the Great Basin.

Although the American fur trappers lost interest in the region southwest of the Great Salt Lake after Smith's ordeal, the Hudson's Bay Company continued its probing. In 1828, Ogden led another party south from the Columbia River basin and discovered the Humboldt River in the vicinity of Winnemucca. Under a pleasant November sky, the trappers enjoyed a few days of snaring and skinning beaver. Not troubled by the worries or needs which plagued Smith in the previous year, they looked forward to a profitable season. But suddenly a bitter blizzard settled over the Humboldt River Valley. The party became frightened and decided to travel eastward along the river, seeking a route to the Salt Lake Valley. One man died on the way, probably in the neighborhood of the present town of Beowawe, but the others managed to move on to their destination in spite of the winter-like weather.

The Humboldt River had confused Ogden's men. They saw it flowing southwesterly, but they believed it must eventually turn north and connect with one of the tributaries of the Columbia River. Once, perhaps twice, they returned to the Humboldt Valley in 1829 to explore further for beaver and to determine where the "unknown river" went. In the spring, they followed it all the way to the Sink, where the Humboldt disappeared into the ground. They camped there for a few days and learned from the Indians that another river could be found by several days' travel to the southwest. However, they were not curious enough then to move onward and discover the Truckee River.

Their second trip into Nevada late in 1829 was a strange journey for which they kept almost no records. They probably returned once more to the Humboldt Valley, proceeded to the Sink, and then started out across the deserts to the south. They probably saw the Carson River and perhaps the Walker River and Walker Lake, but it has not been possible to trace their route with accuracy. Their activities make up one of the unsolved mysteries of Nevada history.

Ogden deserves credit as one of the most important explorers of the state's past. No town or prominent natural feature in Nevada is named for him. Later explorers won more honor and fame than this rugged Britisher.

A Late Fur Trader: Joseph Walker

Men of the Hudson's Bay Company who ventured into the Humboldt region in the next two or three years made no important new discoveries and had little luck in trapping beaver. It was now the turn of the Americans to explore the unknown land once more, and they may have been looking for something other than beaver.

One of the most famous fur-trapping expeditions ever made into the American West was that of Captain Benjamin Louis Eulale de Bonneville. He led a well-financed expedition of more than a hundred men into the Rocky Mountains with the best equipment and supplies available at that time. Although the party did some trapping, it became more famous for its explorations. Captain Bonneville was an officer of the Army officially on leave, and he may have been prompted by a desire to obtain more information about some of the lands controlled by Mexico.

Captain Bonneville's chief lieutenant was Joseph Walker, a tough frontiersman who had once been a Missouri sheriff. In midsummer of 1833, while Bonneville's party was north of the Great Salt Lake, Walker and about forty men left the main party supposedly to search for beaver west of the lake. Instead of returning soon, they went all the way to California—by way of Ogden's "unknown river." Captain Bonneville pretended to be displeased, but he may have wanted Walker to obtain information for the Army.

Walker's party crossed the barren, salty flats of northern Utah and entered the northeastern section of Nevada in search of the Humboldt. When they found its tributaries and then the river itself, they were struck by its small size and by the poverty of the Indians who lived near it. In some places they could not find enough wood for fires, and grass for the animals was scarce along part of the river bank. The men had carried buffalo meat on their pack horses when they left the main party, but their supply ran low as they crossed Nevada, and they could not find enough game to replace it.

To complicate matters, the Indians began to annoy the trapping party. At first they stole traps, later, as the group continued westward day by day, they built fires and sent smoke signals in the nearby hills when the party passed down the river. Then, near the Humboldt Sink, the natives gathered in large numbers—800 or 900 strong—and some of them sought permission to enter Walker's camp. When the white men refused, the Indians threatened to approach anyway. Walker's men then shot several ducks sitting on the water, to demonstrate they had weapons which could kill at a distance. The Indians were impressed and withdrew.

The next morning, however, they returned, threatening and challenging once more. The white men, outnumbered twenty to one, decided they must act decisively. They mounted horses and made a firing charge on the Indians. Nevada's first battle between white men and Indians was underway, but it lasted only a few minutes. The fur trappers killed thirty or forty Indians, and the remainder fled in terror. There was no more trouble from the Indians in this first crossing.

Determined to reach California, Walker's party continued southward past the Carson Sink, up either the Walker or the Carson River, and then into the Sierra Nevada mountains. Severe hunger handicapped them until they reached the mountains; game was scarce, and for a few days they lived on insects, as the Indians had done in this region for generations. Snow had already fallen in the mountains, and the crossing was a miserable ordeal. Not knowing a good trail, they struggled with starving and rebellious horses against heavy snowbanks and rugged cliffs, and even at times against rebels in their own party who wanted to turn back. But Walker led them across the wild slopes not far from Yosemite Valley and into the lush valleys of central California.

Although Walker was officially an intruder, the Mexican authorities at Monterey treated his men well. The Americans stayed from November until February before starting back. For the return trip Walker had obtained some Mexican horsemen to accompany him. In addition, he had 365 horses, 47 beef cattle, and 30 dogs, which had been obtained from the Mexicans. This time he had Indian guides to help his men through the mountains, and they crossed in the southerly Sierra over the opening later named Walker's Pass. Walker decided to travel northward along the eastern side of the mountains until he discovered the river (the Carson) which had guided him into the mountains the previous fall. They struggled for days in the barren desert without success.

Then Walker became confused and, believing that he recognized a landmark, ordered the party to proceed out into the desert, away from the mountains. He hoped for a shortcut to one of the rivers, but instead he must have strayed into the barren region east of the present town of Hawthorne. After three days without water, their animals dying, they stumbled upon the river which one day would be named in honor of Walker. They apparently did not see Walker Lake.

After refreshing themselves, they moved northward again, discovering the Carson River, the Carson Sink, and the Humboldt Sink. They had come back to their old route and to the region of their earlier encounter with the Indians. Once more Walker's men regarded the Indians as dangerous; the fur traders took the initiative, attacked, and killed fourteen natives. One account of this incident in later years by an Indian said that members of the tribe were seeking friendship when they were assaulted in this second encounter. At any rate, Walker's group had no more trouble with Indians as they proceeded up the Humboldt River toward the Great Salt Lake.

On this return trip, Walker established a new trail from the Humboldt Basin to the Great Salt Lake, via Goose Creek and Raft River. This trail left Nevada in the extreme northeast corner of the state and eventually became the road which many later emigrant trains used. It proved to be a far better route for men and animals than the trail across the salt flats which they had initially used.

Walker's travels across the Great Basin proved that the western deserts could be mastered by determined men. It was dangerous and difficult to cross the sprawling desert, but Walker had established a route which followed rivers most of the way. The American novelist Washington Irving wrote an account of Captain Bonneville's adventures and gave credit to Walker's daring exploration. As thousands of people read it, many became interested in the Far West; soon some of them would be pushing westward along the trail Walker had blazed.

Walker returned to travel the Humboldt route again as a guide in one of the earliest of these emigrant parties. We will delay the story for later pages and first consider the accomplishments of the last of the great explorer-discoverers, who also benefited from the work of Joseph Walker.

John Frémont

The fur-trading business was dying in the western mountains in the 1830's and early 1840's. In American history men have often attacked nature's resources with such greed that they have destroyed the source of their profits; so it was with the fur trappers after the first few years. Walker found very few beaver along the Humboldt River, and settlers who came later were attracted to the valley for other reasons.

As the fur-trading declined, the interest of the United States government increased. Some senators in Washington began to feel that the Americans should gain control of the lands west of the Rocky Mountains for future settlement. At least, they felt, the government should learn more about it. In 1842, the influential Senator Thomas H. Benton of Missouri made arrangements for his son-in-law to lead exploring expeditions into the little-known region. This son-in-law was John Charles Frémont, a lieutenant in the Army Topographical Corps, who had considerable experience as a surveyor and mapmaker.

John C. Frémont

Christopher (Kit) Carson

Frémont's first trip took him only into the central Rocky Mountains; he did not come near Nevada. In 1843, however, he planned to go all the way to the Pacific, to the Oregon country and the Columbia River. He was well prepared for this expedition, having some valuable instruments—a telescope, a barometer, thermometers, and a small cannon for protection—as well as two of the best guides in the West, a man named Christopher (Kit) Carson and Thomas (Broken Hand) Fitzpatrick. They had explored and trapped beaver in the western wilderness for more than a decade, and were known as hardy mountain men.

Frémont made his trip to the Pacific Ocean via the Columbia River Basin, but in doing so he was crossing land that had already been explored. He was eager to get into some of the lesser-known lands to the south—the desert region through which the San Buenaventura River was said to flow. He knew of Ogden's River (the Humboldt) and he knew that Joseph Walker had followed its course for many miles, but he retained the belief that another great river remained to be discovered. So, late in the year, he started southward across eastern Oregon, searching.

Frémont never found the legendary San Buenaventura, of course. Entering the northwestern corner of Nevada on the day after Christmas, members of his party were the first men of their race to see the vast, open stretches of northern Washoe County. They passed southward, saw the picturesque High Rock Canyon, and camped in the vicinity of the present town of Gerlach. In January, 1844, Frémont's men encountered some snows which hindered their travels and for four days the fog was so heavy they were not certain where they were going.

Pushing southward, hoping to find the Humboldt River or the San Buenaventura, Frémont discovered Pyramid Lake, which he named for the giant pyramid-shaped rock which stands in the water near the eastern shore. "It was set like a gem in the mountains," Frémont wrote in his journal. "For a long time we sat enjoying the view, for we had become fatigued with mountains." Exploring the east side of the lake, the party passed southward, arriving a few days later at the south end, where the town of Nixon now stands. There was an Indian community, and the natives delighted the explorers with a feast of huge trout.

The Indians told Frémont's interpreters that the river which flowed into Pyramid Lake (the Truckee) came from another lake in the mountains (Tahoe) which was three or four days distant. They talked of other rivers further south, but when Frémont asked them to guide his party there, they only laughed; apparently they knew better than to venture into the desert, leaving their camp and their food, in the middle of winter. Frémont's party went southward without guides, up the Truckee River to the site of Wadsworth.

The party did not follow the river westward from there; instead, the men turned south hoping to find the larger San Buenaventura. They found the Carson River, passed up the river to the vicinity of Dayton, and southward to the Walker River. Having decided that the horses were too lame and weak to make the long trip back to the Columbia River, they prepared to cross the Sierra Nevada mountains—a daring enterprise in late January when the snows were heavy. Indians guided them part of the way, but they were afraid to venture far into the mountains and warned the white men not to do so. Frémont ignored the advice and went on. His men ran short of food; they ate pine nuts which the Indians had given them and killed a dog for meat. They built sleighs to haul their provisions as the weak horses floundered in the snow. They had to abandon their cannon, but they triumphed over the winter and the mountains and emerged in the Sacramento Valley. They had crossed the mountain pass which was later named for Carson, and in doing so, Frémont had seen the blue waters of Lake Tahoe in the distance. He had discovered a second great lake.

After Frémont's party had remained in California for several weeks, he decided to return eastward by a southern route. He knew the northern country, and by now was convinced that the San Buenaventura River did not exist. But he had not seen the southern regions of the American West, and curiosity tugged him in that direction. He decided to see the Old Spanish Trail, which was famous in legend.

The Old Spanish Trail was a looping, 1200-mile-long route between Santa Fe, New Mexico, and the Spanish missions in the vicinity of Los Angeles. The trail did not go directly from Santa Fe to Los Angeles, however; the barren Arizona deserts and the massive Grand Canyon discouraged such travel. Today, the trip by automobile is about 850 miles, but the pioneers added more than 300 extra miles by going northward into Colorado and central Utah, and then southwesterly to avoid the Arizona desert. This path took them along part of the Colorado River and its tributary, the Virgin. Often, it also took them through the valley which the Mexicans called Las Vegas (The Meadows) because of the grassy stretches surrounding a spring of water.

Father Garcés had established the western part of the trail in 1776, and Fathers Dominguez and Escalante had located the eastern portion (in Utah) at about the same time. Jedediah Smith had blazed the central part of the trail in 1826 from central Utah to the lower Colorado River. Later, other parts of the trail had been used by fur traders. Kit Carson had been in a party which trapped westward from Santa Fe to California in 1829. This party probably did not enter Nevada, but at least Carson knew something about the southern region. In 1830-31, a party of fur traders traveled the whole extent of the trail. William Wolfskill and George C. Yount, two enterprising trappers, led about twenty men on this trip, and they probably passed through southern Nevada near the sites of Bunkerville, Overton, and Boulder City. They made no important discoveries, but they helped to establish the Old Spanish Trail as one of the most important in the Far West. By 1844, when Frémont decided to use it, much information was available about how to find and follow it.

Frémont's party came onto the trail in southern California. As they traveled along it toward Las Vegas, the heat became oppressive and the rocky earth damaged the feet of their animals. The explorers met a party of Mexicans who had been ambushed by the Indians; two Mexicans had been killed and two of their women kidnapped. Carson and a companion pursued the Indians and brought back two Indian scalps, but they did not rescue the women.

The Frémont party reached the Las Vegas spring early in May and rested in preparation for another jaunt across the desert to the Muddy River. That was one of the most trying parts of the Old Spanish Trail—fifty-five miles without water. Traveling hard,

Pyramid Lake, as drawn by Charles Preuss, an artist with Frémont in 1844

chewing cactus to ease their thirst, the party made it to the Muddy
River, only to encounter more threats from Indians. Some of the
Paiutes had learned that they could successfully attack and steal
from the parties along the Old Spanish Trail. One of Frémont's men
was killed, but they had to push on, into more pleasant country.
They passed through Utah and across the Rockies. Within a few
weeks they were back in Missouri.

Frémont had circled around the Great Basin, and it was he who
gave that name to the vast region whose edges he had crossed. He
recognized that there could be no San Buenaventura River; all the
water from that interior region must sink into the ground or form
lakes, he reasoned. Therefore, he called it a "basin." The word basin
is not completely accurate, as we have mentioned, but it became
popular and no one bothered to change it.

When Frémont returned to civilization, he wrote a description
of his travels which made him and Kit Carson famous. It also stimulated the interest of Americans in the valleys of California, just as
the stories of Walker's adventures had done.

Frémont was to return to the Far West and to travel through
Nevada again in 1845. By this time, the United States and Mexico
were moving toward war over the question of the Texas boundary,
and the American government was interested in California. A number of Americans had made homes there, and President James K.
Polk wanted to be certain they would be protected from the Mexicans in case of hostilities. Frémont had the assignment to lead a
military exploring unit there.

This time Frémont had both Joseph Walker and Kit Carson with
him. Although it had been twelve years since Walker had discovered the trail down the Humboldt and across the mountains to California, not much was known of the region to the south of the Humboldt Valley—the vast stretches of south-central Nevada through
which Jedediah Smith had once wandered. When Frémont's party
entered northeastern Nevada and came into the Humboldt Basin,
Frémont decided to send part of the group with Walker down the
river, but the remainder he led farther south, through the Ruby
Mountains and into the center of the state. Going south and west,

Frémont passed near the site of Eureka, went through Smoky Valley (between Austin and Tonopah) and, turning westward, came to the north edge of Walker Lake. There, Frémont's party met Walker's group according to a prearranged plan. Then the two sections divided again, Walker taking one party over the Walker Pass and Frémont leading several men northward to the Truckee River and over the Donner Pass.

The river which Peter Ogden had discovered was known by many names: Ogden's River, Mary's River, Paul's River, Barren River, and Unknown River. Frémont gave it the name of Baron Alexander von Humboldt, a German scientist whom Frémont admired (and who never saw the river). Frémont also named the Carson and Walker rivers for his capable guides. No natural features of the state were given his own name, but in later years, he would be memorialized by Fremont Street in Las Vegas, one of the most famous streets in America.

Frémont later became well known in American politics. He helped engineer an American revolt against the Mexicans in California during the Mexican War, and he became a senator when California became a state. About a decade after his 1845 trek through central Nevada, he became a candidate for President of the United States. In 1856, when the modern Republican party was in its first presidential campaign, he was so popular that he won that party's nomination for the presidency. The reputation which he had made from his adventures in the West did not get him elected to the highest political office in the nation, but it did make him one of America's most influential men.

4. Emigrants West, 1841-1850

MUCH OF THE STORY OF AMERICA is the description of a massive westward movement. The earliest colonists from England came westward across the Atlantic. Their descendants left the Atlantic seacoast in large numbers to break new land and build towns in the Appalachian foothills. As the nineteenth century opened, they had crossed those mountains and were pouring into the Ohio Valley. By 1840, the restless Yankees had pushed west of the Mississippi River; Independence, Missouri—nearly in the center of the United States of today—was one of the westernmost outposts of American civilization.

Half a continent still lay before the Americans, and if they had filled it in an orderly, regular way perhaps the Pacific Coast would still not be settled. But suddenly, in the 1840's, a burning desire possessed hundreds of Americans to rush beyond the Great Plains of Kansas and Nebraska, through the mountains of Wyoming and Idaho, across Oregon or the desert of Nevada to the Pacific Coast. The first emigrants, few in number, were attracted by the rich lands which the earliest explorers and fur trappers had described. "California" and "Oregon" became magic words, and it did not matter that California was a possession of Mexico and that Oregon was part-British. The adventure lovers and land hunters wanted to be there.

Magnetic California drew the first party of settlers across Nevada in 1841. Thereafter, a few settlers crossed the region each year, some with good luck and some with gruesome disaster. In 1848, gold was discovered in California, and in the next year a stumbling, confused migration of thousands went via the Humboldt or the Old Spanish Trail to the slopes of the Pacific. The westward surge has never stopped since 1849-50; let us summarize its beginnings.

THE BARTLESON-BIDWELL PARTY, 1841

No good road or trail existed across the western wilderness when the first party of emigrants set out to find homes in California; in fact, the Far West had not even been thoroughly explored when the first daring pioneers decided to cross the continent with wagons.

It was the stories of abundant land in California which drew the original emigrants. An American, Dr. John Marsh, had taken up land in the Sacramento Valley and wrote letters back to his friends in Missouri, telling of wonderful opportunities. Another man who had seen California and testified to its wonders was a former fur trapper named Antoine Robidoux, whose remarks were read in many parts of the Middle West and East. By the autumn of 1840, hundreds of excited persons had formed a Western Emigration Society, which planned to make a great trek westward in the spring of 1841.

When spring arrived and it was time to depart, only sixty-nine persons appeared at the designated meeting place near Independence, Missouri. One of the organizers of the party was John Bidwell, a young man who had almost no knowledge of the hardships of the trail or the route to follow. "We knew that California lay west," he said later, "and that was the extent of our knowledge." Another leader was John B. Bartleson, an ill-tempered character who demanded and got the title of captain of the party. He knew no more about how to get to California than Bidwell.

As they started up the Missouri River along the trail established by fur traders, they met a group of missionaries headed for Oregon; their guide was "Broken Hand" Fitzpatrick, who had trapped in the Rockies and knew that region well. This was a marvelous piece of good luck, because he guided them all the way to the Bear River (north of the Great Salt Lake). When they reached this point, however, the missionaries and Fitzpatrick turned north toward Orgeon, and the emigrants had to decide whether to follow them or to turn southwesterly over the little known road to California. They had only vague reports about the trail which Walker had followed eight years before. About half the party decided to change their plans and go to Oregon, but thirty-four emigrants decided to try for California in spite of the dangers. Among them was one woman, Mrs. Benjamin Kelsey, and her small daughter.

As they crossed the desert northwest of Salt Lake, their troubles began; their wagon wheels often became stuck in the sand and tangled in underbrush. The animals were soon exhausted and water became scarce. After a few days of slow progress, they were delighted to find a towering mountain. At its base was water and grass to refresh their horses and oxen. This later came to be known as Pilot Peak (in eastern Elko County almost on the Nevada-Utah boundary); it guided thousands of later emigrants who followed in the footsteps of Bartleson and Bidwell.

Beyond Pilot Peak, the heavy wagons again slowed their progress and wearied their oxen, so the emigrants abandoned them and most of the belongings they had been hauling to California. They pushed on to the Humboldt River, many of them walking because only a few had horses. It was a long, slow procession down the river in the chill October days, and some of the men became impatient at the pace. Bartleson and a few other men who had horses did not want to stay with the slow-moving hikers and oxen. One day, probably near the site of Winnemucca, they divided the food; eight men, including Bartleson, went on ahead.

Bidwell and cool-headed Benjamin Kelsey led the remaining slow party past the Humboldt Sink to the Carson River, then south-

Artist Craig Sheppard's watercolor conception of Gravelly Ford on the Humboldt River

Pilot Peak, near the Emigrant Trail

ward until they found the Walker River, and on toward the awesome Sierra Nevada. Unexpectedly, they encountered Bartleson
and his seven companions, who had taken a wrong turning and had
wandered out into the desert. Some Indians had befriended them,
giving them pine nuts and fish; many of Bartleson's group were ill.
They now were willing to take their chances with the main party,
even if it could not move rapidly.

It took about two weeks for the party to struggle across the snow-
packed mountains, probably by way of Sonora Pass. The story of
their crossing is like the account of Walker's experience; they ran
out of food, killed their last living oxen, and then slaughtered horses
for meat. Indians stole some of their precious animals, and steep
hillsides caused a few painful falls. But the ending was happy: on
the last day of October, they emerged into the San Joaquin Valley
and found much antelope and wild fowl. Soon they reached the
rich Central Valley, where they made their homes. They arrived at
the ranch of Dr. Marsh, whose letters had first persuaded them to
make the dangerous trip. Without a map and without a guide
across the desert and the Sierra Nevada, they had traveled hundreds of tortuous miles to their destination.

In spite of their ignorance and errors, the Bartleson-Bidwell
party made the first successful emigrant crossing of the Great Basin.
No lives were lost, and there had been little trouble with Indians.
Mrs. Kelsey and her young daughter proved that even women
could stand the arduous journey. It took six months to make the
trip, but when it was finished, the trouble seemed to be justified by
what they found. Soon, back in the heartland of America, more
were ready to follow.

More Emigrant Trains, 1841-1845

The numbers in the first parties were small; no stampede to the
West followed on the heels of the successful Bartleson-Bidwell
party. However, that group did provide some of the experience for
the next group of emigrants across Nevada. Joseph B. Chiles, one
of the members of the 1841 party, had gone back to Missouri in
the following year, and by 1843 was ready to lead another group

westward. Joseph Walker, the veteran of the Humboldt Route, had also been persuaded to join them.

This caravan had many wagons, loaded with furniture, farm equipment, and other machinery; Chiles was convinced they could get wagons across the Great Basin. Most of them got to California, but the Sierra Nevada range took a heavy toll of the wheeled vehicles and their contents. Once more, the obstacles of the desert—the sand and sage and insufficient feed for animals—caused suffering, but they made the voyage successfully. Much of the credit went to Walker, who led them down the Humboldt, then south to Walker River and eventually to Walker Pass, where they surmounted the Sierra.

In the next year, another member of the Bartleson-Bidwell party, Andrew Kelsey, led thirty-six persons to California across the rough western terrain. But the group which gained more fame in that year was led by Captain Elisha Stevens, Martin Murphy, and Dr. John Townsend. In the party was a rugged old man named Caleb Greenwood, often called "Old Greenwood" because he was in his eighties and had spent half a century in the Western wilderness.

The Stevens-Murphy-Townsend party had good luck going down the Humboldt River. The grass was good that year and the Indians gave no trouble, because Old Greenwood knew how to keep them happy with small gifts. When they came to the Humboldt Sink, they decided to go westward to the river which the Indians described. It was this party which first used and gave its present name to the Truckee River. They had to cross a parched alkaline section of desert to get to the Truckee near Wadsworth, but they had less trouble with that barren stretch than many later travelers.

Today, the drive up the Truckee River from Wadsworth to Reno is a smooth, pleasant experience in a comfortable automobile on a modern freeway. In 1844, it was a miserable, painful ordeal. In places the canyon was so narrow that the party had to walk in the middle of the river; in other places it was so rocky that it made the feet of men and animals bleed. The fertile Truckee Meadows (where Reno and Sparks are now situated) were easier to cross, but to the west travel was even harder than before. The most challenging problem came after the party reached the site of Donner Lake; there, the westward path seemed to be ending with the mountains towering above the men. But Old Greenwood was equal to the test; the emigrants tore apart their wagons, build windlasses, and hoisted their equipment piece by piece up the most difficult faces of rock. More than once they had to assemble and disassemble their wagons, and at one place they even had to hoist their oxen up the sides of a severe cliff. In the end the talent and determination of the emigrants mastered the dangers and obstructions of the snow-covered highlands. The Stevens-Murphy-Townsend party was the first which succeeded in getting its wagons all the way to California's Central Valley. After this triumph, the Truckee River route competed with the Carson and Walker River route for the attention of the emigrants.

Two parties crossed Nevada by the Humboldt route in 1845; travel was picking up, but it still had no important impact on Nevada. Only about 250 persons crossed the future state in wagon trains in that year besides the Frémont-Walker party which made their explorations of the center of the state and reexamined the Humboldt later in the season. Otherwise, the silence of the centuries hung over the sagebrush desert. The curious Indians who watched and sometimes troubled the struggling men and beasts of burden could not have known that members of this strange race would soon transform their lands and lives.

One thing was certain: none of the white men who crossed Nevada in these years wanted to stop here. Who would consider making a home in such a land? The common goal was California, which was known as a place of verdant promise with much rich land, handy timber, wild game, and a wonderful climate. The desert regions around the Humboldt seemed to offer nothing but death or savagery; there was a common fear among the emigrants of getting caught by the winter, when snow blocked the mountain trails. The worst fears of the pioneers became realities for one party—the most famous of them all—in the winter of 1846-47.

THE DONNER PARTY, 1846-47

The story of the Donner party begins with enterprising Lansford W. Hastings, who had come West in one of the earliest groups and had written a guide for the emigrants, telling how they might best get to California. Hastings had gone from California east in 1845, along the Truckee and Humboldt route and directly across the Great Salt Lake Desert west of the Salt Lake, then around the south end of the lake into the rugged Wasatch Mountains. Most travelers before that time had followed a route further northward (through southern Idaho) to avoid the worst mountains and the threatening salt flats, but Hastings had tried it and made it on the new route. His popular guide for immigrants proposed this as the best route to California.

Two parties of immigrants prepared to follow the Hastings route early in May, 1846. One party, led by an old "mountain man" named James M. Hudspeth, made the trip to California over this route in about four months. The other, led by George and Jacob Donner, met disaster on the deserts of Nevada and in the snowy Sierra.

There were eighty-seven men, women, and children in the Donner party. They had much furniture and equipment, some large wagons, and even a substantial quantity of money with which to start their lives in California. They expected to have Hastings on hand to guide them on the most difficult part of the trip through the Salt Lake desert country, down the Humboldt, and across the Sierra. But Hastings rushed on ahead with another group, leaving the members of the Donner party to make their own way according to his guidebook.

They became lost traveling through the Wasatch Mountains and wasted many days trying to find the path. The party was already depressed and exhausted when it reached the Salt Lake Valley and prepared to cross the Salt Flats. Hastings had initially told them that it would take only about a day to cross the flats; it required nearly six days and six nights over the terrible wastes, and many were without water for three days. They saw all kinds of mirages and fantasies in the distance. Oxen went mad and stampeded recklessly. At one time panic seized the party, and some families ceased to help each other. Many wagons and much equipment had to be abandoned before they could all reach Pilot Peak, where the meadows and springs saved them from agonizing death, at least temporarily.

Having recuperated, they tried to find the Humboldt by following Hastings' description and a trail he had made a few weeks earlier. They made a long, unnecessary detour to the south, around the lower end of the Ruby Mountains—a diversion that lengthened their travels by a hundred miles. They then turned northward and reached the Humboldt River near the site of Elko. It was now the end of September and most of the supplies were gone; the first snows had been seen, and a silent hysteria came over the party. Two horsemen, C. T. Stanton and William McCutchen, went ahead to try to get help from California, and the party split into two parts so that the better animals and wagons could move faster. Then, in the rear group, two men named James Reed and John Snyder had a bitter quarrel and a fight, and Reed killed Snyder. Passions and hatreds flamed among the emigrants, and some wanted to hang Reed from the tongue of a wagon. Finally, as a compromise, he was banished from the party although his wife and family remained in it. He and a companion rode ahead into the unknown.

Indians harassed the straggling emigrants at every turn, stealing oxen or horses when they got a chance, and occasionally shooting arrows at the animals. Jealousy and lack of cooperation prevailed in the group. As they pulled slowly down the Humboldt to the Sink, some had no horses or oxen left, and those who did were often not willing to share them. One old man called Hardcoop was left alongside the trail alone, because he was not strong enough to go on; those who wanted to help him could not. Abandoned, he died on the Nevada desert. The emigrants had adopted one of the devices of the Indians, who were known to send their weak elders into the wilderness alone to meet death.

Many members of the party were near starvation as they inched their way up the Truckee Canyon toward the Meadows. Suddenly, in the canyon, they met Stanton, who had been sent on ahead weeks earlier. He had managed to get through to California for supplies

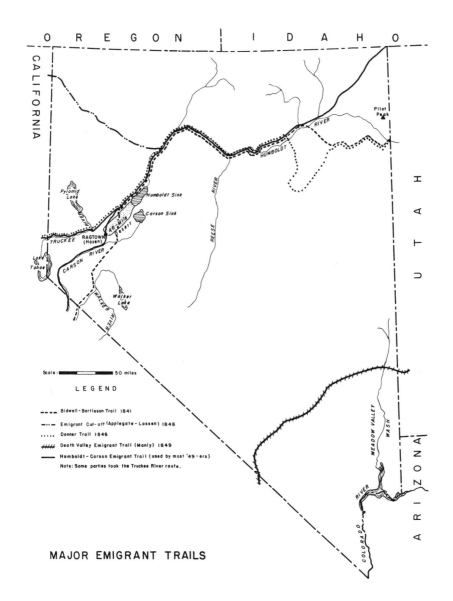

OREGON   I D A H O

CALIFORNIA

CALIFORNIA

Pilot Peak

Pyramid Lake

Humboldt Sink

Carson Sink

RIVER

Humboldt Sink

TRUCKEE

RAGTOWN
(Hazen)

CARSON   RIVER

Lake Tahoe

Walker Lake

WALKER RIVER

REESE   RIVER

HUMBOLDT

U T A H

Scale: ████████ 50 miles

L E G E N D

– – – Bidwell–Bartleson Trail 1841

–·–·– Emigrant Cut-off (Applegate–Lassen) 1846

····· Donner Trail 1846

╫╫╫╫ Death Valley Emigrant Trail (Manly) 1849

—— Humboldt–Carson Emigrant Trail (used by most '49-ers)

Note: Some parties took the Truckee River route.

MEADOW VALLEY WASH

RIVER

COLORADO

A R I Z O N A

MAJOR EMIGRANT TRAILS

and to return with two companions to meet the members of the party. The provisions they brought on mules revitalized the party once more, and when they came into the green Truckee Meadows late in October, their fortunes seemed better. They spent a few days in the Meadows to refresh their few oxen and cows. Once more, Indians stole from them and killed their precious animals, but the respite from travel was welcome.

As they moved up the Truckee River, the heavy snows began. Some of the emigrants came to the site of the lake later named for them and some managed to get to a stream several miles below it. No Old Greenwood was present in their party to show them how to get over the steep mountains, and even he could have done little under the circumstances. The snows of November, December, and January blocked their passage and prevented relief from reaching them. They found one cabin which earlier emigrants had built, and they erected rough shelters of their own. A few made crude snowshoes and decided to walk over the mountains. Fifteen tried, and seven made it. Those who stayed behind hunted animals, and eventually some of them became so desperate that they ate their dogs, harnesses, and shoe leather. In tragic last efforts to stay alive, some were driven to eat their dead comrades.

Finally, in the early months of 1847 as the winter began to wane, rescue parties from the western settlements penetrated the snowy wilderness and saved those who had miraculously survived the winter. Several relief parties had to be sent, and the last of the party did not get over the mountains until April. Of the eighty-seven who had set out for California, only forty-seven reached it; the Humboldt-Truckee trail and the frozen mountains had claimed the rest.

The experiences of the Donner party soon became widely known; the shocking story of the expedition was frequently told, and the Humboldt Trail and Truckee River gained evil reputations. Once again, the Great Basin seemed to most people to be too dangerous, and there was little emigration through that region in the next two years. Then the news of gold in California overcame the bitter stories about the Donner party and the fears of using the Humboldt-Truckee route. In 1849, the western tide was moving across the Great Basin again.

THE GREAT GOLD RUSH OF 1849

In this interlude between 1846 and 1849, some important political and military events occurred which determined the future direction of events in the western desert regions. During those years, the United States fought and won the Mexican War, and as a result of the Treaty of Guadalupe Hidalgo acquired all or parts of the future states of California, Nevada, Arizona, New Mexico, Colorado, and Wyoming. No fighting occurred in Nevada because no white men lived there, but the Americans in California—aided by Frémont—staged a successful revolt against Mexico. The U.S. government was eager to gain possession of the rich region west of the Sierra.

At about the time of the peace treaty, in 1848, a group of men were building a sawmill on the American River near Sacramento when they noticed some yellow specks of sand. Soon they had established that it was gold, and in spite of efforts to keep it secret, the word began to spread. The few people living in California became excited during the spring of 1848, but reports did not circulate widely in the eastern part of the United States until the late summer, when it was too late to start the long trip to California by land. In December, President James K. Polk spoke of the gold fields in a message to Congress. Within the next month, more than fifty ships were on their way toward California, rounding the stormy southern tip of South America. Even London and other European cities had become excited by the rumors. There were stories that a man could get more than $50 a day in gold dust by "panning"—putting gravel or crushed rock in a pan and sloshing water carefully back and forth over it so that the lighter earth would be washed away and the heavier, gold-bearing particles would settle to the bottom of the pan.

It was usually the well-to-do who went by sea to California in the beginning. The poorer people, who could not afford the excessive costs of sea travel, gathered along the Missouri River in the spring and prepared for the land voyage. Most of the thousands who set out for California by foot, by horse, or by wagon were willing to take great chances to become rich, because they felt certain it would be easy to do—in California.

Most of the emigrants followed the so-called California Trail which took them up the North Platte River across Nebraska and Wyoming. Then they would cross southern Idaho, reaching the northeast corner of present-day Nevada. From there, the route for most overlanders went along the trails already established—by way of the Humboldt River and then either the Truckee, the Carson, or the Walker into the mountains. About 25,000 persons, scattered along the trail for about six months, are believed to have made the trip in 1849. By the time they reached the upper streams of the Humboldt River, the men and beasts were already exhausted by weeks—and sometimes months—of weary travel. Cholera and other diseases killed many and weakened others. Grass was poor for the later travelers, because the animals of those who had started first had eaten all that grew near the trail. Most emigrants began the trip with too much equipment; their wagons creaked with excessive loads. But the troubles they experienced between Missouri and the Great Basin were minor compared with what awaited them along the Humboldt route.

It is not easy, in our era of rapid transportation, to put ourselves in the frame of mind which the Forty-Niners must have had when they entered the Humboldt Basin at its eastern end. We motorists still see, along U.S. Highway 40 between Wells and Lovelock, many of the prominent physical features which they observed, usually craggy, treeless hills fleeting by for moments or hours, not for plodding days and weeks. If you had made the trip in 1849, you probably would have been used to the green hills of the East or the fertile fields of the Middle West; the ashen mountains along the Humboldt would have seemed threatening. Remembering the ghastly stories of the Donner party, you would know that the desert ahead could mean trouble with Indians, and the mountains ahead could mean snow, entrapment, and slow starvation.

If you were a latecomer among the Forty-Niners, you would see the debris of many who had had troubles. The trail was lined with the carcasses of oxen, the skeletons of cows, occasional pieces of abandoned furniture, broken wagons, and here and there a human grave. Many gold seekers coughed from the dust, as the storms blew alkali sand into their faces; you would have shared at least a few of these storms. The midday heat would have pulled the water from your perspiring body, and when you tried to drink from a pool along the trail, you might discover once more the bitter taste of the alkali. Imagine blistered feet, chapped skin, cracked and bleeding lips, sore eyes, and upset stomachs for yourself and your family, and you begin—perhaps—to appreciate the lot of the California-bound parties of 1849.

As you came down the river, you saw some of your own animals collapse from exhaustion or lack of grass. Perhaps your family discarded a precious bed or piece of farm equipment to lighten the load. And when, after dreary days and nights, you reached the Big Meadows (near Lovelock), there was reason to rejoice because rye grass grew abundantly and would refresh the animals. But this was also the place of great fear, because the worst trial was probably just ahead.

The crossing of the Forty-Mile Desert—separating the last good water of the Humboldt from the first good water of either the Carson or Truckee—made the trip down the Humboldt seem like a joy-ride to many. If you had been along in '49, and had been lucky enough to get your animals and wagons this far, you would make great preparations at the Big Meadows. Grass would be cut for the animals and every available jug and bucket would be filled with Humboldt water—bitter though it might be. Someone in the group would check the wagons, making what improvements were possible; a breakdown could mean disaster.

Probably you would want to start across the desert in the late afternoon or at night, to avoid much of the oppressive heat. Soon after you had started, there would be thick heavy sand, difficult for walking and almost impossible for the animals pulling wagons. Many beasts could not go on; many would drop in their tracks and die. The stench of rotting animals on the Forty-Mile Desert contaminated the air in a score of places. Here, once more, you would be tempted to throw away all but the vital necessities in order to keep going. Few deserts of Africa or Arabia are more terrible than this for exhausted men and animals. You—like many of your companions—would consider this region cursed by nature and God. One hot spring, with bitter and boiling water, existed in the middle of the desert, but it sickened more creatures than it refreshed.

Some fortunate travelers made it across the desert in a day and a night, but most took longer. You might have been on the desert two or three days, pushing or pulling your belongings through the sand. But suddenly, something would begin to happen to the animals. Sniffing the air, they would raise their heads, begin pulling harder at their loads, or if your wagon had already been abandoned, they would begin a wild stampede. This happened when the half-crazed, half-dead oxen and cattle got a smell of water. Their noses were more sensitive than those of the humans, and they became unmanageable when the air gave them a hint of a river ahead. When your party reached the water, you would have to take care that neither man nor animal drank too much too quickly, because that also could mean death.

To most of the Forty-Niners, the hazards and sufferings of the Humboldt and the Forty-Mile Desert were the worst part of the long trip. The voyage over the mountains was still miserable, and sometimes animals and people lost their lives in the crossing. But no fatal early snow came in 1849; there was no repetition of the Donner tragedy. (Most travelers avoided the Truckee route and Donner summit in favor of more southerly passes through the mountains.) In later years, when the Forty-Niners talked about their sufferings and troubles along the trail, they often described the trip across the northern part of the Great Basin as the worst of all. Later generations have regarded the Forty-Niners—sometimes called the Golden Army—as heroes for their achievements.

In the next year, the gold fever continued in the East and Middle West, and thousands more were willing to take the California trail in spite of the hardships. So 1850 saw another army straggling across Nevada in the summer and autumn months. The story is much the same for this year, except that the Humboldt River ran higher due to an unusual rainy season. This was both good and bad; more fresh water was available, but more mud slowed the animals and wagons. Winter came early in that year, too, and thousands were still on the eastern side of the mountains in the valleys of western Nevada when snow began to block the passes. Rescue missions came across the mountains from Sacramento and managed to get nearly all of the late emigrants to safety, so no great disasters were recorded. In the early 1850's supply stations began to spring up along the rivers—Peter Lassen's at the Big Meadows and Mormon Station in Carson Valley—to serve the travelers. Little by little, the dangers of the trip decreased: within twenty years—as we will see—a railroad spanned the desert by way of the dreaded Humboldt-Truckee route.

THE SOUTHERN ROUTE, 1841-1849

During the years when some pioneers were taking their animals and wagons across northern Nevada to the Pacific, others were using the Old Spanish Trail to reach the fertile valleys of California, a route less famous and less popular than the Humboldt in the 1840's.

The first California-bound settlers apparently used the Old Spanish Trail in 1841. A few persons who had arrived to join the Bartleson-Bidwell party on the Missouri River in that year decided to try a southern route. They went to Sante Fe, New Mexico, and were joined by persons from that community who were ready to move westward. A party of twenty-five persons, headed by William Workman and John Rowland, started along the Old Spanish Trail driving a flock of sheep for food. Four families were included in this party, as well as an engineer, a physician, and scientists. The group was well prepared, and some members knew the trail well. They seem to have passed through southern Nevada—probably through the Las Vegas Valley—without difficulties, and many of them made their homes near Los Angeles. In later years, similar small parties made the same trek, but there was no large migration across the southern tip of Nevada until 1849.

In the first year of the overland rush to California, a number of emigrants came across the Rocky Mountains by the usual route—through southern Wyoming and southern Idaho—and then decided to turn southward toward the Old Spanish Trail to avoid the Humboldt. By this time Mormon settlers had taken up land in the Salt Lake Valley, and the emigrants found a guide there to show them the route to southern California.

The leader of this party was Lewis Manly, and the guide was Jefferson Hunt, a Mormon who knew the trail. In southern Utah, however, Manly and some of his party decided to try a "cutoff" which they had been told about. While part of the group went down the trail safely to Los Angeles, Manly's party started westward in the hope of reaching the gold diggings more rapidly. They wandered in ignorance into the barren region north of Moapa, crossing the rugged Meadow Valley Wash with great difficulty. They apparently struggled with their heavy wagons out into the vast, dreary region which now forms the Las Vegas Bombing and Gunnery Range; perhaps they dragged across the region where atomic bombs have been exploded in recent years. And from there, the panic-stricken, hungry, choking party stumbled into Death Valley.

It was a miracle that any of them emerged alive, but luck was with most of the party. Manly and a companion went ahead for help, finding assistance at the Mission of San Fernando not far from Los Angeles. They managed to return to their stranded companions with a small supply of food and led them out of Death Valley. It was they who gave this region its name. It had taken nearly all winter for them to go from Salt Lake to Los Angeles, but fortunately they had been far enough south not to encounter heavy snows.

The determined pioneers of the 1840's in both northern and southern Nevada expanded the work of the fur trappers and explorers. They proved that large groups of men and animals could move across the desert regions if they planned carefully and if nature was reasonably kind. They proved that wagons could be transported—a fact which their predecessors had not established. It was the emigrants who caused Congress to begin talking about wagon roads—and soon railroads—across the continent.

Nevada was basically unwanted and unloved in those days. It was a barrier to a promised land, rather than an asset in itself. But soon this changed.

5. Mormons and Miners, 1850-1859

THE YEARS BETWEEN 1850 AND 1859 brought big changes to Nevada. The desert region—which had been so forbidding in the 1840's—became a place in which some people wanted to live. Two groups began to settle in 1851: members of the Mormon Church, who wanted to cultivate the land and trade with the emigrants, and the miners, who wanted to find gold in the mountains and canyons.

In a sense, the Mormons and the miners competed for leadership in Nevada in the 1850's, and the miners won because circumstances forced the Mormons to give up their initial plans for settlement. But even though the Mormons who came to Nevada in the 1850's did not create the kind of society they wanted here, they made important contributions to the settling of the state.

MORMONS IN CARSON VALLEY, 1851-1857

No group of American pioneers was more daring or more devoted than the members of the Church of Jesus Christ of Latter-Day Saints (Mormons) who established the first settlements in Utah and later in Nevada. There had been much suffering and many sacrifices among the Mormons before they came to the Far West; they had fled into the western deserts to escape the hatred and the attacks of their fellow Americans.

The religion of the Mormons seemed strange to most Americans of the 1830's and 1840's. They claimed to have newer and better revelations than the traditional Christian churches, and they believed that their leader, Joseph Smith, was a modern-day prophet, like the prophets of the Old Testament. Joseph Smith, they said, had been visited by an angel, had been given some sacred golden plates, and had translated a new holy message for the world. He claimed that much of the old Christian doctrine was in error.

The Mormon converts not only accepted Smith's spiritual messages enthusiastically, but they also organized their daily lives around his teachings. They were ambitious, hard-working people who prospered nearly everywhere they settled. They worked together well and cared for the needy within their group. They spent so much time together in their work, worship, and social activities that they had little time for the non-Mormons, or "gentiles." Many persons resented their unusual religious ideas and their clannishness when they established their first community in Kirtland, Ohio. Because of the resentment against them and the threats to their lives and property, many Mormons moved from Ohio to Missouri, only to find more trouble and resentment from their neighbors. They moved once more, this time to Illinois, where they created the city of Nauvoo.

The Mormons had good fortune at Nauvoo for a while. They built a pleasant and successful city; in the early 1840's it seemed likely to outgrow Chicago. But once more many "gentiles" suspected the Mormons and envied their success. The Latter-Day Saints were becoming politically powerful; they were eagerly seeking to win converts to their church, and wild rumors were circulating about them. All this provoked raids on Mormon homes and property, and the Latter-Day Saints in turn wrecked some of the property of their enemies. Eventually, Joseph Smith was arrested, thrown into a jail at Carthage, Illinois, and murdered by an unruly mob. The community which the Mormons had established at Nauvoo was no longer safe for them by the middle of the 1840's.

The new leader of the Mormons was a strong, exciting man who had made a reputation as a missionary in England. Brigham Young had a natural talent for leading men, and most Mormons accepted him as the successor to their original prophet. Young had read some of Frémont's reports about the Far West and decided that the Mormons must travel there—across a thousand miles of uninhabited land—to gain peace and safety. In 1846 he moved part of his followers into Missouri and Iowa—at the edge of civilization—and in 1847 their first great migration across the plains and mountains began. Young and the first group of Mormons reached the valley of the Great Salt Lake in July, 1847. They had gone so far to the west that they were beyond the borders of the United States; Mexico still controlled the region, although she was to lose it in the following year. Mexico had done nothing to explore or settle this part of the Great Basin.

The story of the Mormons in the Salt Lake Valley is one of dedication, courage, and hard work. There was hunger and suffering in the beginning, but the leadership of Young and the coöperative spirit of the members enabled them to conquer the desert. They soon had established themselves so completely that they could encourage thousands of additional converts to join them. For two years they had little contact with non-Mormons, but in 1849 they were visited by the famous Forty-Niners rushing to California to seek their fortunes. The Mormons sold food to many of the gold-rush parties. Some of Brigham Young's flock even joined in the rush, but he managed to keep most of his followers in Salt Lake City in 1849 and in subsequent years as more gold hunters passed through Utah. In 1850, one group of residents in Salt Lake City set out for California, but part of them decided on their way that they could make more money by selling supplies to the travelers than by searching for gold. These men established the first settlement of any kind in Nevada—a crude trading station near the eastern slopes of the Sierra Nevada. The clerk of the group was a man named H. S. Beatie.

Beatie's station was established near the present town of Genoa. He chose this location because it was near the Carson River, which most of the emigrants of 1850 followed. This was a good place for a trading post, because most emigrants needed supplies after they

had crossed the desert and before they entered the rugged mountains. Beatie and his companions could buy bacon and flour in
California for a reasonable price, carry it across the mountains to
their station on mules, and then trade it or sell it to the tired,
hungry travelers. At times, the emigrants were willing to trade a
horse or cow for some food, because many animals which they had
brought were exhausted after their trip across the desert.

Beatie and his companions did not plan to stay in Carson Valley
permanently; they did not even build a permanent house. They got
along with only a small log enclosure without a roof or floor. They
lived in the open during that summer season when the emigrants
were traveling, and then they left. But they had learned that there
was a need for a station near the eastern slopes of the Sierra
Nevada. A year later, another party of Mormons profited from this
lesson.

Before this second group of Mormon traders went to Carson
Valley, some important political events had occurred in Washington. In 1850, Congress decided that California had enough people
to be admitted as a state. At the same time, the territories of Utah
and New Mexico were created by Congress in the desert regions
which had recently been obtained from Mexico. The Territory of
Utah was extremely large, including the present state of Utah, most
of Nevada, and parts of Colorado and Wyoming. Congress included
all of this land in Utah Territory because it seemed best to govern
it from Salt Lake City. Brigham Young became the first territorial
governor.

In the spring of 1851, about twenty Salt Lake City businessmen,
including a man named John Reese, established another trading
station near the Sierra Nevada. They reached the Carson Valley
on Independence Day and began to plow the land, build fences,
and erect a fort against Indian raids, and perhaps even against
some of the emigrant trains. This fort was the first substantial building to be erected in Nevada. A replica of it can be seen on the site
of the original fort, where a state park is presently maintained.

The busy settlers got some of their supplies from California to
sell to the emigrants, and augmented them by planting a garden.
Soon they had a little community which they called Mormon Sta-

tion, and in a few weeks they had an important trading post in operation. They found a ready market for their merchandise and vegetables among the emigrants from the east and among prospectors from California who were beginning to search for gold near the Carson River.

One party of men who had come over the mountains from California had been disappointed with the results of their panning and decided to establish another station. In the fall of 1851, they settled about ten miles north of Mormon Station in an adjacent valley. They claimed some land, although it was late in the year for crops. Settling approximately where the Nevada state capitol building now stands, they called the region Eagle Valley when they shot an eagle and nailed its feathers to the door of their crude house.

Only a few men now lived in the extreme western part of Utah Territory, but enough to create a need for law and order. The settlers in western Utah were so far separated from the territorial capital in Fillmore City that they could not depend on the authorities there to enforce laws; it required several weeks to travel to the territorial capital. Sacramento, the capital of California, was beyond the mountains over a difficult road, and the officials there had no right to enforce the law in western Utah anyway. Thus, the pioneers in and around Carson Valley were beyond the reach of the law.

If a settler decided to cultivate some land and build a house, how could he prove that it was his property? How could he file a claim to it, unless he went to Fillmore City; then how could he describe where it was? If someone stole his horse or his tools, how could the settler get legal action? No sheriff or court existed and no record books were being kept in the region. The first Nevadans had to be pioneers of government and law, as well as pioneers of the land.

Just as the pilgrims who came to America in the Mayflower in 1620 signed an agreement for self-government—the Mayflower Compact—because they could not depend on the laws or officers of England, so the first settlers in Nevada had to arrange for a government that would suit their needs. In November, 1851, they held three meetings at Mormon Station and established a plan for surveying the land, for making formal records when they claimed some ground, and for settling disputes in a small court which they

Mormon Fort, Genoa, built in 1851

created. This was a "squatters' government" with a few officials appointed to keep the peace and to settle land disputes. It was a crude government in many respects, and some prospectors and settlers outside Carson Valley ignored it, but the Mormons in Carson Valley found it useful for several years.

Many residents wanted Congress to create a separate territory of western Utah. They sent a message to Washington asking for this, but since so few people lived in the region, no one in Washington took this petition seriously. In the next few years, however, as more people moved into the valleys on the eastern edge of the Sierra Nevada, the demand for more government became greater. Some newcomers who arrived from California after 1851 felt they could get better laws and officers from Sacramento than from the "squatters' government" or from the territorial government of Utah. In 1853, forty-three settlers signed a petition asking the California legislature to annex their valleys and to enforce California law.

When Governor Brigham Young and other Mormon leaders learned of this petition, they realized that some of Utah Territory might be lost, reducing the amount of land under Mormon jurisdiction. To prevent this, Young decided to establish a county government in western Utah to provide more official services for the residents, and to send more Mormons into the region near the Sierra Nevada to make the claim of the Territory of Utah more secure. In 1854, the Utah legislature created Carson County in the extreme western part of the territory.

Next, Governor Young selected Orson Hyde, one of the most prominent men in the church, to serve as probate judge, to organize Carson County, and to act as spiritual leader of the communities within it. Judge Hyde reached Carson Valley in June of 1855 and arranged for an election under the laws of Utah Territory. The old "squatters' government" disappeared, although some of its records were recognized by Carson County.

Judge Hyde quickly began to change things in the new region. He and the new Mormon settlers were soon making claims all along the California boundary near the main emigrant trails. Hyde surveyed the old Mormon Station in Carson Valley and renamed it Genoa, which became the county seat. He founded the new community of Franktown in Washoe Valley, about 25 miles north of Genoa, and he built a sawmill to provide lumber for homes. About sixty or seventy Mormon families came into Carson County in 1855 and 1856, settling a number of the rich valleys near the Sierra Nevada. The members of the church now outnumbered the non-Mormons who had wanted separation from Utah Territory. Many of the non-Mormons resented Hyde and his county government, and some disapproved of the Mormon religion in general. By the time Judge Hyde had been in Carson County for a year, much antagonism had developed between the church members and the "gentiles."

In spite of the tension, matters seemed to be going well for the dozens of Latter-Day Saint families in Carson County in 1856. Successful gardens had been planted and prosperous homes were appearing. In the autumn of that year, however, Judge Hyde was suddenly recalled to Salt Lake City to assume new responsibilities and the Utah legislature soon abolished most of the government at Genoa and decided that Carson County would be governed from Salt Lake City.

The reason for this change of policy was that Governor Young and the Mormon Church were having difficulties with the federal government in Washington. Federal authorities felt that the Mormons were defying national laws, and some emigrants had complained that the Mormons had cheated or mistreated them. Also, the Mormon leaders were practicing polygamy, which provoked much resentment in the East. Many rumors circulated about the "wickedness" of the Latter-Day Saints, and no one in the national government bothered to check on these matters. Governor Young expected more serious trouble with the federal government and did not want church members scattered too widely. In the summer of 1857, the Mormons learned that part of the United States Army was marching from the great plains toward Utah to enforce federal law.

Most Mormons believed the army was coming to destroy their homes and to kill their leaders. Confusion and excitement spread through Utah Territory, and the church members prepared to fight for their land. Among the preparations was a call to all of the Saints living far from Salt Lake City to abandon their homes and farms and return to that community. Such a message went to the settlers near the Sierra Nevada in the late summer.

All faithful Mormons in western Utah hastened to help their leader. On September 22, 1857, about one hundred thirty loaded wagons began the long trek from Carson Valley toward Salt Lake City, carrying most of the Mormon population of Carson County. They left valuable property and bountiful gardens, which were taken over by Indians, "gentiles," and the few Latter-Day Saints who would not obey the call.

The scores of families who left their homes in 1857 were never needed in Salt Lake City. The Mormon leaders and the federal government settled their differences peacefully and the army caused no serious trouble for the church. Brigham Young was removed as governor of the territory, but he retained his great prestige and authority as president of the church.

Most Mormons who went back to Salt Lake City, however, did not return to western Utah. They made new homes elsewhere, and most of them lost their property in Carson County. They had left Carson County without any effective government, and for the next two years only about a hundred to two hundred people—mostly prospectors looking for gold—remained in the region.

LAS VEGAS MISSION, 1855-1858

During part of the time the Mormons lived in western Utah, some of their fellow church members were operating a different kind of outpost in another part of the region which would eventually become Nevada. In 1855, during the same week that Orson Hyde and his companions arrived in Carson Valley, another group from Salt Lake City entered the Las Vegas Valley, more than 400 miles to the southeast, to establish a settlement.

The Mormons who settled in Las Vegas Valley had a different kind of assignment than Judge Hyde's party. They had no responsibility to form a county government; their primary work was to be religious, not political. Those who went to Las Vegas had been instructed to build a mission and to teach their faith to the Indians.

Undoubtedly, the church leaders hoped that the establishment of the mission would give them a claim to the region, and they also intended this settlement to be a rest station for persons who traveled between Salt Lake City and southern California. Primarily, however, it was a unit of the church, directly controlled by President Young.

In the spring of 1855, the church sent twenty-nine men to found the mission although this meant that they would have to leave the homes which they had started only a few years before. Church authorities said that wives and children must be left behind while the mission was being established. President Young selected William Bringhurst to act as president of the mission, with complete authority over all affairs. Bringhurst, like Hyde, proved to be an energetic leader.

The trip from Salt Lake City to Las Vegas required thirty-five days—approximately the same length of time as a journey from Salt Lake City to Genoa. With today's automobiles and highways, the same trip takes about eight hours. The most difficult part of their trek was the crossing of 50 miles of arid land northeast of the Las Vegas Valley, which resembled the dreaded Forty-Mile Desert between the Humboldt and Carson rivers. The cool waters of Las Vegas spring were most welcome when the missionaries arrived in mid-June.

On the first day after the twenty-nine pioneers arrived, they built a small bower for religious services. On the next day, they began to divide the land for farming and to build a fort. Each man had a small plot for a garden, but each also had responsibilities for building the fort and performing other duties for the mission. Almost immediately Bringhurst and his men became friendly with the Indians; the entire history of the mission was peaceful, even though the Indians often stole food and cattle.

These hardy church men had to overcome a host of difficulties in building a settlement in this hot, isolated valley. For the first few weeks, they had little to eat except bread. The high temperatures made it impossible to work for many hours of the day, and there were no trees nearby for shade or shelter. Bringhurst sent a party of men into the mountains to the west in search of timber, which they found about twenty miles from the Las Vegas spring. Since no roads existed, it was tedious work to haul the timber to the mission site. Most of the original fences for gardens and fields were constructed with mesquite brush, and the missionaries used adobe mud as the main building material for their fort.

Aside from the physical difficulties, these first settlers found Las Vegas to be a depressing place because it was so isolated. The mail arrived from Utah only once a month, and many missionaries longed for their families. Bringhurst constantly urged them to keep busy with their gardens and other improvements; he presided with a firm hand and managed to get most of the men to work well together. A few quarrels and disagreements occurred, and a very small number left the mission before the end of the year, but most of the original settlers remained, steadfastly devoted to their assignment.

The harvest of this first year brought several disappointments. On one occasion, a party of emigrants had gone through the valley on its way to California, and some of their cattle had broken into the Mormons' fields and eaten much of the corn. Blackbirds damaged other crops, and the Indians took even more of the precious vegetables. In spite of this, the mission harvested enough food to sustain its members during the winter, and they felt they had been blessed.

The missionaries only managed to build part of their fort during the first year, but they erected houses before winter and they won praise from President Young for their diligence.

In the following year, the mission began to take on an appearance of permanence. The fort was completed and several missionaries brought their families to the valley. They cultivated two crops of grain and vegetables, and this would have assured an adequate surplus if there had not been a new, heavy burden placed on the little community.

While exploring the desert and mountain regions around Las Vegas in 1856, the Mormons had learned that lead ore existed in the vicinity. (They did not know that the ore also contained silver; this was only discovered in later years.) When the church authorities in Salt Lake City heard about this natural resource, they decided to develop it so that the Mormons would not have to transport lead from the East. President Young sent five men to Las Vegas, led by Nathaniel V. Jones, with instructions to mine the ore and to obtain the necessary workers from the mission. Bringhurst disliked this arrangement, because it would take his men away from their tasks at the mission. Soon he and Jones were engaged in a bitter quarrel. For several weeks the dispute continued, until a message came from President Young, ordering Bringhurst and his mission to give supplies and aid to Jones; it was evident that Jones had more authority than Bringhurst in this case.

This incident was an important turning point in the history of the mission. From this time until the mission was abolished two years later, the church made heavy demands on its members. The missionaries could not produce crops for themselves and the mining operation and carry on extensive religious work among the Indians and still have a thriving mission; fewer than a hundred persons lived at the mission. Insects and Indians continued to damage the crops, and by the late summer, Bringhurst told Jones that he could not supply any more provisions for the mines.

To add to his troubles, Jones learned that the lead ore would not be easy to mine or refine. He had expected to build a furnace near the mines by using rocks, but he found it could not be built without equipment from Salt Lake City. Late in 1856, he returned to church headquarters and made a report to President Young. Much of the blame for his failure must have fallen on Bringhurst, because President Young promptly removed him and placed another missionary, Samuel Thompson, in his place.

These quarrels and the troubles with the crops discouraged some of the missionaries and caused many of them to want to leave. This was about the same time that President Young began to be disappointed in the colonies near the Sierra Nevada. Early in 1857, he announced that the church members assigned to Las Vegas were released from their mission and were free to leave. Apparently some missionaries were still dedicated to the idea of converting the Indians, and they stayed through 1858, raising more crops and cattle. In the autumn of that year, however, the Indians stole nearly their entire crop, and the last Mormons decided to abandon the mission entirely. The mining operation also proved unsuccessful and was abandoned.

The site of the old mission was acquired by a rancher named O. D. Gass, and for a brief time during the Civil War a few army troops were stationed there to protect the mail route to California from the Indians. For more than thirty years, Las Vegas was only a ranch and had little part in shaping the destiny of Nevada. In one sense, the Mormon mission had failed; but it had proved once more that the remote desert regions could be conquered and cultivated.

Even though the Mormons withdrew in 1857 and 1858 from the area that would one day be known as Nevada, this did not mean they would forget about it. Only a few years later they would send a second wave of settlers to the south and west into the Colorado River basin.

GOLD CANYON MINERS, 1851-1858

The sturdy farmers and traders who made homes in Carson Valley had little in common with the rough miners who panned for gold in the nearby hills. Many miners were neither industrious nor trustworthy, and troubles developed between them and the Mormons. The miners were often disrespectful of government in general and certainly did not want to be governed by members of a religious sect.

It is generally believed that a group of Mormons made the first discovery of gold in western Utah Territory. In 1850, one year before the founding of Mormon Station by John Reese, some men from Salt Lake City were traveling down the Carson River on their way to California. Two young men in the party, John Orr and William Prouse, washed some of the sand in the river near the present site of Dayton and found specks of gold in the bottom of their pans. They explored the nearby gully, later to be named Gold Canyon, and discovered a small gold nugget. But they and their party went on to California, not bothering to pan any more gold or to explore the nearby hills.

The Mormons did not keep their discovery a secret, and soon reports were circulating in California and among the emigrants.

A few people tried to extract some gold near the Carson River at various times during the summer of 1850, but apparently none spent much energy or time at Gold Canyon. All departed before the winter season arrived.

If there was gold along the river and in Gold Canyon, why did no one take it seriously in 1850? If a nugget had been found, why did so little exploring take place in that year? We must remember that most of the emigrants knew little or nothing about panning gold, and they had a strong fear of the desert region. Also, the reports of California's riches were so exciting that no one was willing to be sidetracked by a few yellow specks in a dusty gully. So only in 1851—the same year as the founding of Mormon Station —did some miners from California begin to prospect in earnest in Gold Canyon.

We do not know much about the life of the miners in Gold Canyon from 1851 to 1858; most of them did not keep records or diaries, and they came and went so often that no permanent society developed. Perhaps about two hundred men lived in or near Gold Canyon during the summer months of those years, but they did not form a true community because they wandered widely and had little common activity. The prospectors spent most of their time panning, using the little stream in the canyon. When they had washed all the sand near the stream, they would carry more from nearby gullies to the creek for washing. Of course, this became tedious work, and "pay dirt" became harder to find as the years passed. Until 1858 the average miner could usually pan four or five dollars' worth of gold in a day, and this was an attractive income in the 1850's. By panning this much gold in the summer, a man could live a more idle life in the winter, perhaps in California, and then return to his prospecting in the summer. This pattern appealed to the adventurous, outdoor type of men who roamed the Far West in those years.

Most Gold Canyon miners in the 1850's lived in little huts made of sagebrush and juniper trees, but a few built houses from stones and mud or canvas. Not many of the houses were stable and none could be called luxurious, because no one planned to stay there long. Apparently none of them had glass for windows; usually there was only a door. Some miners had small stoves, but most of them relied on crude fireplaces for cooking or heating. Their diet consisted largely of potatoes, salted bacon, bread, and the meat of wild animals. Potatoes and wheat could be purchased from the farmers in Carson Valley and by the middle of the 1850's a few stations existed along the emigrant trails where items of food could be bought. Eventually, a small community developed at Johntown, about two miles from the mouth of the canyon near the Carson River. Another supply point grew up on the Carson River a few miles away. At first it was called Hall's Station and later miners called it Chinatown. Eventually, it was renamed Dayton. These places became important in serving the needs of the miners, but Gold Canyon was remote from most of the niceties of civilization.

For about seven years, the men who roamed the hills near Gold Canyon were interested only in gold. It did not occur to most of them that silver might exist in the region. Two ambitious young brothers named Allen and Hosea Grosh may have identified silver in some of the rocks in 1856 and 1857, but they kept their findings secret from the rest of the miners. Both men died in the winter of 1857-1858, and only many years later did their letters show that they had searched for silver. Perhaps the Grosh brothers actually found the multimillion dollar Comstock Lode, but if they did, they never informed the world of it and they are not usually given credit for the discovery.

Two odd, unreliable desert wanderers finally got most of the glory for uncovering the fantastic wealth of the lode. One was James Finney, whose real name may have been James Fennimore; he probably was living in the mountains because the sheriffs were after him in California. The other was Henry P. Comstock, a Canadian who had tried his hand at fur-trapping, trading with the Indians, and panning for gold in many parts of the West.

Finney, nicknamed "Old Virginia," was exploring the hills at the head of Gold Canyon in the winter of 1858-1859 when he found a mound, soon to be named Gold Hill, which seemed to be a good prospect. Until then, the miners had not considered the possibility of digging into the mountain for gold; they had been satisfied with panning the dirt on the surface. But Finney and three partners began to excavate and found the earth underneath to be richer in gold. They had to wait until the spring of 1859 to begin serious work, but after they had dug several feet they struck a solid quartzite ledge which contained much gold. They had uncovered the Comstock Lode.

Even before, while they were still panning the earth at Gold Hill, Finney and his partners aroused much excitement. They had staked out placer claims around their discovery and circulated the news at Johntown. Soon dozens of other miners came up the canyon and staked claims, and others began to search elsewhere for similar hills.

Two Irish miners, Patrick McLaughlin and Peter O'Riley, were among those who were looking for new quantities of rich sand and began working in a ravine known as Six-Mile Canyon, a short distance to the north of Gold Canyon. On June 12 or 13, 1859, they discovered a spot from which much flickering gold could be easily panned; it was only about a mile north of the Gold Hill discovery on the side of Sun Mountain (or Mount Davidson). While they were washing the glittering dust, old Henry Comstock, a lazy, loud-mouthed wanderer, appeared. When he saw their gold, he claimed that they were on his "ranch," although no one had ever tried to cultivate or raise stock on that dry mountain. Comstock made such a clamor that O'Riley and McLaughlin decided to give him a share of their claim. But Comstock wanted more; he demanded shares for his friend, "Old Virginia," and for another pal named Emanuel Penrod. Before the meeting had ended, O'Riley and McLaughlin had bargained away much of their discovery.

If this sounds like foolish business on the part of O'Riley and McLaughlin, it should be remembered that they had no idea that this pocket of dirt would be much different from any gold-bearing spot in the region. They could not have known that this ground would soon be famous across America as the fabulously rich Ophir claim. During the 1850's, it had not been unusual for the miners to share ground or to work together in their panning, and the two Irishmen probably thought it would be easier to give Comstock and his friends a share than to have trouble. McLaughlin and O'Riley had unknowingly discovered another outcropping of the

Drawing of Old Comstock discovering silver

lode. They managed to keep their discovery a secret for a few days, but finally when the word spread, Comstock boastfully called it his lode. Although he did not deserve the credit, the name stuck.

As the miners at the Ophir dug into the dry, rocky mountain during the next few days, they began to have trouble; as they washed the dirt they noticed a heavy black mud which made it difficult to separate the gold from the rest of the earth. The miners in Gold Canyon had never encountered mud of this kind, and the prospectors at the Ophir were disgusted. Before the end of the summer, however, they had startling news: some of their rock containing the black earth had been carried to California, and, after analysis, it proved to be rich in silver. The first assays showed that thousands of dollars worth of gold and silver could be extracted from a single ton of Ophir ore. The black mud was more valuable than the gold.

"Old Virginia," Comstock, and their partners had struck it rich; they did not know how rich. It took several months to determine that there were millions of dollars worth of ore in the Comstock Lode, and by that time nearly all earlier discoverers had sold their interests. None of them became wealthy, and only a few of the old Gold Canyon prospectors managed to keep their claims on valuable ground. The old timers were soon outnumbered. Most of the Comstock Lode fell into the hands of new men from California who developed the mines, created a marvelous city, and soon added a new star to the nation's flag.

6. Early Mining Booms, Statehood, 1859-1864

DURING THE DECADE OF THE 1860's, permanence and technology reached Nevada and began to transform it into a segment of civilized America. The explorers and pioneers of the 1840's had merely been travelers, trying to get across unwanted lands. Likewise, the farmers, traders, and miners of the 1850's had for the most part been only temporary residents, coming and going and providing little basis for a permanent society. After the discovery of the Comstock Lode in 1859, however, the pattern began to change and Nevada became important to the nation politically and financially.

In the 1860's, Nevada experienced the beginnings of an industrial and social revolution. The mining and processing of the Comstock's ores required special engineering skills, and the wealth of the mines led to the establishment of exciting, boisterous "Wild West" communities on the slopes of Mt. Davidson. Virginia City became one of the most remarkable places in America. Several men of outstanding abilities were attracted there. Soon prospectors who had arrived too late on the Comstock Lode were spreading out to other areas of the Great Basin, founding new towns and incidentally giving shape to the future state of Nevada.

In the meantime, some of the companions of the miners set about creating a government for the new society. They acted with unprecedented speed. Less than two years after the discovery of the Ophir ore, Nevada had a territorial government, and less than four years after that it was a full-fledged, dynamic state in the Union, contributing important political support to the federal government in the bitter Civil War. Under much pressure Nevada came of age rapidly in the years between 1859 and 1864.

THE RUSH TO WASHOE, 1860-1862

The rush from California to the Comstock Lode began in a small way in 1859. Several hundred men came over the mountains in a frenzy, staked claims wildly, and gouged a few small holes in the mountainside. Some sagebrush and canvas shacks appeared along the lode between the Ophir and Gold Hill, but winter came before most of the miners could find much ore or build suitable homes. Only in 1860 did the first big influx of wealth seekers reach Mt. Davidson. In 1859, they had come by the hundreds; in the following year they came by the thousands.

The problems of trying to bring to this desert land the technology for mastering the ore and the civilization to erect a city were staggering. The silver had to be separated from the worthless rock and then processed, and few men knew how to mine it or to refine it. The mines were high in the mountains—more than a mile above sea level—and isolated by both the forbidding desert and the lofty Sierra Nevada. Almost no water was available near the mines during most of the year, and the few small trees in the region could not supply the need for fuel and lumber. The rocky slopes seemed to defy road building, yet nearly all necessities had to be hauled for considerable distances, and the important equipment and supplies had to come, at great expense, from California.

Of the thousands of men who came to the Comstock Lode in 1860, only a few were miners. Instead, businessmen, gamblers, and speculators began to give the region its first appearance of permanence. As they built saloons, provision stores, and crude hotels, the towns of Virginia City and Gold Hill emerged. Hundreds of freight wagons and pack mules struggled through the mountains during the spring, summer, and autumn, carrying supplies. In California, this exodus came to be known as the "Rush to Washoe," since the entire region was named for the Washo Indians who lived there. By the end of the summer, substantial wooden houses had arisen, and more than a hundred business establishments of various kinds had been erected in Virginia City. Most of the men who came to stake out a rich mine were disappointed, but many of those who came to gamble, speculate, or run a business became prosperous.

The men who poured into Virginia City and Gold Hill came from every state in the nation and from many parts of the world. Nearly all were men with a wandering spirit, and few of them had wives or homes. Many had seen violent, reckless living in the goldfields of California, and there were few tender feelings among them. Many fell ill and died because of bad water, exposure, and lack of proper care, and no one gave the matter much thought. Shootings and brawls were frequent, and there were no marshals or sheriffs to keep order during those early months. Hundreds of men, becoming disgusted or frightened, left with the feeling that there was no future in such a barren, lawless place.

Among the men who swarmed like insects over Mt. Davidson were a few persons of ability and determination who began to bring order into the chaos. One of them was a powerful, 200-pound figure named William Stewart. A lawyer who had been trained at Yale university and who had become prominent in California legal and mining circles, Stewart commanded respect for his knowledge as well as for his husky frame. He won the trust of most mine owners and persuaded many of them to let him settle their differences peacefully. When a judge of Utah Territory, John S. Child, tried to reorganize Carson County in the summer of 1860, he made Stewart the prosecuting attorney. It was during this time that Stewart won a wide reputation for his courage when he faced down badman Sam Brown with a pair of derringers.

The Comstockers did not submit to Utah's authority, but they did show deference to Stewart on most matters. When a federal judge was appointed to hold court in western Utah Territory in the summer of 1860, Stewart was one of the leaders in insisting that the judge's authority be recognized. This brilliant, tough-minded lawyer was to reappear many times in the story of Nevada; he was a leader in territorial and state politics for more than forty years.

Another of the men in the early stampede to Washoe was John W. Mackay, an Irish-born miner. He had been panning for gold in the Sierra Nevada foothills for several years with only moderate success, and his imagination caught fire at the news of silver on the Comstock Lode. Rushing over the mountains, he reached Virginia City with little property and no money. He organized a company with a few other miners, worked in vain on a piece of ground of little value, and finally had to take a pick-and-shovel mining job for four dollars a day. Most of the prospectors who came to Washoe either had to settle for something like this or leave the district. Mackay had more ambition than most of his associates, and he was willing to learn. These traits paid him high rewards in later years.

The first Comstock mines offered many challenges for skilled men. As the Ophir mine extended further down into the earth— reaching a depth of fifty feet in April, 1860—it became increasingly difficult to mine the ore without causing a cave-in. Many accidents occurred as the shafts were sunk, and some miners were killed or injured by falling rocks. Mine owners and workers were groping for a solution to the problem when Philipp Deidesheimer, an engineer from Germany, appeared on the Comstock. Like Mackay, Deidesheimer was an immigrant and a man of imagination. He invented a new system of timbering the mines, known as the square-set method, which safely supported the walls of the excavation while ore was being extracted. This solved one of the earliest problems which troubled the mining community.

Deidesheimer also provided the guidance needed for raising the mineral from ever-increasing depths and for getting rid of the large amounts of underground water which were soon encountered. He told the owners of the Ophir they would have to spend money for heavy machinery to hoist the ore and to pump the water. Although the owners were reluctant at first, they eventually accepted Deide-

Drawing of "The Rush to Washoe"

sheimer's suggestions. Other mines along the lode followed the example, and soon the slopes of Mt. Davidson bristled with hundreds of complicated pieces of machinery. The industrial revolution had come to Nevada.

Philipp Deidesheimer was not the only German immigrant who influenced the history of Virginia City with his ideas. Among the pioneers of 1860 was Adolph Sutro, a brilliant businessman who had spent several years trading and speculating in California. Soon after he arrived, Sutro began to develop theories about how to mine the ore on a larger scale and how to build mills and smelters to refine it. Some of the richest ores were being shipped all the way to England for smelting in 1860, and some of the less valuable ore went to California by costly freight teams. Sutro decided to build a mill and smelter along the Carson River, a few miles east of the mountains.

A few months later, Sutro financed a mill near the Carson River and went into the business of processing ores. Scores of other promoters had the same idea. In 1861, so many mills had been constructed in and around Virginia City and Gold Hill that there was not enough ore to keep them busy. Investors like Sutro had bought much expensive equipment that could not be used, and most of them lost money; Sutro's mill prospered for a time, but eventually became unprofitable. Later, it was destroyed by fire.

Another of Sutro's grandiose dreams was to dig an incredible tunnel from near the Carson River into the heart of Mt. Davidson. The tunnel would be four miles long and would strike the Comstock Lode deep beneath the earth. Sutro argued that this would make it easier to remove the ore by draining the water from the mines. No one paid much attention to him when he first proposed this idea; it seemed too wild and unrealistic. A few years later, however, he made the Congress of the United States and some of the biggest financial houses in the world give consideration and support to his idea and his ambitious dream became a reality.

Few of the early Comstockers were as talented as Stewart, Mackay, Deidesheimer, and Sutro. They became the leaders of the new society because of their special, constructive abilities. By contrast, a totally different breed of men also arrived. Virginia City had its bad men, who for a brief time ranged without respect for law or decency. One of the most infamous was "Fightin' Sam Brown," an outlaw who was said to have killed more than a dozen men in Texas and California. Soon after arriving in the camp, he was reported to have stabbed a man to death in a saloon, carved out his heart, and then gone to sleep on a billiard table. He murdered several other defenseless men without cause, but was not even arrested. Finally, in the summer of 1861, he tried to kill Henry Van Sickle, a Carson Valley innkeeper. This time, he chose the wrong victim. After a wild flight and chase, Sam Brown was shot down by Van Sickle, who became a local hero.

Nearly all early residents of the Comstock, from the brilliant personalities like Stewart and Sutro to the rough desperados like Sam Brown, shared a sense of high adventure. They dreamed of great wealth and expected high drama, and from time to time their expectations were fulfilled.

THE PYRAMID LAKE WAR, 1860

One example of how excitable the early Comstockers were is the story of the Pyramid Lake Indian War. It is a gruesome reminder of the dangerous power of rumor.

On the Carson River about thirty miles east of Virginia City, a man named James Williams had established a trading station. During the spring of 1860, three other men, including a brother of Williams, were living at the station. While James Williams was away early in May, the men kidnapped two young Indian women and held them prisoner. Some of the Indians came looking for the women. They attacked the station, killed the three men, and burned the buildings. When James Williams returned to his station and found the ruin, he sent word to Virginia City that the Paiutes were on the warpath and that a terrible slaughter had occurred.

When the news reached the Comstock Lode and nearby communities, no one bothered to check the details. A few men urged caution and cool-headedness, but their voices were drowned by scores of others who spread rumors that a dozen white men had been killed and that five hundred Indians were on the warpath.

News spread to the nearby valleys—to Genoa and to the young community of Carson City in Eagle Valley. Men began to form military companies to meet the expected attacks from the Indians. When all companies had been formed and assembled, there were one hundred and five men ready for battle. Many were badly prepared for a fight, with poor horses and little equipment, and they had no single leader whom they all recognized and respected. Major William Ormsby of Carson City was an informal commander, but no discipline existed in the ranks. Many were simply rowdy young men, some not yet twenty years old, who wanted an adventure. A few openly said they wanted to steal Indian horses and women. Others felt that their communities were in danger.

As so often in incidents of this nature, one spark ignited a chain of tragic events. Learning that the white men had gathered a volunteer army, the Indians amassed for their own protection. The emotions of fear and revenge brought to the surface all the suppressed ranklings that white men and Indians felt for each other in this frontier day.

The march of the white men toward Pyramid Lake led to the most bloody slaughter in Nevada history. On May 12, advancing down the Truckee River toward the lake, they encountered a band of Indians and made a wild charge. In a few minutes, the little makeshift army found itself in a trap, surrounded by armed Indian warriors. The white men tried to retreat, but those who escaped the trap were pursued by the Indians. Seventy-six men, including Major Ormsby, lost their lives and the other twenty-nine returned beaten and wounded to tell of the horror.

The fright and hysteria multiplied several times over in Virginia City, Carson City, and elsewhere on the eastern slopes of the Sierra Nevada. It was feared that the Indian warriors would soon assault the towns. Women and children were taken to safe places in the nearby valleys or were put in the buildings which seemed most stable. At Silver City, a new community in Gold Canyon, the men built a fort and tried to fabricate a wooden cannon. Pleas for help went out to California, and companies began to form in Sacramento and elsewhere. Hundreds of newcomers to the Washoe region, feeling that these precautions were not enough, fled back over the mountains to California.

In their preparations for the second battle against the Indians, the settlers took more care than the first group had done. They obtained five hundred muskets from the governor of California, they got help from the U.S. Army, and they organized into efficient companies. When the second march toward Pyramid Lake began on May 24, there were more than two hundred regular soldiers and more than five hundred volunteers. The Paiutes were badly outnumbered in this encounter. In the battle which occurred a few days later, nearly one hundred and sixty Indians were killed; the whites lost only three or four men.

The Pyramid Lake Indian War was not an admirable chapter in the history of the early pioneers, but it must be remembered that only much later did all the facts become known. Many who participated felt they were fighting for a noble cause, although others obviously were seeking glory or plunder.

The scare caused by the Pyramid Lake battles did not pass away immediately. For several months, the Indians were still regarded as a menace. Troops of the U.S. Army built a small base near the Carson River which they named Fort Churchill, and garrisons remained there for several years to prevent further trouble. The Indians, however, never sought revenge for the second battle, and the white men had established their supremacy.

THE BUILDING OF TOWNS, 1860-1863

The discovery of the Comstock Lode not only led to the building of Virginia City and Gold Hill, but contributed to the establishment of new communities in other parts of western Utah and to the rapid development of some towns which had already been born.

Among the men who saw the lode and the surrounding area in the early 1860's were J. Ross Browne, a witty traveler who had visited many parts of the globe, and Samuel Clemens, who was at the beginning of the career which would make him famous throughout the world as Mark Twain. Browne came to "Washoe" in 1860 and Clemens arrived in 1861; their books give us priceless accounts of frontier life of that era.

When Browne came over the Sierra Nevada from California, as

thousands of others were to do, the first town he saw was Genoa. He noticed that the little community did not seem very prosperous; since the Mormons had left, it had not quite been the same. Only two or three hundred people lived there, most of them storekeepers, sawmill workers, and teamsters. Some residents of Genoa claimed to have rich silver mines nearby, but they probably told such stories to get the attention—and perhaps the money—of the newcomers.

Browne may not have known that Genoa still had some importance, at least theoretically, as the seat of Carson County. Later in the year, a county judge appointed by the governor of Utah Territory held court there, and a federal judge named John Cradlebaugh tried to keep law and order in Washoe, using Genoa as his headquarters. But the need of life had quickened so much in the newer communities that Nevada's oldest town could not long claim the governmental offices.

As Browne passed north from Carson Valley he came to the young community which would soon replace Genoa as the political center. Carson City, which during the next year would become the territorial capital, seemed to be a "pretty and thrifty little town" in 1860. The silver rush was causing much excitement and prosperity; hotels and stores were under construction in many places. It had several hundred residents.

Carson City had existed for about a year and a half by the time Browne visited it. The founder was Abraham Curry, an ambitious businessman, who had come to western Utah Territory in 1858 to establish a store. When he found lots at Genoa too expensive for his pocketbook, he told the local citizens he would create his own town, and he bought the Eagle Ranch for this purpose. Although few settlers remained in the region in that year (the Mormons were gone and the mining rush was still a year away) Curry surveyed a town and offered lots to emigrants and local residents. In laying out his town, Curry left a plaza in the center, where he predicted a state capitol would someday stand. He was so energetic in publicizing the town that he made his boast come true. He formed an effective pioneer-style chamber of commerce.

So Carson City had a good start when the prospectors of 1860— Browne included—came pouring into Washoe. Browne found that the "city" already had a newspaper, called the *Territorial Enter-prise* (founded in Genoa and later moved to Carson City) which gave a vivid version of the news. Many miners, promoters, and busi-nessmen enlivened the scene. Although Carson City was not on the Comstock Lode, it was only a few miles away, and it shared the turbulent life of Virginia City.

On his way to Virginia City, Browne passed through Silver City, situated in Gold Canyon about two miles below Gold Hill; it was a junior partner among the Comstock towns. Men were digging in the hillsides and building a town when Browne passed through. In 1860, its residents fully expected Silver City to be more impor-tant than Virginia City or Carson City, but no big ore discoveries were ever made there, and it always remained in the shadow of its neighbors.

Browne became disgusted with western Utah and its disorderly little towns and joined the number of those who decided to return to California. He hated the bad-tasting water and did not enjoy the weather. Furthermore, he found the region full of swindlers, raving drunkards, and fighters. As he wrote his memoirs, he may have exaggerated the discomforts to entertain his readers, though much of what he said must be regarded as fact. But if some men left because of climate or chaos, and if others spent their time mining and brawling in the towns, still others explored surrounding mountain ranges, hoping to find another lode. For every person like Browne, who left disappointed, there came several new arrivals willing to suffer the hazards of the desert and mountains.

One such man was Samuel Clemens, who reached the Washoe region not by way of California but from Missouri. Clemens came to the Far West in 1861 because a new territory—the Territory of Nevada—was about to be formed, and he had a job in the govern-ment. However, he soon became more interested in finding a mine than in settling in Carson City. The Comstock Lode offered little opportunity for a prospector by 1861; all the good ground had been claimed.

But Clemens heard wild rumors about two new mining districts —Esmeralda and Humboldt—in the distant mountains. Some In-dians had brought samples of ore into Virginia City from the Hum-

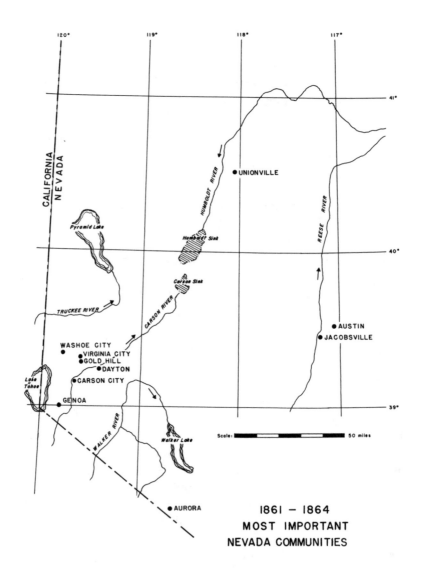

120° 119° 118° 117°

41°

CALIFORNIA
NEVADA

●UNIONVILLE

HUMBOLDT RIVER

REESE RIVER

Pyramid Lake

Humboldt Sink

40°

Carson Sink

TRUCKEE RIVER

CARSON RIVER

●AUSTIN
●JACOBSVILLE

WASHOE CITY
●VIRGINIA CITY
●GOLD HILL
●DAYTON
Lake
Tahoe
●CARSON CITY

GENOA

39°

WALKER RIVER

Walker Lake

Scale: 50 miles

●AURORA

1861 — 1864
MOST IMPORTANT
NEVADA COMMUNITIES

boldt Range, and a few prospectors had rushed to the region. They reported spectacular wealth, and this was exactly the news which the eager young men of the Comstock Lode wanted to hear. Clemens and some of his companions cast aside all other responsibilities and interests to be among the first to get to the Humboldt district. It was more than a hundred miles from Carson City to the new discovery, across the notorious Forty-Mile Desert, which was strewn with the refuse of thousands of emigrants. It required fifteen days to make the trip, and when Clemens arrived several other parties had already reached the district.

When groups of prospectors came into a new region, they often founded small "towns," named them, and then tried to sell property to the later arrivals. Several "towns" had already been established in the Humboldt Range, and Clemens and his companions settled in the largest, known as Unionville. It had eleven houses.

Soon Clemens was prospecting for gold and silver, and he became frantically excited about some glittering fragments of rock. Thinking he had a marvelous gold mine, but afraid someone would discover his great treasure, Clemens sneaked along the mountainside to learn how vast his claim should be. "Of all the experiences of my life," he later wrote, "this secret search among the hidden treasures of silver-land was the nearest to unmarred ecstasy. It was a delirious revel." He later learned, to his bitter disappointment, that he had found only valueless mica. Later, when he and his partners found an outcropping of silver ore, Clemens became discouraged because much heavy work would be required to mine it. Many other prospectors were to have similar experiences on the deserts of Nevada in the years to come. Much of the state's unwritten history belongs to prospectors like Clemens, who had high hopes and moments of intense expectation, and then disappointment.

The prospectors were not, however, easily defeated. When Clemens decided that Unionville did not offer as much as he had expected, he wanted to try the Esmeralda District. Some of the miners stayed in Unionville and eventually built a small but prosperous town. In the 1860's, several hundred persons lived there, mining the ore which had seemed too much trouble to a wandering soul like Clemens.

In the Esmeralda District Clemens had much the same experience. He found there the bustling community Aurora, invested his money in several mines, and lost it. He followed several wild rumors, tried several devices to avoid hard work, and finally left Aurora to become a writer for the *Territorial Enterprise* which had in the meantime moved to Virginia City.

The town of Aurora, as Clemens knew it in 1862, seemed to have much promise for future greatness. It had several thousand residents, and for a few months it rivaled Virginia City in the wealth of its mines. But Aurora was to slip into a depression in the 1870's, while Virginia City became even more rich and famous.

When Clemens gave up his life as a roving prospector to begin his literary career, the prospectors had merely begun to explore the Great Basin. In the next few years, dozens of new rushes occurred and scores of towns were founded. Perhaps if Clemens had not taken a job on the *Territorial Enterprise,* he would have been in the race to the Reese River Valley and the Toiyabe Range in 1862 or 1863. He might have been one of the founders of Austin.

The discovery at Austin was not made by one of the prospectors from the Comstock region; most of them had not extended their activities into central Nevada in 1862. The Pony Express, which had been established in 1860 to carry the mail across the continent on swift-footed horses, used a route across the central part of the Great Basin; the Pony Express company had laid a series of stations along the route where the riders could rest and change horses. Later, after the Pony Express ceased operating, Overland Mail carriers continued to use these stations. One of them was Jacobsville on the Reese River near the Toiyabe Range. During the summer of 1862, a man named William Talcott, while gathering wood in the mountains near the station, found some silver-bearing rock. Within a few weeks, the residents of the Comstock area had heard about it, and soon the roads toward Toiyabe were jammed with wagons and stages. The town of Austin grew swiftly and haphazardly in the little canyon where the silver had been found, and soon it aspired to be as great as Virginia City.

We have seen that many early prospectors were eager to rush hundreds of miles across the desert when they heard of a new strike. The story of Unionville, Aurora, and Austin was to be repeated hundreds of times in Nevada history, but usually the miners

While Samuel Clemens lived in Nevada he adopted the pen name "Mark Twain." After leaving the state he became famous for writing *The Adventures of Tom Sawyer* and *The Adventures of Huckleberry Finn.* This photo shows Mark Twain as a young man

"Tom, Huck, and the Dead Cat" was painted by Nevada artist Richard Guy Walton in 1939. It is now part of the permanent collection of the National Museum of American Art, Smithsonian Institution

found little or nothing when they reached the new "discovery." Even when ore existed, most of the prospectors arrived too late to profit from it, and most ore bodies lasted only a short time. Austin was a producing "camp"—the miners used to refer to their communities as camps—for longer than most towns. It was prosperous in the 1860's, and mining continued for many more years. Most other towns which were founded in this era became ghost camps within a few years.

The great mining excitement of 1860-1863 not only sent droves of nomads wandering through the mountains and desert; it also led to the building of new towns around the Comstock Lode. Since water was needed to mill the ores from Virginia City and Gold Hill and very little water existed on Mt. Davidson, the ore usually had to be hauled to the nearby valleys. Also, the Comstock Lode towns needed much lumber, and this had to come from the heavily wooded Sierra Nevada to the west. So mills for the ore began to appear along the Carson River to the east, and towns grew up around ore and lumber mills in Washoe Valley west of the lode.

The mills east of Virginia City gave birth to Dayton on the Carson River not far from Gold Canyon. Since about 1850, a trading station for the emigrants had operated there, and a few Chinese had established a small community which came to be known as Chinatown. But only when the Comstock Lode began to produce large amounts of ore did an established town develop. Adolph Sutro gave the place a boost by building his mill, as did other promoters and businessmen. Soon there were so many mills along the Carson River that many of them had no ore to process. Still, this impetus helped Dayton to prosper.

Across the mountains in Washoe Valley, the little towns of Washoe City, Ophir City, and Franktown thrived on a brisk milling and lumber business. Scores of teamsters carried ore into the valley from Virginia City and hauled tons of lumber in the opposite direction. Driving through Washoe Valley today, one has trouble imagining that three busy towns once existed there; almost nothing remains of these milling-lumber communities. They prospered only for a few years, and then other cities in other areas became more attractive.

Although a number of towns were getting organized and thousands of men were seeking a rapid fortune in western Utah Territory by 1861, no effective government existed as yet. An attempt had been made to create a government in 1859, and a few men had held a constitutional convention. There had even been an election, and a man named Isaac Roop of Susanville, California (then believed to be in Utah Territory) had become governor. But he had no real authority and was never able to assemble a legislature or to collect taxes.

The officials of Utah Territory could not establish law and order in 1859 and 1860, because most miners and businessmen detested Mormonism. Federal Judge Cradlebaugh had difficulty enforcing his orders at times, and only the prestige of William Stewart kept the judge in business. In addition, the Civil War was beginning in the East, and some men wanted to make Washoe a part of the Confederacy. The majority in most towns favored the Union cause, and although they soon subdued the "rebels," this added to the confusion and anarchy in the region. In short, Washoe badly needed a strong, well-organized government.

NEVADA TERRITORY AND STATEHOOD, 1861-1864

The federal government soon provided the means for filling this need. News of the great silver discovery had aroused interest in Washington as well as in California, and by 1861 Congress was receptive to the idea of creating a new territory in the Far West. On two earlier occasions, delegates from western Utah Territory had gone to the nation's capital asking to be allowed to form a separate government, and many Congressmen had approved of the idea. After the rush of 1860, Congress decided it was the time to act. A bill was passed creating the Territory of Nevada, and on March 2, 1861, President James Buchanan signed it into law.

The establishment of a territory did not immediately give this region a government, because no officials were on hand to assume authority. Abraham Lincoln, who became President two days after the Nevada Territory bill became law, had to arrange for the establishment of a territorial government and designated a political supporter, James W. Nye of New York, for the job of governor.

Governor Nye did not get to Nevada Territory for three months,

James W. Nye, Territorial Governor, 1861-1864; U.S. Senator, 1864-1873

William M. Stewart. U.S. Senator, 1864-1875, 1887-1905

and some of his staff did not arrive until even later. His chief assist-
ant, the territorial secretary, was Orion Clemens, who arrived with
his brother, Samuel, during the latter part of the summer. Both
Governor Nye and Secretary Clemens were spirited men who found
the frontier life of Nevada to their liking. They took seriously their
responsibility of forming a territorial government. Governor Nye
divided the Territory into districts and called for the people to
elect a legislature, to meet on October 1, 1861, in Carson City. Abraham Curry, still promoting his community, provided a room for the
lawmakers in a partly completed hotel, and the first territorial legislature was elected. It gave Nevada some laws for dealing with crim-
inals and for settling disputes, and it established officers to keep the
peace. It borrowed many of its statutes from California, and some
of them remain effective in amended form at present.

The men who came to Carson City for the 1861 legislature were
all eager to get some political advantages for their respective
towns. Each little town had citizens who dreamed of building a
great metropolis, and many of these towns insisted on becoming
county seats. The most ambitious and influential individual was
William Stewart, who had established his law office in Carson City.
Having been elected to the legislature from that community,
Stewart wanted it to become the permanent capital. He mustered
enough votes to accomplish this, but he had to arrange to put
county seats in several small towns in order to get the legislators to
support his proposal. County seats were placed at Genoa (Doug-
las County), Carson City (Ormsby County), Washoe City
(Washoe County), Dayton (Lyon County), Aurora (Esmeralda
County), Unionville (Humboldt County), Virginia City (Storey
County), and Buckland's Station on the Carson River (Churchill
County).*

Many of these communities were so close together that there was
little excuse for creating separate counties; Stewart wrote in later

---

*The first territorial legislature also created Lake County in the northwestern
corner of its jurisdiction, assuming that Susanville and the Honey Lake Valley
were in Nevada. After a dispute with California and a boundary survey, it was
established that this was not the case, and Lake County never became fully organized. Its name was later changed to Roop County in honor of Isaac Roop, and it
was eventually absorbed by Washoe County because it lacked sufficient population
to function properly.

years that it w is unfortunate that western Nevada had been divided into small counties, but it was largely due to his influence that this was done. The results of his political maneuvering had a long-lasting effect on Nevada politics, because most of the boundaries which he arranged in western Nevada are still approximately the same.

The territorial legislature of 1861 met for forty-nine days, and it was one of the most important in Nevada's history. It set the pattern for the territorial government, from which the state government was to grow.

When Governor Nye arrived in Nevada and began to organize the territory, the Civil War was just getting underway. As a Northerner and a supporter of President Lincoln, Governor Nye was eager to keep Nevada on the Union side. A few Confederate sympathizers lived in the state, but Nye and other Union men managed to prevent them from gaining control of the region. For this, Nye and the young Territory of Nevada won the admiration of many leaders in Washington—including the President. This probably helped Nevada to gain statehood quickly.

When the territorial legislature met for the second time, late in 1862, the urge for statehood had become powerful in Nevada. Although the population of the territory was still very small by comparison with other states, the residents of Nevada had great ambition and dreams of grandeur. The increasing wealth of Virginia City, the discovery of new mines in Unionville and Aurora, and the increasing population seemed to prove that Nevada would be more orderly and law-abiding if statehood were granted.

The legislators decided to hold a special election in September, 1863, to choose delegates for a constitutional convention. When the election was held, the voters showed decisively that they wanted statehood. They elected thirty-nine convention delegates.

In a democratic society, no political function is more important than framing a constitution. Just as the United States Constitution is the supreme law of the land, so a state constitution is the most important governmental document within a state. The Nevada Constitution makers of 1863 knew they were assuming an important responsibility.

On most essential matters, the delegates were in agreement.

There was a dispute on what name the proposed state should have, some advocating Washoe, Esmeralda, or Humboldt rather than Nevada, but a majority finally resolved to retain the old Spanish name. The delegates framed a document in many respects like the federal constitution, with a few unique provisions because of Nevada's special interests.

One question caused a serious disagreement among the delegates. Most of them wanted the constitution to establish that mines —including shafts and tunnels—should be taxed in the same manner as all other property, but a minority group, led by William Stewart, demanded that only the production of the mines, and not the mines themselves, should be subject to taxation. In other words, a mine which was not producing could not be taxed, according to Stewart, but one which was yielding ore would be taxed according to the amount of production.

Stewart lost his argument in the constitutional convention because a majority of delegates endorsed provisions that he opposed. When the constitutional document was submitted to the voters for approval or rejection at a special election, however, Stewart campaigned for it. Most mining companies and newspapers opposed it, and the voters defeated it decisively in January, 1864.

The opponents were effective in the mining towns and many persons voted against the 1863 constitution. There was a second reason for rejection. At the time that the balloting on the constitution was held, voters were asked to approve a slate of officers to fill the positions which the new constitution would create. Many persons who had hoped to be nominated were disappointed. Some of those campaigned against the constitution, which was overwhelmingly defeated.

But Nevadans were still eager for full membership in the Union. Besides, President Lincoln wanted an additional state which would send Republican (or Union) senators to Washington. He correctly assumed that Nevada would be such a state. Early in 1864, Congress passed an "enabling act," which authorized the people of Nevada to hold another constitutional convention. President Lincoln signed the act, and the process of electing delegates began once more.

The next constitutional convention met in July, 1864, and adopted most of the provisions of the 1863 session, except for that section referring to the taxation of mines. The delegates yielded to the obvious preference of the people, providing that only the proceeds of mines should be taxed. When this new document was submitted for ratification, the voters approved it overwhelmingly. Stewart, although he was not a delegate to the 1864 convention, had triumphed again.

The elated Nevadans telegraphed their precious constitution to Washington at considerable expense. On October 31, 1864, President Lincoln issued a proclamation making Nevada a state.

It was by far the smallest state in the Union in terms of population, and it remained so for nearly a century. Many eastern politicians complained in later years that Nevada had been given statehood prematurely. For the next hundred years, Nevada was always able to produce men with the wit and willingness to refute such statements.

7. Bonanza, 1864-1881

THE YEARS 1864-1881 were the most colorful and exciting era in Nevada's history. In those years, the great Comstock Lode produced hundreds of millions of dollars worth of silver and gold, helping to change the nature of America's money economy and creating fabulous fortunes. The Big Bonanza was discovered—one of the greatest silver ore bodies ever found. Virginia City and Gold Hill became famous across America and Europe for the financial speculation and the engineering achievements that were associated with their mines.

The Comstock communities became lavish and colorful, contrasting sharply with their bleak surroundings and lowly births. The Comstockers—or at least the rich among them—lived elegantly and insisted upon all the luxuries and fineries of the great cities of the world. Virginia City was like a magnet, drawing men and women— but mostly men—from all corners of the earth until just before 1880, when the wealth of the mines was nearly gone.

The bonanza years also gave Nevada a reckless period of politics. The leaders in the mining industry became the state's most influential politicians, and the great financial leaders occasionally used their money and prestige to win election to the U.S. Senate. Nevada received a bad reputation in the 1870's and 1880's for corruption in politics.

One factor which helped transform the state rapidly during this era was the building of railroads. Most important was the Central Pacific, spanning the northern part of the state along the old Humboldt-Truckee route. The transcontinental rail line was a blessing at first, creating new towns like Reno, Elko, and Winnemucca. Later, Nevadans began to hate it, because its operators tried to charge excessive rates for freight hauling, and they dominated the politics of the state.

There are many dimensions to this magnificent era. No wonder writers have found it a favorite source for historical research and a subject for fanciful fiction.

MINING AND BIG MONEY, 1864-1881

As Nevada assumed the honors and responsibilities of statehood, the Comstock Lode was on the threshold of a new era of mining. The first state legislature chose Stewart and Nye as United States Senators and sent them to Washington. In the absence of Stewart, a new arrival from California rose to prominence on the lode, with important results for the mining industry.

The newcomer was William Sharon, representative of the Bank of California, whose leaders wanted to open a branch in Virginia City. Mining was becoming costly business. Once the mine shafts were extended several hundred feet below the surface, it became necessary to have expensive steam hoists, large quantities of timber from distant hills, large pumps to remove the water in the mines, and elaborate mills for processing the ore. Sharon and his superior —the clever William C. Ralston who ran the bank—knew this and were willing to risk money on mining and milling projects if they could get mortgages and good interest rates.

Sharon managed the bank's money with great skill. During a slight depression in 1865 some of the mill owners who had borrowed from the bank could not pay debts, so Sharon took over their mills. Soon he controlled most of the important mills on the lode and began to extend this control to the mines. By 1869, the Bank of California could actually give orders to the mine owners about how to run their operations. Sharon became a financial dictator, and as new ore bodies were found, he and the "Bank crowd" usually found ways to get a share of the profits because of their monopoly in milling. The bank also had enough money power to influence the prices of mining stocks which sold on the San Francisco Stock Exchange. Its operations were questionable, but they were very successful—for a while.

During his heyday, Sharon had much success in buying and selling Comstock mining shares. As the companies incorporated and sold stock, thousands of Nevadans and Californians were able to get financial interests in the mines. All classes of persons "played the stock market," trying to guess which mining companies would make a profit and which would not, and buying and selling stocks accordingly. Most people—especially the small investors who did not know what was going on—usually guessed wrong and lost money. But Sharon had good information, and he most often guessed right; by the early 1870's he was a millionaire and the bank was prosperous. Sharon made much of his money by the ruse of buying stock in a relatively quiet mine, starting a rumor that the mine had struck an ore body, and then selling his stock when the prices were high.

By 1869, many Nevadans were beginning to hate the "Bank crowd" and its methods. One of these was Adolph Sutro, who continued to talk about and plan for a great tunnel into the lower depths of the Comstock Lode. In 1865, Sharon and most leading mine owners had approved this idea. The tunnel, begun low in the foothills east of Mt. Davidson and extending four miles into the mountain, would make it easier to mine the ore and to drain the excess water. Sutro had received much encouragement for his project; the Nevada legislature gave him a special franchise, and mine owners agreed to pay him two dollars for every ton of ore extracted after the tunnel reached their mines. He planned a neat little town—named Sutro—at the mouth of the tunnel. In a few months it became evident that if Sutro could get his tunnel built, he would be the most powerful man on the Comstock. Sharon did not like this, and soon a bitter contest began.

For several years, Sutro tried to raise money for his project and the "Bank crowd" tried to prevent it. Sutro went to San Francisco, New York, and Europe seeking investors, and Ralston tried to destroy his enterprise at every turn. In 1869, the Miners' Union of Virginia City, which disliked the bank, gave Sutro $50,000 to start his tunnel. This was not nearly enough for such a large enterprise, but he began. He completed the tunnel, but it took nearly nine years, partly because of technical difficulties and partly because Sutro met so much opposition. In 1878 when Sutro finished his project, most of the rich ore of the Comstock Lode was gone. Neither side won in this long and costly battle for the wealth of Mt. Davidson.

Another man who emerged as the foe of William Sharon was John Mackay. Having arrived among the earliest adventurers and working as a pick-and-shovel miner, he learned the underground features and mining techniques of the lode. Like most residents of Virginia City, he bought stock in some mines, hoping to make a profit if new ore bodies were found. In 1865, he and a companion bought stock in the Kentuck—a Gold Hill mine—and managed to get the controlling interest. Mackay then put a crew to work in the mine and found a rich ore body. When Sharon tried to get control of the mine by crafty means, the straightforward Mackay opposed him and Sharon could not execute his plan.

Mackay decided to try to control some of the more promising mines by buying certain stocks in San Francisco. He formed a partnership with three other men whose names were soon to be famous across the nation—James G. Fair, James C. Flood, and William O'Brien. By careful and quiet purchase of stocks over a period of several months, they won control of the central part of the Comstock Lode in 1872. This was the Consolidated Virginia property, which had produced little silver in the early years of Virginia City. In the spring of 1873, Mackay's men discovered the top of a massive ore body which proved to be one of the richest in the history of the world. It was nearly a quarter-mile beneath the surface, directly under Virginia City. The world soon came to know it as the Big Bonanza. Sharon's position on the Comstock Lode was badly shaken, because the bank could not control this vast new wealth.

In 1874, Sharon became desperate and began to buy large amounts of stock in various Comstock mines, using the money of people who had deposited in the Bank of California. With reckless daring, he bought shares in mines that were only moderately valuable, and soon thousands of investors were following his lead. Prices of stocks went up and up, and people borrowed money to get into the act. In the hysterical money market of 1874, everyone seemed to be getting rich in Virginia City and San Francisco. Persons who had bought shares of stock in the Consolidated Virginia Mine for $15 each in 1872 saw the value of each share rise to $176 in November, 1874, and then suddenly rise to more than $700 per share in January, 1875. Those who rushed to haul in the riches drove the prices still higher. The same pattern existed for other mines and their stocks, but suddenly bad rumors began to come from the Comstock and prices fell as rapidly as they had risen. Thousands hurried to sell their stocks, and the millions of dollars which shareholders thought they owned suddenly disappeared. And so did millions of dollars worth of savings which depositors had placed in the Bank of California. Sharon's scheme had backfired. In the summer of 1875 the bank had to admit it could not pay creditors and temporarily closed its doors.

After this incident, the power of the "Bank crowd" was never quite the same in Virginia City or Nevada. The "Bonanza Firm"— as Mackay and his associates were called—had formed another banking institution, called the Nevada Bank of San Francisco, and they became the unquestioned leaders of the mining and financial circles on the Comstock Lode. The next two years—1876 and 1877 —were the most prosperous in the history of Virginia City as the wealth of the Big Bonanza was mined at rapid speed by a thousand men. In those two years, the mines produced more than $75,000,000 worth of ore.

Before the end of 1877, however, the Big Bonanza was exhausted of high-grade silver and gold ore, and no new bonanzas were found. Some mines were eventually extended about a mile below the surface in a frenzied search, but without success. Stockholders and other investors spent millions in new explorations beneath Mt. Davidson, but they continually faced disappointment. By 1881, the Comstock's ore production had fallen below $1,500,000. The great treasure house of silver had been removed and the poorer ore which remained was bringing a lower price. The Comstock mines had helped to flood the world silver market, and the price of the white metal had fallen sharply. The era of fabulous riches had ended.

Life on the Comstock Lode, 1864-1881

What was life like for the average residents of Virginia City and Gold Hill during the boom years? While Sharon, Sutro, Mackay and the other wealthy figures fought the great financial battles, hordes of miners did the actual work of drilling, blasting, transporting, and milling the ore. What of these men? What did it mean to be one of Virginia City's residents in the 1860's and 1870's?

Working in a Comstock mine was not a pleasant experience. The underground caverns were extremely hot, and men could labor only for short periods before stopping to rest. The heat was caused by underground reservoirs of near-boiling water, and at times miners accidentally drilled into such reservoirs, starting a flood in the mines that sent them fleeing for their lives. It became most difficult to pump the water and to brace the walls of the mines with timber as the shafts went deeper. One reason for the interest in Sutro's tunnel was the hope that such a project would drain the water from the mines and make them cooler.

Aside from the heat and water, there was great danger in the mines because of the speed with which the companies worked. Many superintendents were reckless, and some miners knew little about the hazards of underground work. Dynamite used in blasting the rock took a number of lives, and falling timbers killed others. But the most dreaded danger of all was fire.

Thousands of trees were cut in the Sierra Nevada and hauled to the mines to hold up the roofs and walls of the ore chambers, and by the time the excavations had become large, virtual cities existed

John W. Mackay, Big Bonanza owner. Because of the generosity of his wife and son, the Mackay family became benefactors of the University of Nevada

The statue of John Mackay on the Reno campus, executed by the famous sculptor Gutzon Borglum

William P. Sharon, Comstock promoter; U.S. Senator, 1875-1881

beneath the surface, with stairs, ladders, working platforms, bins for holding ore, and untold tons of timber for bracing. This was a special menace because the miners used candles for light.

One night in the spring of 1869, a fire started in the Yellow Jacket Mine at Gold Hill, trapping dozens of miners in the network of tunnels underground. Firemen and miners descended the shaft with hoses and tools to try to save the victims, but the heat and smoke repelled them. For three days, Comstockers witnessed a ghastly scene in which the flames roared furiously, and charred bodies were recovered from the lower levels. Thirty-seven miners lost their lives either by burning, suffocation, or falling, in the worst mine disaster in Nevada's history. Finally, when the flames could not be stopped by water, the shafts of the Yellow Jacket and adjacent mines were sealed. The fire raged in some sections of the underground workings for more than a month.

Little wonder that the miners felt a keen sense of apprehension as they extracted the silver-bearing ore. When they returned to the surface after a perilous, exhausting day shift or night shift below, most of them sought exhilarating entertainment. Virginia City was well prepared to provide it.

Elaborate saloons, ornate gambling rooms, and elegant restaurants had replaced the old tent shanties by the middle of the 1860's. Freight wagons over the Sierra Nevada—and later the railroads— gave Virginia City a variety of foods and clothing equal to that of some of the world's largest cities. Jewelry and fine carriages appeared, and the narrow streets of James Fennimore's old town soon showed the miners much to admire and desire. They lived wildly and spent recklessly with little thought of tomorrow—when they would have to descend into the mines again.

Virginia City and Gold Hill were mainly men's towns until the late 1870's. When the state government took a census count in 1875 (just before the peak of the Big Bonanza), the Comstock communities had 19,528 residents of whom 13,415 were males. The men, then, outnumbered the women about two to one; the disparity had been even greater in the 1860's.

Not all men, of course, were miners. The huge mills of the Comstock Lode employed many laborers, and thousands of others

Drawing of early Austin

Virgina City at its peak

worked in related occupations like wood-chopping, freighting, assaying, stock selling, and blacksmithing. The towns were filled with gamblers, entertainers, merchants, and lawyers of all descriptions, most of them looking for ways to build a fortune quickly. The industrious Chinese had their own section, which seemed like an exotic foreign city to the miners. Indian settlements developed around the edges of Virginia City, where the natives often lived upon the refuse which the white men threw away.

Many who saw Virginia City in its glorious days testified that it was one of the most fascinating places in the world. It was the liveliest city between Missouri and the Pacific Coast, since most of its population consisted of gold and silver seekers or adventure hunters of another kind. Fully half of its citizens had been born in foreign lands, having left their homes in search of fortune or adventure. For a few years the Comstock gave it to them. They and their American-born companions found excitement in stock speculation and dreams of wealth, in gambling and drinking, in reading the witty *Territorial Enterprise* and the *Gold Hill News*, in dog fights and human fights, in the famous opera houses (where many comedies and few operas were performed), and in prospecting for new mines. "The life of the Comstock in the old days has never been written so that those who did not share it can understand," one resident wrote in later years. "It can never be so written."

Not all Comstock life was wild and rowdy; some families lived in conservative, richly furnished homes and entertained themselves quietly with literature, formal parties, balls, and church functions. Some of the elegance that was the ideal of their lives can be seen today in St. Mary's of the Mountain Catholic Church or in the Episcopal Church, in Piper's Opera House, the Fourth Ward School, and the Mackay mansion. The ornate furnishings and beautiful chandeliers of the past century continue to delight tourists as much as they delighted Nevada citizens of nearly a century ago.

As we look at the surviving monuments of the Comstock's past glory, we should remember that most of them were built during Virginia City's greatest years—1875, 1876, and 1877. A fire destroyed most of the city on October 26, 1875, roaring through the main streets with such terrible force that it destroyed churches, business buildings, mills, and hundreds of homes. By desperate effort, Mackay and his men prevented the flames from going down the shaft at the Consolidated Virginia Mine. This achievement protected the source of wealth which was to rebuild much of the city. We would have many more interesting reminders and precious records of the Bonanza days had not other fires taken their toll over the years.

The residents of Virginia City and Gold Hill lived wildly or quietly, elegantly or crudely, as their individual tastes suggested. But in some matters they shared experiences. One of these common concerns was politics, because most Comstockers took representative government seriously. To a large extent, they controlled Nevada state politics for more than thirty years.

POLITICAL INTRIGUE IN GOVERNMENT, 1864-1881

Mining and politics were closely intertwined during much of the first seventy-five years of Nevada's history. Several of Nevada's most successful political figures made their starts in mining or won their initial reputations by serving the miners.

When Nevada became a state in 1864, members of the United States Senate were chosen by the legislature. As we have seen, when the first state legislature assembled, it chose the popular William Stewart and the much-admired James W. Nye. Neither was technically a mining man, but both knew the industry well and both had the respect of most Comstock residents. Stewart was an expert on mining law, and this gave him widespread support from Nevada's people. After getting to Washington, he became the author of the first national mining law and an outstanding advocate of the miner's cause.

Senator Nye won reelection in the 1867 session of the legislature and served for six more years, but by the time he sought a third term in 1872, the great wealth of the Comstock was beginning to be spent in the political arena. Although the legislature made the final selection of senators, it was customary for a senatorial candidate like Nye to campaign widely among the voters, trying to get them to vote for state senators and state assemblymen who would be favorable to his candidacy. In 1872, William P. Sharon was near the peak of his influence and power, and he decided to seek Senator Nye's seat. Also, Adolph Sutro wanted the office in order to promote his tunnel scheme. And still another well-known candidate in Virginia City entered the race: John P. Jones, the superintendent of one of the Comstock's largest mines.

All these opponents had more money than Nye, and Sharon and Jones had the greatest fortunes. They spent money lavishly, trying to please the mining-camp residents across Nevada. Newspapers of Nevada and California took sides. The *Territorial Enterprise* accused Sharon of dishonesty and greed, and the *San Francisco Chronicle* implied that Jones started the terrible Yellow Jacket fire. But this story about Jones was obviously false, and most voters on the Comstock knew it. During the campaign, Jones was often called "the Commoner" by the citizens and newspapers of Nevada, and he steadily gained support from this name. When the election came, the voters showed their affection for Jones and their dislike of Sharon by electing a legislature favorable to "the Commoner." Senator Nye, now old and ill, got little support.

With the election, Senator Jones began a long career in the upper house of Congress, winning election four more times—in 1877, 1885, 1891, and 1897. For thirty years he defended the interests of the silver mining companies, speaking specifically for the Comstock long after its greatest wealth had been mined.

Senator Stewart won a second term to the United States Senate in 1869, but, while serving this term, he decided not to seek re-election. He was to return to politics in the 1880's, regain his seat in the Senate, and eventually spend a total of twenty-eight years there. His decision of 1874 to retire, however, provided another opportunity for Sharon and Sutro to fight for the powerful office.

Neither Sharon nor Sutro was primarily interested in the welfare of Nevada's people. Sharon wanted to extend his domination and that of the Bank of California over the financial wealth of the Comstock. Sutro hoped to get a huge loan from Congress to push his tunnel more rapidly. Sharon spent a fortune in Nevada to win the voters and bribe the legislators; he undoubtedly distributed hundreds of thousands of dollars, and it worked. The 1875 legislature

Fourth Ward school, Virginia City, a century ago

elected him to the Senate. His term began shortly after the great
stock-market crash which caused the Bank of California to close
temporarily. He remained one of the most hated men in Nevada in
spite of his election to the Senate, and even some who had voted
for him soon regretted it. Senator Sharon spent little time at his
duties in Washington and demonstrated no real concern for the
welfare of Nevada. His main energies continued to go toward the
building of his own financial empire. He could not, however, stop
the progress of Sutro's tunnel.

In 1880, when Senator Sharon's term was coming to an end,
Nevadans were eager for a change. Until then, they had always
elected Republicans to the Senate, but now Sharon had discredited
his party as well as himself. The Democrats nominated James G.
Fair, and the great wealth of the Big Bonanza thus became involved
in politics. Once more Sutro tried to win the election, but Fair's
prestige and money were more effective; he won the election in
1881 after Democrats had won control of the state legislature with
his help.

This period of Nevada's political history—from 1864 to 1881—
was not one of which the state can be proud. There was much corruption, and the money of the wealthy rather than the will of the
people decided the outcome of senatorial elections. Nevada politics
became a scandal across America; many unfavorable articles were
written about the state. This era showed that in a democracy the
people must be alert to the danger that wealthy men or companies
may use political office to get special, personal benefits, disregarding the welfare of the public.

There was not nearly as much extravagant spending by candidates for the House of Representatives or for the governor's office.
These offices seemed less important to the Comstock financiers.
Nevertheless, influential mining men often sought and won these
positions.

Nevada's first elected governor was Henry G. Blasdel, a well-
known mine superintendent and mill operator of Virginia City.
Governor Blasdel was an honest and energetic chief executive and
won reelection in 1866 by a large majority. He was a religious man
and tried to use his office to improve the morals of the mining com-

James G. Fair, Big Bonanza
owner. U.S. Senator, 1881-1887

Adolph Sutro

The Virginia & Truckee trestle at Gold Hill

munities. When the Nevada legislature voted to legalize gambling in 1867, he vetoed the bill. Two years later, the legislature again endorsed gambling and Governor Blasdel used the veto once more. This time, the legislature overrode the veto and games of chance became a legal part of Nevada's social and political scene.

When the much-admired Governor Blasdel decided to retire from politics in 1870, the voters elected L. R. Bradley—widely known as "Broadhorns" Bradley because he was a cattle rancher from northeastern Nevada. He had driven herds of cattle from Missouri to California in the 1850's and had come to Nevada in the 1860's, settling first in Austin. From there he operated a cattle business which extended into Elko County. Later, he entered politics. After his first election, he became a forceful governor and won the respect of most voters in the state. He was elected to a second term by a large majority in 1874.

In 1877, while serving his second term, Governor Bradley became the enemy of some of the richest mining companies on the Comstock Lode. The Consolidated Virginia and other companies tried to get their taxes reduced and persuaded the state legislature to pass a bill which would decrease their property tax assessments by about one-third. This would have substantially reduced the state government's revenue and would have meant that nonmining property would have to bear a larger share of the tax burden. Governor Bradley vetoed the bill with a strong statement that was virtually a declaration of war on the large mining companies. In the next election, when he tried to win a third term, the mining firms opposed him and he lost the election. The winner was John H. Kinkead, a well-known mining and milling man who was more acceptable to mining interests.

Governor Kinkead was typical of the pioneers who displayed wide interests—ranging from mining and milling to merchandising and politics. His term in the executive mansion climaxed a long career in the West. He had come to Carson City in 1859 and had served as treasurer of Nevada Territory under Governor Nye in 1862. He participated in the constitutional conventions of 1863 and 1864. Between 1867 and 1871, he had been a government officer in Alaska, returning to Nevada during the boom years of mining. He was known as one of Nevada's earliest mill builders, as one of

Henry G. Blasdel. Governor, 1864-1870

Lewis R. (Broadhorns) Bradley. Governor, 1871-1878

John H. Kinkead. Governor, 1879-1882

the constructors of the Virginia and Truckee Railroad, and as the founder of Washoe City. He served as governor from 1879 to 1882.

RAILROADS AND POLITICS, 1868-1881

While the mining interests played a dominant role in Nevada politics during the Bonanza years, they were not the only powerful group to exert pressure on the democratic process. During Nevada's young years, the railroad builders also did much to transform the state and to shape governmental policies.

Mining was mainly responsible for the settlement of western and central Nevada, but railroad construction brought about the establishment of several new towns in northern Nevada along the old Humboldt-Truckee route of the pioneers. The Central Pacific Rail Road Company built part of the transcontinental rail line along this route in 1868 and 1869.

As early as 1862, President Abraham Lincoln had signed a bill providing for the construction of a railroad from Council Bluffs, Iowa, to Sacramento, California. This seemed like a bold, almost unrealistic scheme at the time; it had been only a few years since pioneers had begun struggling across the vast plains and mountains of the West. But men with imagination took up the challenge and the Union Pacific Company began building westward from Omaha while the Central Pacific started in California.

Work began in Sacramento in October, 1863, but it took four years for the line to reach Nevada. Heavy equipment had to be hauled from the eastern states to California by sea, and construction through the steep, rocky Sierra Nevada was most difficult. The first train crossed the Nevada state line on December 13, 1867; in May of 1868, tracks had reached as far east as the Truckee Meadows.

The builders of the Central Pacific decided there should be a town in the Truckee Meadows because there was much water and a rich valley. In this valley, the railroad was only about twenty-five miles from the Comstock Lode, and it was expected that much freight would be loaded and unloaded here for the mining and milling communities.

A number of farmers had taken up land in the Truckee Meadows, but no town existed as yet. The valley's most enterprising businessman was Myron C. Lake, who owned a small inn and a bridge across the Truckee River. Aware that the railroad could mean business for him, Lake offered to give the company some land north of the river for a townsite if Charles Crocker, the construction superintendent, would put a station there and make it a distribution center. Crocker agreed, and on May 9, 1868, an auction was held at Lake's Crossing, which soon came to be known as Reno.

The auction was a lively event; the railroad had advertised widely that it was creating a new town and more than 1,500 people appeared from the surrounding regions to buy choice property or to watch the fun. Some of them paid as much as $1,000 for a lot.

For a time Reno was as crude and rough as a new mining town, with its tents and sagebrush shacks, its saloons and gamblers. When trains began to arrive regularly from Sacramento in July, Reno became a bustling place where stagecoaches stopped frequently from Virginia City and Carson City, and where freight wagons gathered to load needed supplies for the nearby towns. No longer was it necessary to haul western Nevada's supplies over the Sierra Nevada by slow, rocky wagon roads. Both the railroad and Reno soon prospered.

But the railroad builders, of course, pushed on. Crocker and his partners wanted to lay as much track as possible, because the farther east they got, the greater their bonuses and their land grants from the federal government would be. Construction of the line across the Forty-Mile Desert and up the Humboldt, however, was no simple chore. The desert seemed no more friendly now than it was to the Forty-Niners.

Crocker's men, of course, were better prepared for their assignment than the struggling emigrants of 1849. They built the railroad up the Truckee River to the point where it turns northward toward Pyramid Lake, and there they established a supply center and a town. The railroad workers were never far from a good supply of food, water, and equipment.

The town of Wadsworth was established by the railroad company not long after Reno was founded, and for a brief time it was as busy. It became the main supply point and freighting center for central Nevada in 1868, and remained one of the state's most important railroad maintenance centers and watering stations for almost forty years.

The building of the line from Wadsworth to Winnemucca progressed with remarkable speed, considering the difficulties. Industrious workers—many of them Chinese—often laid three miles of track in a single day in fierce mid-summer heat, and once they recorded eight miles of construction in twenty-four hours. At times water had to be hauled fifty miles or more to the sweating workers, and trains kept puffing constantly along the new track to bring rails, ties, and food. The frenzy of Crocker's crews matched the desperate struggles of the frantic pioneers who had struggled westward along the same trails a few years before.

The railroaders built another small station on the lower Humboldt River, at the site of an emigrant trading post owned by George Lovelock. The small town which developed here did not become a main distribution center, like Reno, or an important maintenance center, like Wadsworth. Many years were to pass before extensive cultivation of the nearby lands made Lovelock an important community.

When the Central Pacific crews reached Winnemucca, a town was being built there. The location had been the site of a trading station for several years, and many emigrants with their ox carts had forded the Humboldt River in this region. Originally known as French Ford, the town was renamed for the Paiute chief, Winnemucca, before the railroad arrived. The first train entered the little community on September 16, touching off a wild celebration. Winnemucca soon became an important freighting point for goods destined to be delivered in Oregon.

Farther up the Humboldt, the Central Pacific founded another town, Argenta. It was initially established about sixty miles east of Winnemucca in the fall of 1868, but its residents decided they liked another site a few miles to the west. In the winter of 1870, they moved to the new location and called their community Battle Mountain. They prospered there not only because of the employment which the railroad offered but also because their town became a supply center for the nearby mining region in the Battle Mountain Range.

Crocker's crews pushed swiftly eastward toward their connection with the Union Pacific, giving life to the towns of Carlin and Elko. At first they were little more than construction camps, but the enterprising Crocker managed to sell lots, and soon the buyers were building homes and stores. A rich silver strike at Hamilton in the White Pine Mountains, 120 miles to the south, generated a big demand for supplies and transportation services; Elko and Carlin became the jumping-off points for men and freight bound for Hamilton.

So the iron horse made its way eastward across Nevada for the first time, preceded by an inter-racial band of laborers working at top speed. The hundreds of nameless trailblazers spanned the desert northwest of the Great Salt Lake in the early spring of 1869, and by early May they had connected with the Union Pacific at Promontory, Utah, directly north of the lake. On May 10, a golden spike from California and a silver spike from Nevada were driven into place to symbolize the completion of the first transcontinental railroad.

The young communities back along the line in Nevada celebrated with enthusiasm as the news of the connection was telegraphed to them. They rejoiced wildly once more when the first trains arrived from the East. Within four months, Reno, Winnemucca, and Elko were among the most prominent towns in Nevada. They could not yet compete with Virginia City or Austin in wealth, but they soon became almost as lively in terms of rowdy men and rough frontier living.

Like the pioneer residents of the mining camps, those who lived in the railroad towns could not feel content until they had their own county governments. A self-respecting town wanted its court house. Thus Reno demanded the county seat of Washoe County, and Washoe City was unable to resist the change. Winnemucca likewise began to outshine the mining town of Unionville and became the seat of Humboldt County. The legislature created a new county to satisfy the Elkoites, detaching part of Lander County for this purpose.

The forming of new county governments did not immediately bring civilized society to the railroad towns. Reno became the center for a group of ruffians and troublemakers for several years. In the early 1870's, burglars, cheating gamblers, and robbers conducted their operations boldly with little interference from the sheriff. In July of 1874, however, a group of citizens formed a vigilante committee which they called the "601" to chase undesirable residents out of town. Formal notices were sent to unwanted individuals. A few who did not heed the warnings were chased from the region.

Although the railroading life was hectic, Nevadans generally regarded the Central Pacific as a great blessing in the beginning. It brought supplies to the mining camps much more rapidly than the old freight wagons and it made agriculture much more profitable than in the days when oxen and horses supplied the only sources of power for transportation. Soon the trains became a vital part of everyday life in northern Nevada, and their exciting novelty disappeared.

Little by little during the 1870's, the public attitude toward the railroad changed. The manager of the Central Pacific began to impose costly freight rates for the goods they hauled to Nevada, and before long Nevadans were complaining bitterly. Railroad freight rates were still less costly than team-and-wagon rates, but the railroad managers made certain they got the highest possible fees for their services. And they discriminated openly against Nevada towns.

The cost of hauling a carload of machinery from New York to San Francisco by train in 1877 was about $600, but if the machinery were going from New York to Reno, the charge would be $818, and if it were unloaded at Winnemucca, the charge was $996. In other words, Nevada towns were charged a "back haul" rate—a fee equal to the charge for hauling the machinery all the way to San Francisco and then back to Reno or Winnemucca, even though it would never go to San Francisco. The railroad company charged such fees because the towns along the line depended upon it for existence, and no laws yet prohibited such unfair treatment.

For many years, the Central Pacific's well-financed representa-

Elko in 1876

tives operated in Carson City and persuaded the legislators not to pass any laws which would restrict the company. On a number of occasions, the railroad refused to pay taxes which the county assessors and treasurers tried to collect. After the company had been operating in Nevada for about ten years, the state's Congressman in Washington said: "Nevada is an orange which for ten years these railroad vampires have been sucking in silence. . . . Their object seems to be to crush, not to develop, the industries of Nevada."

The state and county governments of Nevada fought the railroad owners with little success until 1910. By then, the Central Pacific company no longer operated the transcontinental line; the Southern Pacific company had replaced the much-hated founders. Also, the United States government had instituted an Interstate Commerce Commission and had passed laws against rate discrimination. In 1910, the state government won a reduction of rates which ended nearly forty years of exploitation.

So the railroad was partly a blessing for the state, and partly a money-hungry monster. It helped open some new regions of Nevada to settlement and growth, but it also retarded the commercial development of the state by excessive fees.

THE LITTLE RAILROADS, 1869-1881

The Central Pacific was the most important railroad in Nevada from the 1870's through 1900 but many smaller lines supplemented it in serving Nevada. The Central Pacific was the spinal cord for a network of rails which served the state's mining regions.

One of these railroads was the Virginia and Truckee, promoted largely by William Sharon. The wily Comstock financier had conceived the idea of a railroad between Virginia City and the Carson River before the Central Pacific ever reached Nevada. Such a railroad would reduce the cost of hauling ore from the mines to mills on the river (and incidentally it would annoy Sharon's enemy, Adolph Sutro, who planned to extract the ore through his proposed tunnel). It was a costly and difficult enterprise to build a line down the slopes and canyons of Mt. Davidson, but Sharon persuaded the unsuspecting residents of Storey and Ormsby counties to donate $500,000 in bond money for the project. By the end of 1869, the railroad connected Carson City and Gold Hill; it was called the "crookedest railroad in the world" because of the number of twists and turns required to get the engines up the mountainside at a proper grade.

Soon the Virginia and Truckee was extended northward from Carson City into Washoe Valley and eventually to Reno, where it could receive and dispense freight hauled by the Central Pacific. The quaint and sturdy engines and cars of the Virginia and Truckee were familiar to residents of Virginia City, Carson City, and Reno until modern times, and for many years a branch line extended southward even into Carson Valley. The Virginia City portion of the line was abandoned in 1939, and the remainder, between Reno, Carson City, and Minden, ceased operation in 1950.

The mining population of Austin, although not as prosperous as that of Virginia City, was just as eager to have railroad service. The citizens of Lander County got permission from the legislature to issue bonds for the construction of ninety-three miles of line between Austin and Battle Mountain. It was completed in 1880 and served not only the mining community but also ranches along the Reese River Valley through which it passed. This line, the Nevada Central Railway, operated until 1938.

Before the Austin-Battle Mountain railroad had been completed, another line had penetrated into the region of central Nevada farther east. A new mining strike in 1869 had opened the town of Eureka, about sixty-five miles east of Austin (see Chapter VIII), and tracks were laid from Palisade—which is near Carlin—to Eureka in 1873, 1874, and 1875. Part of the financing came from the Bank of California. The Eureka and Palisade Railroad, like its neighbor to the west, continued to operate until 1938.

Another region of Nevada to hear the chug of locomotives in the early years of statehood was the section southeast of the Comstock Lode—toward Walker Lake and beyond. The men who built the Virginia and Truckee were pleased with their profits in the 1870's and felt that an expansion of the railroad system could mean more riches. It was believed, in the late 1870's, that a track into Nevada's southern desert would reap rewards. The financiers formed the Carson and Colorado Railroad Company, ambitiously indicating that they planned to construct a line more than 400 miles long to the Colorado River.

In 1880, construction of the Carson and Colorado began at Mound House, a few miles east of Carson City on the Virginia and Truckee line. The superintendent was H. M. Yerington, a skillful construction expert who had also supervised the building of the Virginia and Truckee about ten years earlier. Mining booms seemed to be developing in Bodie, California, not far from Aurora, and farther to the east at Candelaria, and the immediate objective was to take railroad service to those areas.

The news of this construction caused excitement in those towns and also in the sparsely settled areas through which the line would pass. One of these regions was Mason Valley, through which the Walker River flows. A tiny town had grown up in the valley in the 1870's, because the water made it possible to raise crops and cattle there; the first residents called their community Pizen Switch, but by the late 1870's some preferred the more respectful name of Greenfield.

When construction of the Carson and Colorado began, the residents of Pizen Switch wanted to make certain that the line would go through their town, and they felt a compliment to the railroad superintendent might do the trick. So they renamed the community Yerington. It was a vain effort, however, because the practical railroad boss was more interested in a direct line to the mining region than he was in the flattery of a few farmers. The railroad bypassed the town of Yerington by a dozen miles. In later years, however, a spur line went into Mason Valley.

Superintendent Yerington had decided that a better location for a railroad town would be at the south end of Walker Lake. The railroad was to pass down the eastern side of this body of water. Beyond the south end was a broad, open valley. At this point, the wagon roads forked to the mining camps at Candelaria, Aurora, and Bodie; it was one of the crossroads of Esmeralda County, and this influenced Yerington to designate this spot for a railroad town.

The railroad company advertised widely. Remembering how

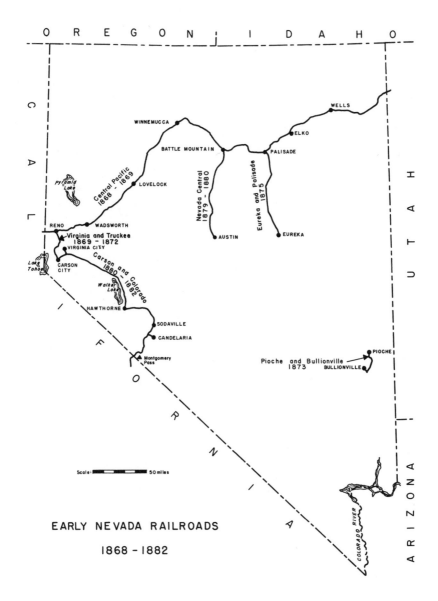

EARLY NEVADA RAILROADS
1868 - 1882

profitable the sale of lots had been for the Central Pacific at Reno about a dozen years before, they urged businessmen to come to Mound House, get on the Carson and Colorado train, and ride on dusty flatcars and coaches to the spot. More than eight hundred men responded on April 14, 1881. They went to the townsite, which was then only parched, barren desert. A few men had been enterprising enough to establish tent saloons and gambling facilities for the occasion, so some of the visitors were induced to buy lots. The town of Hawthorne began to flourish. For many years, it was an important freighting center for the mining operations in the nearby Sierra Nevada and the central Nevada ranges.

The Carson and Colorado railroad never reached the Colorado River, nor did it even get halfway there. During the construction, its builders decided it would be more profitable to point the line southward into California's Owens Valley, rather than farther to the southeast, across the forbidding wastes. Little did the builders know that a generation later, two of the West's richest mining towns—Tonopah and Goldfield—would spring up near the route they had originally planned. About fifty-five miles east of Hawthorne, the Carson and Colorado was turned southward into California. It did reach far enough east to give service to the little mining camp of Candelaria, but its engines never broke the silence of the rest of southern or south-central Nevada.

Such railroads as the Central Pacific, the Nevada Central, the Eureka and Palisade, the Virginia and Truckee, and the Carson and Colorado changed the character of western and northern Nevada. This mechanized form of transportation made it much easier to reach those regions, and it became less difficult to supply the miners, cattlemen, and ranchers with the necessities and comforts of life.

No railroads, however, yet served most of the southern and southeastern sections of the state. It is time now to trace the developments in those regions.

8. Opening Southern, Eastern Nevada, 1864-1881

WHEN THE COMSTOCK CITIES were most prosperous and the Central Pacific was in its prime, settlements were also established in eastern and southern Nevada; towns appeared near ore bodies or on rich agricultural land.

The struggle between the mining society and the Mormons, which was a feature of the 1850's, was reenacted under different circumstances in the 1860's. When the Mormons abandoned their outposts in Carson Valley, Washoe Valley, the Truckee Meadows, Las Vegas, and elsewhere, they seemed to have forsaken forever the regions distant from Salt Lake City. In the next few years, however, as the church's internal problems eased, the desire to expand revived. In 1864, Mormons became again interested in colonizing the southern and eastern parts of present-day Nevada. Soon there were outposts at Panaca, Callville, St. Thomas, St. Joseph, and Moapa.

However, miners appeared also in this general area. The discovery of ore near the Pahranagat Valley brought men from the camps of western and central Nevada, and a dispute arose over jurisdiction. Largely as a result of the miners' claims, the state of

Nevada was enlarged at the expense of Utah Territory; thousands of square miles were added to the Silver State's eastern edge. After many years of disputes, Mormon settlers began once again to leave their outposts, although not permanently.

Meanwhile, new mineral discoveries were made at Hamilton, Pioche, and Eureka—far from the center of the state's mining and political activity. Each of these towns had an era of glory before the ore gave out; life was much different there from that in the Mormon towns to the south and from that in most civilized parts of the world.

NEW MORMON SETTLEMENTS

When Nevada achieved statehood in 1864, her territory did not extend as far east and south as it now does. The eastern boundary was about fifty miles west of its present location, and the extreme southern triangle of the state was part of Arizona Territory. The miners and politicians of Nevada had not yet developed an interest in regions so far from the Comstock Lode; the present sites of Wells, Ely, McGill, Pioche, Caliente, Las Vegas, Henderson, and Boulder City were all beyond the borders of Nevada, and no towns yet existed in any of those places.

The Mormons of Utah, however, were showing new interest in expanding their area of settlement. In May, 1864, Brigham Young sent a group of colonizers into Meadow Valley, where they built homes and began to cultivate the land. Shortly before, a Mormon missionary to the Indians had discovered an outcropping of silver ore in a canyon ten miles northwest of Meadow Valley, which stimulated interest in the whole area. The site where the ore was discovered later became Pioche, and the Mormon community later formed the township of Panaca.

Panaca is the oldest town in eastern Nevada. Its founder was Francis Lee, who acted as presiding elder of the church mission. The pioneer settlers were troubled by Indians during the early years, who posed such a threat that almost no development occurred at the site of the ore discovery for several years. The settlers of Panaca persisted with their farming, however, and the land yielded

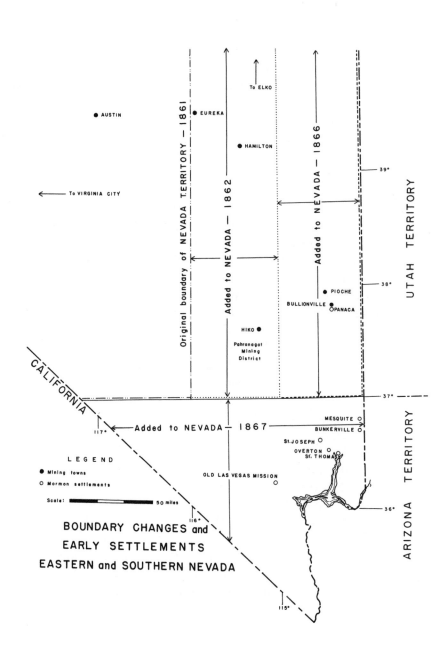

To ELKO

AUSTIN ● EUREKA

HAMILTON

To VIRGINIA CITY

Original boundary of NEVADA TERRITORY — 1861

Added to NEVADA — 1862

Added to NEVADA — 1866

39°

UTAH TERRITORY

38°

PIOCHE
BULLIONVILLE ● OPANACA

HIKO ●
Pahranagat
Mining
District

37°

CALIFORNIA

117°

MESQUITE ○
—Added to NEVADA — 1867— BUNKERVILLE ○

St. JOSEPH ○
OVERTON ○
St. THOMAS ○

ARIZONA TERRITORY

LEGEND
● Mining towns
○ Mormon settlements

OLD LAS VEGAS MISSION ○

Scale: ▬▬▬ 50 miles

36°

116°

**BOUNDARY CHANGES and
EARLY SETTLEMENTS
EASTERN and SOUTHERN NEVADA**

115°

good crops. By 1866 the town was firmly established, and the mission was elevated to the status of a church ward.

In the fall of 1864, more church members were sent further south, some to make plans for navigation of the southern Colorado River and others to establish colonies where cotton and other hot-weather crops could be grown. The Mormons on this occasion did not try to send settlers back to their old location at Las Vegas, because the property there was now owned by an Arizona rancher.

In October, President Brigham Young nominated Anson Call to lead a party which would explore the Colorado River canyon and choose the site for a warehouse and shipping center. It was felt that goods might be hauled more cheaply to Salt Lake City if they came most of the way by water. President Young wanted to try shipping goods into the Gulf of California and up the Colorado by boat, and then overland northward to Salt Lake City, rather than all the way overland by wagon from San Francisco or Omaha. Anson Call was to find a way to make this practical.

Call established a community, which he named Callville, on the big bend of the Colorado River approximately due east of the present town of Henderson. (The location is now covered by the waters of Lake Mead.) For a short time, steamers operated up and down the river, carrying goods that had been brought by water all the way from San Francisco and New York. But the operation was not a success; the river was too dangerous. A few years later, in 1869, the transcontinental railroad provided better overland service, and the water route was not needed.

In October, 1864, another group was dispatched to the Muddy River Valley, about fifty miles northeast of Las Vegas. Under the guidance of Thomas B. Smith, they reached the valley in January, 1865. They founded the town of St. Thomas, named for their leader. The church called this the "Cotton Mission," since it was expected to supply the older Mormon towns with an abundant supply of the white fiber. Despite some trouble with the Indians, the mission succeeded in the early years. Later, other towns—St. Joseph, Moapa, West Point, and Overton—were established farther up the river.

The settlers produced enough wheat, corn, and cotton to justify the construction of a mill to grind the grain and operate a cotton gin. Thousands of pounds of agricultural products went northward into Utah, and the church regarded the Muddy Mission as a promising venture. But by the late 1860's, a serious political problem placed the whole development in jeopardy. The boundary lines between Utah Territory, Arizona Territory, and Nevada were uncertain, and all three were trying to claim the valley. Nevadans got into the act because miners had discovered ore about seventy miles to the northwest.

THE PAHRANAGAT MINES

The Pahranagat Range runs north and south in southern Nevada; along its eastern edge is the rich valley which bears the same name. The ore found in these mountains in 1865 did not prove to be important, but the political consequences of that discovery were significant.

When news of the new lode reached Austin early in 1866, the usual excitement spread among the miners. There was no road from the Nevada towns to the Pahranagat Range, but scores set out from Austin anyway. Soon four small towns sprang up in the new district, and even though there were fewer than two hundred men, they soon began to demand a county government. The mining-conscious legislature in Carson City, encouraged by a mining-conscious governor, moved quickly to create Lincoln County, providing that the county could be formally organized when persons had signed a petition.

Governor Blasdel was still a mining man at heart, although he had gone into politics, and he had a prospector's desire to see the new mining district. He may even have wanted to invest some money in Pahranagat property. In the spring of 1866 he decided to make a trip to the region, saying that he wanted to help organize the county.

No one had ever traveled from the western Nevada towns directly across the southern Nevada deserts to the Pahranagat region. All travel had been through Austin, then almost due east toward the site of the future town of Ely, and then south. This allowed the travelers to avoid the worst part of the parched southern desert. Governor Blasdel and several companions, however, decided to take a southern route, coming near the Amargosa Desert and Death Valley. Like many pioneer explorers before them, they almost perished. Running short of food and water, the party decided to divide. Governor Blasdel and one companion, being stronger, went ahead to one of the Pahranagat towns for help. When they sent a rescue party back into the desert, they found that some of the men had been killing lizards for food; one man had died.

For Governor Blasdel, the Pahranagat trip was a disappointment even after he reached the tiny mining towns. He was dissatisfied with the property, and he could not find three hundred persons to sign a petition for a county government. So he returned to Carson City—this time by the northern route through Austin—without having accomplished his mission. Not until the following year were there enough people in the Pahranagat region to create Lincoln County.

Governor Blasdel's personal discouragement, however, did not destroy the interest in Pahranagat. While he was on his trip, Congress in Washington considered a proposal to move the Nevada boundary one degree of longitude—or about fifty miles—to the east. A strong argument presented in the House of Representatives was that the discovery of the Pahranagat mines made the area a mining region, more suited to government by Nevada than by Utah. Congress accordingly added this large slice of territory to Nevada in the spring of 1866. Ironically, the Pahranagat mines were in Nevada anyway, but no one knew it because no survey had yet been made. Panaca was in the region which Nevada annexed in that year.

In addition to giving Nevada much of the former Utah Territory, Congress also shifted land from Arizona Territory to Nevada. An extension of the southern boundary of Utah westward to the California state line shows that all of present day Clark County and parts of Lincoln and Nye counties lie below the line. This entire region belonged to the Territory of Arizona until 1867, and within it were the Mormon settlements of St. Thomas, St. Joseph, and Callville. For more than two years after this area was transferred from Arizona to Nevada, no boundary survey was made, and Mormon residents did not know whether they were in Nevada, Utah, or Arizona. They believed they were in Utah Territory and resisted the government officials of Nevada.

Meanwhile the wandering miners were penetrating other areas of eastern Nevada. Pahranagat was not the only region which prospectors opened in the 1860's; most of the ranges south and east of Austin were visited by the fortune hunters. Austin became a focal point for prospectors in the middle 1860's. They would meet there to get their supplies for long treks into the distant mountains and to exchange information about the outcroppings they had seen to the south and east. While Virginia City had been the main jumping-off place in 1860, Austin replaced it about 1865, because it was closer to the unprospected lands.

Austin was the home of the *Reese River Reveille*, a pioneer newspaper that was the best source of information on the mining prospects of central and eastern Nevada in the 1860's. It was also the seat of Lander County, which covered all of northeastern Nevada until the late 1860's. Lander County has sometimes been called the "mother of counties" because three other counties were later formed from its eastern and northern sections. Austin might also be called the mother of some eastern Nevada communities, because important discoveries were credited to men who set out from there.

THE SHORT LIFE OF HAMILTON: WHITE PINE COUNTY

After the Pahranagat discovery, the next mining boom in eastern Nevada was on Treasure Hill in the White Pine mountains, about 100 miles east of Austin and about 120 miles north of Pahranagat. The town of Hamilton, which grew up high on the slopes of a towering mountain, was one of the most remarkable camps in the state's history. It had some of the richest silver ore ever found in Nevada, but not a great quantity of it. The usual conglomeration of miners and money chasers began to arrive in the district in 1868. Within two years the peak of the boom had passed, but those two years were filled with adventure.

The ore of the White Pine district was discovered on the side of a lofty mountain range, and accordingly the towns were built there. In 1868-1869, the communities of Hamilton, Treasure City, Eberhardt, and several other smaller camps were scattered over the slopes near miners' diggings. Treasure City, on the most elevated part of the mountain, was nearly 10,000 feet above sea level, and Hamilton, 8,000 feet.

The miners who succumbed to the White Pine fever had to cross wide expanses of desert and to learn to live in the severe climate. The earliest arrivals found it easier to dig caves than build houses for living quarters, and for a time Hamilton was known as Cave City. During the first winter, thousands of fortune hunters defied snows, winds, and disease to search for mines or to dig out the rich ore, and the towns grew under circumstances more trying than those which the Comstock pioneers had faced in 1859-1860. Eventually, impressive little cities were established.

As in all mining districts, a recorder was appointed immediately to keep track of claims; he was soon overwhelmed by the hordes of men wanting to establish their ownership of a rocky ledge. Thousands of filings came to him in a few months, and he took three assistants. Even then, the officers could not avoid overlapping claims and fierce disputes. By the spring of 1869, one hundred seventy mining companies had been created in California to extract the White Pine ore, and they claimed to have capital of nearly a quarter of a billion dollars.

Some of the foremost mine experts in America contributed to this excitement about White Pine. Rossiter W. Raymond, commissioner of mining statistics for the U.S. government, called the silver mines near Hamilton and Treasure City the richest that had been discovered in the century. Not until the high-grade ore of Goldfield was discovered more than thirty years later were Nevadans to see richer rock.

The ore at White Pine, however, did not extend deeply into the earth. The early developers felt certain they had found a whole mountaintop of the most precious silver ever known to man. This led to indiscriminate investment not only by Nevadans and Californians, but also by wealthy businessmen in New York and London.

Like the Comstock Lode, the White Pine district had a period of hasty, expensive mill building. Most investors lost more money than they made in these ventures. A San Francisco company, expecting to see a city of forty or fifty thousand people develop at Hamilton, built a huge and costly water system. Another investor built the elaborate Withington Hotel from sandstone, plus lumber which had been hauled laboriously from Oregon. These speculators were confident of a marvelous future for Hamilton and Treasure City.

The men of Treasure Hill loved horseracing, gambling, and celebrations of all sorts. Perhaps the high mountain air and the bitter, restricting winters gave the camp more zest during the pleasant seasons of the year. "It is a faster camp than the Comstock," one resident wrote in 1869, and he was probably right at the time.

Of course, the earliest prospectors and settlers in the boom period insisted that the district must have its own county government; no town with the expectations of Hamilton could long tolerate having the county seat a hundred miles away, at Austin. So the 1869 session of the legislature once again responded to the mining rush by creating White Pine County, and Hamilton became the site of a fine courthouse.

The year 1870 was the richest for the White Pine district in terms of the value of ore produced. Even by this time, the excitement had passed, and in later years production declined as the rich pockets of ore were rapidly exhausted. In 1873, fire, the enemy of so many hastily built camps, wrecked a large part of the town. Thereafter, Hamilton and the neighboring towns swiftly declined. The migrant miners and businessmen had nearly all left before the fire, and after that tragedy the emigration increased. Later prospectors never found rich ore in quantity in the lower depths of Treasure Hill. In 1885, another fire swept through the town, destroyed the courthouse, and removed most of the evidence that a rich camp had once existed there.

The heyday of Treasure Hill communities drew to a close while the Comstock was still booming; their troubles could not be blamed on the decline in the price of silver that occurred in the 1870's.

Even as early as 1870, the men who made Hamilton a lively, exciting town were drifting to new discoveries—westward to Eureka and southward to Pioche.

TRIAL AND ERROR IN EUREKA

The ores of Eureka were discovered in 1864, but several years passed before they could be mined and processed successfully. Problems arose largely because the metals could not be refined easily; much lead, as well as substantial quantities of silver, appeared in the Eureka ores, and the early developers went through a period of trial and error before they learned how to process the ore.

In 1870, a new technique for smelting was developed, and the town began to grow. Not until 1871 did the mines report substantial ore production, but soon the Eureka district had surpassed both Austin and White Pine—the nearest important neighbors. Eureka's growth was more gradual than that of Hamilton, but the era of prosperity lasted much longer. Eureka remained reasonably prosperous for about fifteen years, and in the early 1880's, with the Comstock in decline, it was Nevada's most productive mining camp. By the end of that decade, however, Eureka felt the pinch of depression.

Eureka had less trouble with gunmen and fighters than some of the other towns, probably because the vigilante committee "601" chased out those who were bent on making trouble. Law-abiding citizens had the upper hand here to a greater extent than in the early days of White Pine. Nonetheless, Eureka did not completely escape violence.

The most serious trouble occurred in the summer of 1879 and was known as the "charcoal burners war" or the "Fish Creek war." Because the ores of Eureka had to be smelted in furnaces at extremely high temperatures, charcoal was in great demand. Hundreds of men made their living in the mountains around the town by gathering wood from the pine and juniper trees and carrying it to special outdoor ovens where it was transformed to charcoal for the furnaces in Eureka. The business of chopping wood and making charcoal was important in many Nevada mining towns, but it was especially significant in Eureka.

In August, 1879, Eureka's mine and smelter owners wanted to

Eureka County court house

reduce the price for the charcoal from 30 cents to 27½ cents per bushel basket. The Charcoal Burners' Association, which represented the interests of the workers, refused to work for this price, and they decided to prevent charcoal from being hauled to Eureka. For a time, citizens of Eureka feared the charcoal burners would swarm into town from the mountains and destroy property.

The local sheriff became so alarmed that he telegraphed Governor Kinkead in Carson City, asking for a militia to keep the peace. The charcoal burners did not make any trouble, but after a week of tension, an over-eager sheriff's posse went to the Fish Creek charcoal camp about thirty miles south of Eureka. The posse attacked a group of workers and killed five of them. None of the sheriff's men were hurt. This was another example of reckless conduct by the early mining camp settlers.

Eureka, like its distant neighbors, wanted to form a county government of its own as soon as the boom got underway. In 1873, the legislature created Eureka County from the eastern part of Lander County, and in a few years an attractive red-brick courthouse was erected. This building is still one of the landmarks of central Nevada. The legislature fashioned a long, narrow county, stretching far enough north to include part of the route of the Central Pacific Railroad.

Eureka was fortunate to have a railroad connection with the Central Pacific and thus with the outside world during the boom years. The Eureka and Palisade Railroad was constructed in 1873-1875, partly by the financing of wealthy men associated with Virginia City and the Bank of California. This gave Eureka an advantage which Hamilton and Pioche did not have in the 1870's and 1880's.

BOOM AND BUST IN PIOCHE

Although ore had been discovered in the hills northwest of Panaca in 1864, no important mines had been developed. Indians were troublesome throughout the region. Also, the ore was difficult to process. When the rush to White Pine began in 1868-1869, it brought new interest to the Panaca region, 110 miles to the south, just as it focused attention on the Eureka discovery. By the spring of 1870, a rush had begun from Hamilton to the south, to the area then known as the Meadow Valley district.

F. L. A. Pioche, a financier from San Francisco, was one of the first successful investors in the region, and the early settlers honored him in the name of their town. It was a questionable honor in the beginning, however, because Pioche inherited some of the worst characters of the White Pine district. No camp in Nevada had a more disgraceful reputation than Pioche for gunmen and troublemakers. In 1873, the Nevada State Mineralogist reported to the state legislature that, "for a time Pioche was a scene of lawlessness and horrid murders, which have scarcely ever had a parallel in the history of this coast." But the town's many stable, peaceful citizens within three years gained control of the situation. After 1873, the toughs moved away in search of other bonanzas. In its early years Pioche was prosperous, producing more silver and flourishing longer than Hamilton, even if the initial discovery was not as rich.

Pioche, too, wanted its own county government. Instead of creating another new county, however, the legislature in 1871 moved the seat of Lincoln County from Hiko, the main town in Pahranagat Valley, to Pioche. The Pahranagat mines were dormant by this time, and there was little objection to the transfer.

The county officers in Pioche had a tendency to live lavishly and immediately planned a courthouse and jail. Although they initially agreed to spend only $26,400, the final cost was much more than that. In addition, large debts occurred when a sheriff stole county money and the public officials borrowed carelessly. Mining became less profitable after 1873, but the debts continued to rise. Soon Lincoln County had an obligation of several hundred thousand dollars which it could not pay. This county's experience became a lesson to all Nevada in the need for careful governmental financing. Eventually it cost the taxpayers of southern Nevada nearly $1,000,000 to make up for the reckless policies of early county officers in Pioche.

No other mining region in Nevada except the Comstock Lode was beset by more financial schemers in such a short period of time. Many lawsuits were initiated by men trying to get part of a rich mine without having any legitimate title to it. Leading mine owners faced a long list of court actions against persons or companies trying to get their ore legally or illegally.

Pioche was more than 200 miles from the Central Pacific railroad line, and all freight had to be hauled by wagon across the desert at considerable cost. Since there was a strong desire for a railroad to connect the town with the Central Pacific, financial manipulators saw this as another opportunity to make a quick profit. On two occasions, groups of promoters nearly succeeded in getting the county government to issue large amounts of bonds to obtain money for the purchase of railroad stock. There was no assurance that the railroad would ever be built, and if the financial transaction had been carried out according to the original plan, the taxpayers would have been cheated once more. An alert district judge and Governor Bradley prevented this scheme from maturing.

The men who wanted a quick and dishonest fortune had less opportunity in Pioche after 1873, because the camp began to decline in prosperity. Most of the rich ore down to the level of 1,200 feet had been extracted, and underground water made mining almost impossible below that level. In addition, the price of silver declined sharply as more came onto the market from western mines. By 1876, the boom period had passed, and before the end of the decade the major companies had sold their interests and nearly all mining had ceased. A railroad had been built from Pioche to Bullionville in 1873, but by the time it began operations, the decline had already started. In a few years it was discontinued. The nearby milling communities at Bullionville and Dry Valley began to wither and die. It was the old Nevada story of boom and bust.

THE MORMON TOWNS, 1868-1880

Events at Pioche had an important impact on the Mormon towns that had been settled in the 1860's. Panaca was ten miles from Pioche and only a mile from Bullionville, and the industrious, reverent Mormons usually had little regard for the rowdy mining and milling workers. Serious difficulties arose when Lincoln County officials tried to collect taxes from the residents of Panaca, St. Joseph, St. Thomas, and other little settlements of the Latter-Day Saints.

Pioche in the 1870's

Even before the county seat had been moved to Pioche, when the county assessor operated from Hiko, he had had differences with the Mormons. These settlers believed their towns were in Utah and refused to pay taxes to Lincoln County or Nevada. Nevada taxes were higher than those in Utah Territory. When the Lincoln County assessor-treasurer presented a tax bill, the Mormons presented receipts for taxes already paid to Utah Territory. Sometimes, they chased the tax collector away with threats of violence.

Finally, in 1870, an official survey was made of the Nevada-Utah boundary line established by Congress in 1866. The survey showed Panaca to be about twenty miles inside Nevada; the Moapa-Muddy Valley communities were also well within Lincoln County.

This dissatisfied the Mormon settlers and their Utah leaders. However, the discontent was eased in Panaca when the development of the Pioche mines brought prosperity. The Mormons had a good market for their products and many of them earned high pay for hauling ore from Pioche to Bullionville. (This practice ended after the construction of the Pioche and Bullionville Railroad.) In spite of their distaste for the way of life of the mining camp, the citizens of Panaca generally benefited from the boom, and most of them accepted Nevada jurisdiction quickly.

In the southern Mormon settlements, the situation was different. The higher Nevada taxes and the fact that the settlers were beyond the jurisdiction of Utah seemed unacceptable. At the town of Overton, many persons could not make enough money from their crops to buy tools and clothing because there was no ready market for agricultural surpluses. Also, in the summer of 1870 a flood hit the town of West Point, causing much destruction. The church decided to abandon this town on the upper Muddy River, sending the settlers to other parts of the valley.

The tax collectors of Lincoln County were required by state law to obtain the taxes in coins rather than in paper money, and the Mormons were unable or unwilling to pay hard money. Besides, the Mormons were afraid Nevada would try to collect back taxes, which they had refused to pay.

In the face of these problems, President Brigham Young advised the settlers at the Muddy Mission that they could abandon their settlements if they wanted to return to Utah. As a possible solution the settlers asked the Nevada government to create a separate county for them, and also sought to have Congress return the area to Utah Territory. But these efforts were unavailing, and, early in 1871, the Mormons abandoned their settlements along the Muddy River and returned to Utah. About six hundred persons had been living in the valley at that time, and they left much rich, cleared land and an excellent irrigation system, as well as their homes. Others, not of the Mormon Church, came into the region, tore down the houses, and made a profit from the property the Latter-Day Saints had left behind.

The rich lands of the valley remained in non-Mormon hands for nine years, but in 1880 members of the Church once more became interested. Within a short time, the town of Overton revived, and some of the old Mormon settlers returned. Nevada officials did not trouble them seriously over back taxes. As the years passed, Mormon families reacquired most of the property that members of their faith had owned before. They reestablished the town of St. Thomas; the former St. Joseph became Logandale.

Meanwhile, another group of Mormons claimed the fertile land of the Virgin Valley, about thirty miles east of the Moapa communities. In 1877, settlers from Santa Clara, Utah, decided to take up this valley to practice a cooperative program of community living. They were members of the "United Order" within the church, a sect which believed that a community should supply as much of its own needs as possible. This experiment, then, was not fostered at the suggestion of church authorities, as the missions at Las Vegas and along the Muddy River had been.

The original "company" of twenty-three persons that undertook to settle the valley was headed by Edward Bunker, Sr., who led the party into the valley in January. The first building to be constructed was a community dining hall, which also served as a church. The members spent the first spring and summer building an irrigation canal and preparing the land for cultivation; only in the late summer did they establish their permanent town, Bunkerville. The returns from the land were impressive; cotton, grain, and vegetables flourished in the warm climate. The members built mills to process flour, cotton, and molasses, winning the respect of neighboring communities.

Under the United Order's system of operation, all grain and hay went to a single yard, all produce went into a single storehouse, and all teams of animals were fed by one man. Each member had duties to the community and shared in the profits and losses. Parcels of land were assigned by lot to various settlers, and they were instructed on how to use it. Meals were served to all settlers together.

For about two years, this system operated well and the town began to attract additional members to the United Order. By 1879, however, some members became dissatisfied, because a few of the community did not do their share of the work. Church records show that discontent grew, and that the Order began dividing property among its members on a permanent basis and making allotments dependent upon labor. By 1881 the United Order was dissolved, and the company's stockholders were paid a portion of the produce. Today, Bunkerville remains as a picturesque reminder of a pioneer experiment.

During the period of the communal undertaking in Bunkerville, another Latter-Day Saint community was established by authority of the church leaders. On the north side of the Virgin River, opposite Bunkerville, lies the Mesquite Flat, a narrow strip of fertile land. The church sent several families to settle that area in 1879, and a few months later a community, Mesquite, was established.

A severe flood on the Virgin River struck both Bunkerville and Mesquite in 1882, and the latter settlement was badly damaged. After more floods and problems, the earliest settlers of Mesquite abandoned their colony in 1891, and another group colonized the region in 1895. Since that time, residents of this town have learned to cope with the troublesome river, and the valley has been productive for more than two generations.

MORMON TOWNS AND MINING TOWNS

Once again, in eastern Nevada, we become aware of the great differences between the two main currents of emigration which settled Nevada. Those who originally settled the Pahranagat camps, the towns on Treasure Hill, Pioche, and Eureka were silver seekers, eager to make a quick fortune and enjoy a luxurious life, usually somewhere beyond the borders of Nevada. The Mormons, on the other hand, did not come to exploit the land, but to cultivate it. They came to make homes and, as a rule, to stay.

The mining camps eventually became stable and produced some of the state's leading citizens, but their beginnings were chaotic. Many were rowdy and violent, and most of the pioneer operations were badly organized. The Mormon communities of Panaca, St. Thomas, Overton, and Bunkerville were essentially quiet and well-organized from the beginning.

Perhaps there was a greater degree of freedom in the mining camps than in the towns where the Mormon church was so strong. The mountain towns had more variety; they had newspapers, theaters, and diverse social groups. In the Mormon valley towns, the church substituted for all such institutions.

Hamilton, Pioche, and Eureka were essentially men's towns in the early days, with few traditional homes and families. Panaca, Bunkerville, and St. Thomas were family towns, with a high percentage of women and children. Even the appearances of the two types of communities emphasized this fact. The mining towns usually had a few attractive and elaborate homes, and many shacks and cabins. Civic pride did not extend far enough to make the towns attractive, and the lack of water made most camp residents despair of greenery. The Mormon settlers built stable, modest, comfortable homes and often supplemented their verdant fields with flowers. As a rule there were no bars or gambling rooms in the Mormon towns, and little of the hectic speculation which characterized the mining communities.

As the years and the mining booms passed away, a conservative class of people remained. The mining towns became more peaceful, more suited to family life, and—as far as nature would permit—more green. But in appearance and attitude they still remain unlike the church-founded communities to this day.

9. The Twenty-Year Depression, 1881-1900

THE DECLINE OF THE COMSTOCK LODE in the 1880's and the passing of the other Nevada mining booms caused serious problems. No new industry arose to replace the mines, and people began to drift away because there was a shortage of jobs. In 1880 Nevada had a population of 62,000; twenty years later it had only 42,000.

The story of this era between 1880 and 1900 is largely one of frustration and disappointment. Thousands were spent in Virginia City and Gold Hill in futile efforts to find another Big Bonanza. From time to time there was hope for another boom in some of the old mining camps, but such hopes nearly always collapsed.

The depression in the mining towns hurt Nevada's small ranchers and farmers also. As the miners had spread out across the Great Basin, they had provided a ready market for agricultural products; scores of Nevada valleys had been settled by hardy families who produced hay, grain, vegetables, and—in a few places—fruit. But it became more difficult to operate at a profit in the 1880's and the 1890's.

Many Nevadans believed their troubles came not from the exhaustion of the silver mines but from the decline in the price of silver on the world market. Since the federal government had stopped minting silver dollars in 1873, there was less demand for the "white metal"; so Congress was blamed for the low price of silver. Nevada senators tried to get legislation passed which would raise the price of silver or require unlimited coinage. In the 1890's, Nevadans became so disgusted with Congress that most of them denounced the Democratic and Republican parties to join a newly formed Silver party.

NEVADA IN DEPRESSION, 1881-1900

"The fever period is fortunately passing away," a famous visitor to Nevada wrote in 1879. "The prospector is no longer the raving, wandering ghoul of ten years ago, rushing in random lawlessness among the hills, hungry and footsore."

The visitor was John Muir, the great student of nature who became famous for helping to establish America's National Park system. He was impressed by the fact that there were so many "dead towns" on the Nevada landscape. In his book *Steep Trails* Muir said there were about five deserted towns for every one that still had ordinary life. "Nevada is one of the very youngest and wildest of the States; nevertheless it is already strewn with ruins that seem as gray and silent and time-worn as if the civilization to which they belonged had perished centuries ago. Yet, strange to say, all these ruins are results of mining efforts made within the last few years."

Most of the decaying camps which John Muir saw had never been important towns. They had grown rapidly after the discovery of a small outcropping of ore and had disappeared almost as rapidly when no great ore body materialized or when another discovery was reported elsewhere.

But even the more important towns of Nevada were beginning to look forlorn and troubled by 1879 or soon after. We have already seen that all big mining camps had extracted the richest ores at the higher levels, and the search for new wealth was unavailing. For the next twenty years, the population of these camps gradually dwindled when efforts to find more bonanzas failed.

The most extensive ventures, of course, were made on the Comstock Lode. Diligent explorations continued in the main mines of Virginia City after the decline began in 1877. Another drastic underground fire broke out in the Consolidated Virginia mine in 1881, and it became necessary to close the mine for three years, and then reopen at great cost. Senator Jones, when he was not serving the state in Washington, directed the search for more high-grade ore during part of the 1880's, but finally gave up the attempt. Some investors spent millions sinking deep shafts to explore the lode nearly 4,000 feet below the surface of the earth, where extreme heat and excessive water hindered their efforts. People said the Comstock miners were "chasing a dollar to the gates of hell." Although some ore was mined, its value was low and the quantity was small, by comparison with the boom days.

The "Bonanza kings" sold much of their stock in the Virginia City mines when the decline began and gradually passed from the scene. Mackay, the most modest and brilliant of the mining leaders, held his interest in Comstock mines until 1895, but in the meantime he invested part of his fortune and his talent in the laying of a cable across the Atlantic Ocean, making possible rapid communication between Europe and America.

Across Nevada, the story was essentially the same. In Austin, the prosperity of the 1860's never returned. Only the railroad and the fact that it was a county seat kept the town alive. In Pioche and other camps, water flooded the lower levels of the mines when work ceased, and the underground workings caved in as timber decayed or burned. In Eureka, moderate prosperity lasted until the middle 1880's and then vanished. Hamilton, once the pride of eastern Nevada, shrank to a tiny village after the fire of 1885.

Prospectors continued to roam the hills during these discouraging years. The bearded "desert rat," coaxing his stubborn, overloaded burro across the desert in search of a new bonanza, was a familiar sight.

How did the prospector manage to survive for weeks or months in the wilds, far from the comforts of the towns? He carried on his donkey or mule a slab of salt pork, some flour and baking powder, beans and coffee, and perhaps a few other small supplies of food.

Most of his load consisted of a bedroll and the equipment necessary for probing the mysteries of the rocks—a pick and shovel, a mortar and pestle for crushing samples, a pan, canteen, a spoon, and maybe—if he were well equipped—some dynamite for blasting and bottles of chemicals to test for silver.

Such a man—part hermit and part wandering pilgrim—often preferred loneliness to the society of his fellow men. Most prospectors had dreams of finding a marvelous ledge like the one Peter O'Riley and Patrick McLaughlin found on Mt. Davidson. Once in a while they would find a promising spot, chip some samples from it, and carry the fragments of rock to the nearest towns. So residents of Virginia City, Austin, Pioche, Elko, and other towns frequently heard rumors about a new strike or a promising lode. A few prospectors even found places that could be mined at a profit, and some of them made a meager living. Others managed to find a businessman in town who would "grubstake" them with the understanding that the profits of any mine must be shared with the donor.

Nevada's mining hopes did not die during the long depression years. From time to time, as prospectors turned up small deposits of precious metals, the newspapers reported these events in ways which aroused the expectations of the patient residents of the mining camps.

The most important discovery of the 1890's occurred in southeastern Nevada, about fifty miles southwest of Pioche. An outcropping of gold led to a small rush and to the founding of the town of Delamar, which became the most important producing camp in the last years of the nineteenth century. Delamar produced $15,000,000 worth of ore, but it did not substantially change the economic situation for the state. It became infamous in Nevada history because the choking dust of its mines and mills killed or injured scores of workers in the 1890's. By 1900 Delamar had passed the peak of its prosperity. In another decade it was rapidly becoming a ghost town.

Delamar and other less important discoveries of the 1890's proved to be preludes to the revival of mining after 1900. Two other discoveries in southern Nevada at the beginning of the twentieth century rewarded the patience of the residents of the Silver State.

RANCHING AND STOCK RAISING, 1851-1900

It was not the limited mining and the prospecting spirit alone that kept Nevada alive in the last years of the nineteenth century. As we have seen, men had been tilling the soil and raising stock in some of the valleys even before mining began, and this activity increased with the mining booms. After the bonanza era had passed, some stockmen and ranchers operated successfully because the railroads enabled them to ship their cattle and sheep to distant centers of population. Thus rapid transportation opened the way to new markets.

Nevada's climate and topography would not permit the intensive farming which Americans of the Middle West and California knew. Few valleys and mountains had water, and therefore greenery was sparse. Nevada's pioneer agricultural activities were often performed on lonely ranches nestled on the edge of a stream-producing mountain range or the side of a barren-looking valley. By the middle of the 1870's, nearly every life-giving stream big enough to support a garden and a field of hay had been claimed.

The pioneers soon learned that Nevada's soil was rich, if only enough water could be put on it. Marvelous crops could be grown, if only unseasonal frosts did not strike. But the dangers of drought and frost were great, and Nevada farmers preferred to raise cattle, sheep, hay, or those vegetables that did not require a long growing season. We have mentioned that Mormons in Carson Valley raised gardens and fattened cattle for sale to the emigrants in 1851; Eagle Valley had settlers late in the same year and produced its first crops in the next year. Other areas along the Carson and Humboldt rivers were minor cultivation areas in the 1850's, but only after the discovery of the Comstock Lode did large scale ranching seem feasible.

Even before the period when ranches were established in Nevada, stockmen knew that the valleys of the Great Basin offered excellent grazing land. A band of sheep was driven from California into the Carson Valley as early as 1851, and in the next few years more emigrants were favorably impressed with the valleys on the eastern edge of the Sierra Nevada. By the late 1850's a few cattle owners were driving their herds into Carson Valley and the Truckee Meadows for the winter months because the range in western Utah Territory was preferable to that of California during the cold season. Even though snow sometimes covered the bunch grass and low brush on which the cattle thrived, the animals learned to paw through the snow to reach the feed.

One of the first California cattlemen to profit from this knowledge was H. N. A. Mason, who had become familiar with Nevada's resources in 1854 when he had first crossed the Great Basin with a herd. In 1859 he drove a band of cattle from California into the Walker River region which later came to be known as Mason Valley. This was the beginning of a vast cattle and ranching empire, since Mason and his California partners became large landowners, with holdings in the Quinn River area of Humboldt County as well as in Mason Valley.

Another large ranching enterprise which started in the 1850's was that of Fred Dangberg, who settled in the Carson Valley about five miles east of Genoa and eventually became the owner of more than 35,000 acres of land. He provided much hay for the Comstock communities and was one of the first Nevadans to grow alfalfa for the market. He managed and expanded his lands for nearly a half century. After his death in 1904 his sons established the attractive town of Minden, which soon became the seat of Douglas County.

In 1859, another group of cattle owners from central California drove their animals into the area immediately west of Mason Valley, through which flows the west fork of the Walker River. Two of these herdsmen were R. B. Smith and T. B. Smith, and the region was called Smith Valley in their honor. The ranchers prospered especially after Aurora boomed in the early 1860's, and a freighting station, Wellington, began to function. Smith Valley never had a large population, but it has remained a rich agricultural region for the past century, much like Carson Valley immediately to the west.

At about this same time, or perhaps even earlier, the foundations of Nevada's extensive sheep industry were laid. Among the earliest herders who chose to settle permanently in the western Great Basin was Pedro Altube, a Basque who recognized a similarity between Nevada's mountains and his native Pyrenees. In 1859 he established the Spanish Ranch in the Elko region and in later years brought scores of his fellow countrymen to Nevada to help with the herding. The Basques became a picturesque part of northern Nevada's landscape, standing lonely watch over their flocks. The sheepmen preceded the cattlemen on some of the desert ranges.

As the seasons passed and California was afflicted by a few drought periods, more stockmen from that state drove their herds into other parts of Nevada. The winter of 1862-63 was especially dry on the western slopes of the Sierra, and many cattlemen tried Nevada's northern ranges. A few established permanent homes in the Reese River Valley and along the Humboldt River. The expansion of the mining industry provided a nearby market for part of the cattle and sheep produced locally, and the livestock industry grew during the boom years.

The northern areas now included in Elko and Humboldt counties did not produce mineral wealth equal to those regions across the center of Nevada, but they had some of the state's best grazing land and they became leaders in the production of livestock. In the middle 1860's, cattlemen were bringing increasing numbers of Texas longhorn cattle to the northern ranges. These sturdy, hearty animals became standard along the Humboldt in the boom years, but they required a long time to mature and they had to compete with the herds of sheep for the range grasses. Cattlemen eventually learned that they could make more profit from faster maturing Hereford cattle than from the Texas longhorn.

When the Nevada mining towns declined in the late 1870's, the livestock industry did not suffer greatly because it did not depend to any large extent on the Nevada market. (In some cases ranchers who produced hay and grain or vegetables for sale in the mining towns did lose business.) By the early 1880's, stockmen were shipping their animals by rail to Omaha and San Francisco. Although these shipping rates were high, the sale of cattle and sheep would, as a rule, bring a profit because it had cost little to fatten the animals on the open range. Before 1890, Nevada ranchers generally did not raise enough hay to feed their cattle in the winter, and relied heavily upon the range forage.

Humboldt County ranching: Cattle drive (above) and branding

A severe winter in 1889-90 changed their policy. Northern Nevada was struck by one of the coldest, snowiest seasons in history, and thousands of cattle and sheep perished in blizzards. Stockmen were taken by surprise; they had no way to get feed onto the range, and the snow was too deep for the animals to paw for grass. Although most cattlemen and sheepmen survived this loss, a depression troubled the industry in the 1890's. It became difficult for the ranchers, unless they had large-enough holdings, to weather the economic storms. Some stockmen experienced financial disaster; others survived to build great ranching empires.

Two Ranching Empires

Some of the men who became successful ranchers and stockmen had first been associated with Nevada's mining camps or mining operations. Two examples were Jewett W. Adams and William N. McGill, pioneers who managed to build large cattle businesses even though the economy of the state was suffering in the later years of the nineteenth century.

Adams had arrived in Virginia City as a young man in 1864 after several years in California. Clever and imaginative, he first made a living by gambling, but he abandoned this to go into the freighting business. His teams and wagons hauled supplies into Virginia City in the days before the railroads were built.

In 1873, Adams began to shift his attention to cattle, and for a number of years his herds grazed in northern Nye County in central Nevada. He did not restrict his interests to cattle-raising, even though he constantly enlarged his land holdings and his herds in the 1870's. He spent time in Carson City, where he entered politics and in 1874 won election as lieutenant governor. His first term coincided with the second term of Governor Bradley; on several occasions during the boom years, Adams acted as governor of the state when Governor Bradley was ill.

By 1882 Adams was well known throughout the state and was persuaded by his friends to run for the office of governor. He won the election and became Nevada's second Democratic chief executive, following Governor Kinkead. He was regarded as an honest

Nevada's foremost creative writer, Walter Van Tilburg Clark (1909-1971). He used Nevada's ranches and mining towns as settings for his best known stories. Two novels, *The Ox-Bow Incident* and *The Track of the Cat*, reflect life in remote parts of northwestern Nevada; another novel, *The City of Trembling Leaves*, draws on Clark's childhood experiences in Reno in the 1920's

A memorial to Walter Van Tilburg Clark has been established in Morrill Hall on the Univeristy of Nevada campus in Reno; it features a bust created by noted Reno sculptor Yolande Jacobson Sheppard

and competent governor, even by many of his political opponents. In 1886 he ran for a second term but was defeated in a Republican landslide.

Even while serving as governor, Adams continued to build his agricultural business. He began to buy ranches in White Pine County and had thousands of cattle driven into the adjacent valleys. He also invested in mines in Nye County during his years as governor, and for a short time realized a profit from the production of silver. This was only a minor part of his interest, however, since most of his resources were in cattle.

After his retirement from political office in 1887, Adams continued to spend much time in Carson City, leaving the management of his cattle herds to foremen. For a few years he was director of the United States Mint at Carson City. An important event of his later life was the forming of a partnership with William McGill.

McGill had also begun his Nevada career on the Comstock Lode, arriving there in 1871. A trained engineer, he immediately gained employment on the Sutro tunnel, which had been started about two years earlier. After a year, he moved to Hamilton where he became a surveyor. Later, he engaged in mining near the present town of Ely and at the briefly prosperous town of Taylor. He made a profit, but sold his interest in 1885 and invested some of the money in ranching. This proved to be a wise move in the 1880's when mining was unprofitable.

McGill and a partner bought a ranch in Steptoe Valley near where the town of McGill was later to develop. In the late 1880's, he rapidly acquired other lands in White Pine County, soon becoming one of the largest landowners in eastern Nevada. After 1892, however, a severe depression hit much of the West, and McGill's business had several difficult years. He was able to continue partly because he had part interest in one of Nevada's first electric power plants, which served Ely in the late 1890's, and because he owned a meat business in Ely. His cattle empire did not expand significantly between 1892 and 1897.

In 1898, Adams and McGill decided to merge their lands and cattle herds, since each felt it would be more profitable to cooperate. They went into the sheep business and made large profits, and soon after the turn of the century their cattle business improved. Together, the two men acquired many more properties in White Pine, Nye, and Lincoln counties. After 1900, the state of Nevada as a whole was to emerge from its long depression, and the Adams-McGill partnership profited from the improved economic climate.

Another famous ranching partnership in Nevada's cattle industry was that of John Sparks and Frank Tinnan, both former citizens of the Confederacy who built a huge empire in Elko County. Sparks came to Nevada with a herd of Texas longhorn cattle in 1868; he and Tinnan began acquiring land in the lush valleys of the northeast as the railroad began to serve that area. Later, Tinnan sold his share to Jasper Harrell, a Californian, but Sparks remained the main operator and policy maker for their company.

By the turn of the century, the Sparks-Harrel Company owned ranches and rangeland stretching for about 150 miles north and south and almost the same length east and west. Sparks was largely responsible for introducing Hereford cattle to Nevada, and eventually they became the most common type of range animal in the state. Scores of cowboys rode the range under his supervision, branding calves and herding fattened animals to the rail heads.

The Sparks-Harrel herds, like so many others, were severely reduced in the winter of 1889-90. After the bitter experience of that year, their ranches began to raise and keep large quantities of hay for future difficult seasons.

Sparks, like Adams before him, became interested in politics and used his ranching reputation as a stepping stone into the governor's office. He was elected first in 1902 and again in 1906; the main events of his political career belong to later chapters. Also like Adams, Governor Sparks had interests other than cattle raising and politics. He became the owner of the Wedekind Mine north of Reno, which caused excitement shortly after 1900. Because of his activities in this area the newly developing railroad town just east of Reno was given his name.

The stories of Adams, McGill, and Sparks are not typical of the history of the ranching and stock-raising business in Nevada. Other operations were smaller, and few of them were as rewarding as those of the great cattlemen.

In the last twenty-five years of the century, too many cattlemen and sheepmen had driven their animals onto the Nevada ranges, and overgrazing became a serious problem. The cattle owners regarded the sheepmen as wandering intruders, and the sheepmen— many of whom had been on the ranges ahead of the cattlemen— had an equally intense dislike for the cattle owners. There was not enough grass and water for the animals of both.

History does not tell us how often cattlemen and sheepmen shot it out with rifles or tried to destroy rival herds. Basque sheepherders —silent, hardy men who often operated from ranches in northern Nevada or Oregon—became the bitter enemies of the cowmen of Elko County, and their intermittent sniper warfare made life dangerous for both. Not until 1934, when Congress passed the Taylor Grazing Act, was this problem partly solved by limiting the number of animals which could be grazed on the open range. Here, as in many other cases, government regulation was essential to prevent chaos.

In many parts of the Middle West, the cattle and sheep owners eventually lost their best ranges to the small farmers who had followed them onto the plains and plateaus, eventually taking up the land and restricting the operations of the free-ranging stockmen. In Nevada, this happened only in relatively isolated areas; on the contrary, the tendency in this state has been for the large stockmen to buy the property and the water rights of the small farmers, some of whom had tried to make a living by raising vegetables and fruits for the market. More than 90 per cent of the harvested crop acreage in Nevada is used for raising hay and grain for livestock feed.

Nevada is the seventh largest state in the Union, but it is forty-ninth in the value of the farm products that it sends to market. Only tiny Rhode Island, the smallest of our states, has less income from farming than Nevada.

Scattered through Nevada are the remnants of farms and homesteads where pioneering families once made a living. Now many of these sites are abandoned, except for occasional cowboys or cattle feeders who use them temporarily. Today, a large livestock company may own several ranches and farms because such ownership gives it rights to graze on the range and places to take cattle during roundup. The trend toward the absorption of the small cultivator by the large cattlemen and sheepmen began between 1880 and 1900, and it was a slow, gradual process.

THE SILVER CONTROVERSY, 1873-1900

The depression in the mining camps and the hard times on the ranches and farms created an unhappy political mood in Nevada; other parts of the West shared this discontent. To understand how Nevadans thought about their problems in the last years of the nineteenth century, we must review some of the acts of Congress which had a bearing on their troubles.

During the early years of Nevada's history, the price of silver had been high, but by the early 1870's it was declining. The falling price coincided with an act of Congress passed in 1873 which did not provide for the minting of silver dollars. Smaller silver coins were still to be minted, but this did not satisfy the western mine owners and miners. They wanted silver dollars to be coined freely, as in the past. They referred to this new law as the "Crime of '73."

The western states as a whole objected to the "Crime of '73," but they could not reverse the situation. Congress did pass the Bland-Allison Act in 1878, which provided for the purchase of a small amount of silver and the minting of dollars from this; but it was not enough to help the silver producers, who already were beginning to curtail their production. When the depression in the mining industry became acute in the 1880's, the mining people bitterly condemned the national legislation, even though part of their problem stemmed from the depletion of the rich ore bodies.

Senators Stewart and Jones became two of the West's leading spokesmen in the fight for free coinage of silver. They argued that the low price of silver was artificial, and that it was a conspiracy of eastern businessmen and bankers—"gold bugs" who wanted to deflate the economy by having a gold standard (a money economy based entirely on gold).

Among the ardent "Silverites" on the local level was C. C. Stevenson, a pioneer of Gold Hill who had arrived there soon after the discovery of the Comstock Lode. He had been part owner of one of the early mills and had also invested in the livestock business, importing some herds of Jersey cattle to Nevada. When the Nevada Silver Convention was formed in 1885 to press for a more favorable silver policy, Stevenson became chairman.

The Nevada Silver Convention was an unofficial body and could do nothing to change the national government's policy. But Stevenson became widely known to Nevadans by his work for the Convention, and in 1886 the Republican party persuaded him to run for governor. He defeated incumbent Governor Adams and became Nevada's fifth chief executive. Governor Stevenson did not live to complete his term of office; when he became disabled and could not serve in the last weeks of his life, Lieutenant Governor Frank Bell succeeded him. Bell also was a pioneer of Nevada, having arrived in 1858. He had invested in the Comstock mines, and, like Governor Stevenson, was a "Silverite." So was his successor, Governor Roswell K. Colcord, a mechanical engineer and mining superintendent who was elected in 1890.

People throughout the western states were demanding legislation for higher silver prices in the late 1880's, and their agitation bore fruit in 1890 when Congress passed a new money law. This was the Sherman Silver Purchase Act, which seemed to hold out hope for western miners and farmers, even though it did not provide for free coinage of silver. In a short time, however, it became obvious that the new law would not give much real assistance to the western states. Ranchers and miners began to feel that the Democratic and Republican parties were not interested in them, and started a new political movement. In 1892, the People's party emerged in defiance of the two old parties, and its leaders demanded free and unlimited coinage of silver.

Although most Nevadans were in sympathy with the People's party (or Populist party, as it was usually called), they did not rush to join it. Only a small People's party developed in Nevada, because the political leaders decided to form the Silver party instead. Organizations known as "Silver Clubs" began to appear in 1891, replacing the old Nevada Silver Convention, and, in the following year, Senator Stewart helped to form the Silver party. In the election of 1892, the Populists nominated James B. Weaver of Iowa as their candidate for President, and the Silver party supported him. He received more than twice as many votes as the Democrats

Francis G. Newlands. Con-
gressman, 1893-1902; U.S.
Senator, 1903-1915

William M. Stewart. U.S. Senator,
1864-1875, 1887-1905; shown as a gladiator
fighting for the free coinage of silver in 1892

and Republicans combined in Nevada, but he lost the election nationally.

A new political leader appeared in Nevada in the early 1890's during the campaign for free silver, and he soon became one of the state's most admired figures. He was Francis G. Newlands, an attorney from San Francisco, the son-in-law of William Sharon. He had been a legal advisor to Sharon and had made many trips to Virginia City in the 1870's and 1880's, but he did not move to Nevada until 1888. In 1892, he became the Silver party candidate for the House of Representatives and won the election. This launched him on a political career that was to include ten years in the House of Representatives and fifteen years in the U.S. Senate.

Many leaders of the Democratic and Republican parties in Nevada hesitated to leave their old parties and join the new Silverites, but Senator William Stewart led the way in his typically dynamic manner. When the state legislature elected him for a new term in the Senate in 1893, he declared he was a member of the Silver party—no longer a Republican. Senator John P. Jones soon did the same.

In the next two years, Nevada's voters remained dedicated to the Silver party. During the election of 1894, the Silverites won every election contest on the state level; the Republicans—who had been Nevada's leading political party most of the time since 1864—ran second, and the Democratic candidates received only a few hundred votes. The Silver party's choice for governor in 1894 was John E. Jones, a well-known mining figure (not related to Senator John P. Jones), who had been a pioneer of the White Pine and Eureka regions and had served for eight years in the office of surveyor general in Carson City. Governor Jones was one of the first political officers in Nevada to leave the Republican party and join the Silverites, which won him the praise of most Nevadans in the 1890's. He died after only about a year in office, and Lieutenant Governor Reinhold Sadler finished his term.

Governor Sadler was also typical of the "Silver Men" who led the state in the 1890's. He had arrived in Nevada in the 1860's, an immigrant from Germany. He lived briefly in Virginia City, Austin, and Hamilton during his first years in the state, operating stores in the booming mining camps. In the 1870's he raised cattle for a few years and lived in Carson City, and in the 1880's he became involved in milling in Eureka. Known throughout the state and devoted to the Silver cause, he won election to another term as governor in 1898 and was in office as the nineteenth century ended.

The year 1896 found most Nevadans still ready to shout and vote for Silver, but in that year a new political alliance developed. The Democrats and Populists throughout the nation were uniting behind William Jennings Bryan, a famous orator from Nebraska, as their candidate for President of the United States. The Silverites and Democrats of Nevada also joined to support him. Bryan became a hero to Nevadans, who hoped that he would change the course of history, restore the free coinage of silver, reopen their mines, and give the state prosperity once more. The Republicans suddenly became weak in Nevada since they supported William McKinley of Ohio, a gold-standard man. The election of that year brought bitter disappointment to most Nevadans, because Bryan lost to McKinley.

To many Nevadans it seemed that the world was collapsing. The Sherman Silver Purchase Act had been repealed in 1893, the great hope of the Silver Democrats in 1896 had been lost, and most Nevada mines remained dormant. The free-silver movement gradually lost its appeal. In 1900, Bryan and McKinley opposed each other for a second time, again most Nevada voters favored Bryan, and again President McKinley won. The silver cause seemed completely dead when Congress passed a gold-standard law. Senators Jones and Stewart shifted back into the Republican party, abandoning their Silver party label. In a few years, even the Silver-Democrats dropped the "Silver" from their party name.

The era of the Silver party was sad and frustrating in Nevada politics, just as it was discouraging in mining and agriculture. Yet Nevadans of that time showed much political spirit and much interest in their governments. They did not completely forget the Silverite cause, and forty years later another Nevada senator would once more wage the fight which Bryan, Stewart, Jones, and others had tried to advance. In the 1930's, Senator Key Pittman won part of the battle that the Silverites of the 1890's had lost.

10. The Tonopah-Goldfield Boom, 1900-1915

THE YEAR 1900 marks the end of an epoch in Nevada history. No one could have known in 1899 that remarkable new mineral discoveries were about to be made, or that the federal government would soon irrigate part of the desert, or that a new machine, the automobile, would shortly revolutionize transportation.

Thoughtful persons in Nevada in 1899 must have known that the old times were quickly fading. Virginia City had lost its splendor; Pioche, Eureka, and Austin were dormant. William Stewart and John P. Jones, those two Comstockers who had been in the United States Senate for nearly a generation, were about to step down. The battle for free silver had been lost, although some would not yet recognize it. Nevada's population had been declining during the previous twenty years; it was probably only about half as large as during the boom of the 1870's.

Even if the past era was waning, it was not easy to estimate the shape or dimension of the future; men instinctively expect more of the same, rather than something strikingly new. So when word began to spread about a new silver strike at Tonopah, some of the old excitement revived among the prospectors and speculators who were still looking for another Big Bonanza. A couple of years later, when Goldfield was discovered with its magnificent high-grade ore, the enthusiasm increased, and for a few years there was a scramble over the Nevada desert reminiscent of the 1860's. It seemed that the world was right again with the mining fraternity. Little by little, from 1900 to about 1920, it became evident that Nevada did not have another Comstock era, but a different type of mining activity, a new group of problems, and a more complex society.

THE DISCOVERY OF TONOPAH

The mountain ranges and arid valleys of central and southern Nevada had little part in fashioning the history of the state before 1900. The region east of Walker Lake, south of Austin, and west of Pioche and Hamilton had never revealed great mineral secrets to the wandering prospectors.

Most of this huge south-central desert was in Nye County. Back in 1864, the territorial legislature had heard of the discovery of a silver-bearing ledge in the Toyiabe Mountains and had created a county government for the new town of Ione. But Ione had not prospered. Soon ore was discovered at Belmont, fifty miles to the southeast. Belmont became the county seat in 1867 but never became a boom camp. Several other small mining districts produced precious metals, but none could compare with even Pioche, Austin, or Eureka before 1900.

At the turn of the century Nye County seemed better suited to ranching than to mining. In the Smoky, Reese River, and Monitor valleys of northern Nye County several families had built homes and had raised crops and livestock. One of the ranchers, James Butler, in Monitor Valley was a part-time prospector who like many other Nevadans of that period had turned away from mining to make his living in agriculture.

Butler had been born in a California mining camp and had come to the White Pine district in his teens, when the Hamilton rush was underway. He had lived in Eureka and Austin and shared the hopes and disappointments of those towns. He loved mining and prospecting, but the depression and the need to support a family kept him on his ranch most of the time. Although he had no special legal training he had been elected district attorney of Nye County.

In the spring of 1900, Butler took a prospecting trip southward into the desert. He had heard of some men exploring in a new district which they called the Southern Klondike, a prospectors' camp about a hundred miles south of his ranch. Butler walked most of the way, leading his burros, and on the way he camped near a jagged "sawtooth" mountain. When one of his burros strayed away during the night on May 19, Butler went to find him and discovered some rich-looking rocks.

Butler went on to Southern Klondike, showed some of the ore to other prospectors, and then returned north along the same route. He got some additional samples and went to Belmont. Since he did not know anyone there who would assay the ore free of charge, Butler gave a sample to Tasker L. Oddie, a young attorney, and promised him a share in the mine if he could get the sample checked.

This incident transformed the lives of Butler, Oddie, and thousands of other Nevadans and opened a new chapter in the history of the state: Butler was to become a millionaire, Oddie to be swept into a mining and legal career which eventually would make him Governor and U.S. Senator, and Nevada was to become a mining center once more.

Oddie was not able to get the assay made in Belmont, so he sent the sample to Austin, where a school principal agreed to test it if he could have a share in the mine. His assay showed the ore to be rich in gold and silver, worth more than $300 a ton. He notified Oddie, and Oddie tried to notify Butler, but by this time the prospector had returned to his ranch and was tending to summer chores. When Butler eventually heard the news he did not get around to returning to his discovery until August, and work did not begin on the ground until November, 1900.

Butler, Oddie, and a merchant named Wilson Brougher mined the first shipment of ore under harsh conditions. With little money and almost no equipment—they did not even have a tent—they extracted two tons of ore and hauled it to Belmont. From there, they had to ship it by wagon to Austin, since no railroad came near Belmont, and then their cargo went by train to Salt Lake City. Like the early miners on the Comstock Lode, the three men had to wait for their proceeds to come from the distant smelter. When they finally received their payment, it amounted to $500, the beginning of a million-dollar fortune.

Butler had located eight claims for himself, his wife, and his partners, but it soon became evident that three men could not mine all the ground. Hundreds of men soon began to arrive, wanting rich claims of their own or seeking a way to share the wealth of Butler and Oddie. The owners leased small portions of their property to miners, with the understanding that one-fourth of the ore mined would go to Butler and his companions. Butler granted more than one hundred leases in this manner, without any contracts or written documents. He did not survey the ground of the lease-holders, and no one insisted on technicalities. Everyone trusted Butler and he trusted the men who worked on the ground. No law suits ever developed between Butler and the lessees.

As the newcomers clustered in the canyon near the mines, a new town arose, which Butler called Tonopah, an Indian name for a spring of water about three miles away; Butler wanted to honor the Indians. The name soon became famous throughout the West.

Tonopah was not as isolated in 1901 as Virginia City had been in 1860, but it was not easy to get supplies there. The Carson and Colorado Railroad came southeastward from the Comstock country, past Walker Lake and Mina, and then southward into California. It did not enter Nye County, but came within sixty miles of Tonopah. The easy solution was to haul ore by wagon westward to Sodaville, on the Carson and Colorado, rather than northward to Austin, which was 120 miles away. The desert west of Tonopah soon became a thoroughfare, with huge wagons and teams of twenty horses hauling ore in one direction and freight in the other. All lumber, tools, and talent for building a city had to be brought from distant places. This team-and-wagon freighting continued to supply the region until 1904, when the railroad was extended into Tonopah from the west; within a few years Tonopah had rail connections with the south as well.

The isolation of Tonopah was also ended by the automobile. On July 4, 1903, Tasker L. Oddie and some companions drove a car from Sodaville to the new camp and proved that such a machine could cross the desert, even without good roads. In another two years, automobiles became common equipment in and around the camp. Tonopah benefited too from new methods in milling ore which had been developed on the Comstock Lode. Since the days of the Big Bonanza, mechanized inventions had created new equipment for miners.

Tonopah gained the reputation as a more peaceful town than some of the older camps. Men had ceased to wear guns, as a rule, and Tonopah did not have as many frontier rowdies as Virginia City or Pioche. Its growth was orderly and quiet, for a boom town.

In 1901 Butler sold his mining interests to eastern investors for a high price; he was one of the few prospectors in Nevada history who became wealthy from his discovery. The investors organized the Tonopah Mining Company, which produced tens of millions of dollars worth of ore during the next forty years. Several other companies also operated profitably, extracting large quantities of silver, and Tonopah became one of the most prosperous towns in the state. It had the appearance of a frontier camp only in its earliest years; after about 1908 it was stable and sedate. For another decade and a half it was one of the West's leading producers of precious metals, and it had some of the most elegant hotels and saloons in the state.

Tonopah was designated as the county seat of Nye County in 1905. When the era of highway construction began, U. S. Highway 95 was routed through the town. This served to keep the community active after the mineral production declined sharply in the late 1920's. With the best ore gone, and with the price of silver dropping, the once-wealthy town took on the look of other fading camps. In later years, however, military operations of the U.S. government gave Tonopah new life.

Goldfield, July 4, 1907

In a sense, the Tonopah boom of 1900-1905 generated enthusiasm for prospecting as the Comstock discovery had done forty years before. Nearly a hundred new camps were established, and many rushes occurred in scattered parts of Nevada during the next decade, but most of them failed to produce rich mines. Only one town, Goldfield, proved to be as important as Tonopah in the early years of the new century.

THE GROWTH OF GOLDFIELD

In Tonopah's early days, it was not unusual for a businessman or investor to "grubstake" a prospector—to furnish supplies and provisions to a miner on promise of a share in his discoveries. After Butler became wealthy, he grubstaked a few prospectors, as did other businessmen in Tonopah.

In 1902 Butler grubstaked William Marsh and Harry Stimler when they went southward looking for more outcroppings. About 25 miles south of Tonopah, in a region which prospectors had seen and ignored for many years, they found a showing of gold ore and staked some claims. On this site the town of Goldfield quickly grew.

For several months Goldfield did not seem to be unusual; the wealth-seekers built a typical tent city, but most of them gave up during the extremely hot summer of 1903. Marsh and Stimler stayed on to develop their ground and discovered high-grade gold. As soon as they had shipped some of it, a frantic rush began. Men who had been inspired by the story of Tonopah, as well as men who had failed to make money in that town, hurried to Goldfield.

Nevada's important mining booms had been based largely on silver; the older districts had produced some gold, but the "white metal" had been regarded as the typical Nevada resource. Goldfield changed this belief and made the "yellow metal" respectable in the state once more. Goldfield produced some of the richest ore in the history of the world. Millions of dollars were extracted from small sections of earth no larger than a baseball field.

The worth of Tonopah ore averaged about $40 per ton in the

early years. By comparison, the ore of the Comstock Lode at the peak of the Big Bonanza had an average value of about $65 per ton. But in Goldfield, the ore exceeded $100 per ton in value, and a few shipments brought an unbelievable $12,000 for each ton. The individual rocks were so precious that some miners carried them away in their pockets or lunch buckets; the mine owners lost tens of thousands of dollars to dishonest employees in this manner. Goldfield became famous as a high-grade camp, or one in which the ore was very rich. The stealing of valuable pieces of ore was called "high-grading."

For this reason, Goldfield had a reputation for toughness and had more trouble than its neighbor to the north. It attracted some of the most skilled financiers ever to operate in Nevada as well as a rougher class of laboring men than any other camp of the modern era.

The two financiers who made the greatest impact on Goldfield and Nevada were George Wingfield and George S. Nixon. They became the most successful and most powerful mine owners in Goldfield.

Wingfield came to Nevada from Oregon, where he had been a cowboy. He arrived in Tonopah during its early boom period and proved himself to be a skillful and daring gambler. When the Goldfield strike occurred, Wingfield quickly became interested and shifted his attentions to that town. He was young, alert, and boldly willing to take big gambles.

Nixon was older than Wingfield. He had come to Nevada many years earlier to work as a telegraph operator, and from this inauspicious beginning he eventually went into the banking business in Winnemucca and Reno. He became prominent and prosperous, entered politics during the years of the Silver crusade, and later joined the Republicans. In 1905, when Senator Stewart stepped down after serving for three decades, the state legislature elected Nixon to replace him. By this time, Nixon was already well known in Tonopah and Goldfield and had become Wingfield's partner for the purchase of Goldfield mines.

Wingfield and Nixon began building a mining empire by buying the interests of the discoverers Marsh and Stimler. They continued to add other claims, incorporating them into the Goldfield Consolidated Mining Company in 1906. The company produced tens of millions of dollars worth of gold in the next few years, and the stockholders became wealthy. Since Nixon was in Washington much of the time after 1905, Wingfield had most of the responsibility for running the mines—and the town.

The one-time cowboy and gambler found Goldfield well suited for his talents and temperament, and so did many other spirited men. Miners from as far away as Coeur d'Alene, Idaho; Cripple Creek, Colorado; and the Klondike came to Goldfield in those years, men who had little fear of mine bosses or law-enforcement officers. Many of them had belonged to radical labor unions and had seen violent strikes in places like Cripple Creek and Coeur d'Alene. The Western Federation of Miners and the Industrial Workers of the World (IWW), labor unions which had made a reputation for striking in other camps, grew strong in Goldfield.

In 1907 Wingfield and Nixon decided to put an end to "high-grading," because workers were stealing thousands of dollars worth of ore. The owners announced that they would place "change rooms" on their property and require all miners to change their clothing in the presence of a company inspector before entering and after leaving the mines; in this way, they could prevent the workmen from carrying away precious rocks in secret pockets. The miners went on strike in protest, and the company soon agreed to a compromise which allowed union men to inspect the changing of clothes. Under this arrangement, the high-grading continued; tension between the miners and Goldfield Consolidated increased.

During the same year, a depression hit the economy of the United States, and Goldfield felt the impact. Gold and silver coins had been in general circulation, and the miners expected to be paid with such money. The depression, however, made the "hard money" scarce throughout the country, and the mine operators soon found they could not obtain enough coins to pay their men. They began to issue "scrip," an unstable paper money. The miners' union refused to accept such payment and went on strike. The atmosphere in Goldfield became as tense as in a city preparing for war.

Wingfield and a few less important mine owners held a meeting with Governor John Sparks, telling him that the union men might dynamite the mines or wreck the town. The governor wired President Theodore Roosevelt, asking him to send troops to Goldfield because serious dangers existed and the state government was unable to protect the people. President Roosevelt acted quickly to send Army units to Goldfield.

All this activity was surprising, because there had been no violence or lawlessness in Goldfield as a result of the strike. Residents of the town were startled when they learned that federal troops had been dispatched to keep the peace. Although there was tension, the local sheriff had never found reason to call for outside help. Troops arrived, discovered no immediate danger of violence, and settled down for several weeks.

While the Army units remained in Goldfield the mine operators were in a strong position, and they took advantage of it. They decided to import miners from other areas, hire them at lower salaries than the Goldfield workers were getting, and destroy the union. Wingfield had strike-breakers hired in California and Utah. The strikers soon realized that their jobs were lost and that their union's power was broken.

When President Roosevelt felt that the troops were not needed in Goldfield, he prepared to withdraw them. Governor Sparks managed to persuade him to leave the soldiers in the camp for several more weeks, until a special session of the legislature could be called. When the legislature met, a new Nevada State police agency was created to handle the problem.

Neither the union nor the mine operators were free of blame for the Goldfield trouble of 1907-1908. Some miners had been stealing ore and the union had defended them in the practice. But the mine owners, headed by Wingfield, acted in a questionable manner when they obtained federal troops to destroy the union. This was the most serious labor dispute in Nevada's history.

After the departure of the troops, Goldfield passed into a new phase of its existence. For the next two or three years it was at the peak of its boom. Goldfield's mines during these years surpassed those of Tonopah in the value of the precious metal produced, and the population of the town was probably about 15,000 for a brief time. The high-grade ore, however, was becoming scarcer, and, after 1910, returns became gradually smaller. In January, 1919, the Goldfield Consolidated Mining Company closed its mill because the known ore bodies were exhausted, and no new ore was found. Like many other towns, Goldfield existed for a few more years on the profits of companies that reprocessed the tailings of the earlier operations, but this occupied only a few dozen men, instead of thousands.

Goldfield had become the county seat of Esmeralda County in 1907, taking the honor away from Hawthorne. Four years later, Hawthorne's residents demanded a division of the county, and Esmeralda lost more than half her territory to the new Mineral County. In the 1950's, Esmeralda had one of the smallest populations in the state. Goldfield survived into the 1960's primarily because it was a county seat and situated on U.S. Highway 95.

Disastrous cloudbursts and fires destroyed most of the city in later years. In 1923, a fire razed fifty-two blocks of former homes and businesses, and blazes in 1943 and 1945 wrecked more buildings. Goldfield did not revive with the help of installations of the federal government, as Tonopah did. A few of its residents continue to hope for a revival of mining, even though a half century has passed since its greatest mining era.

Tonopah-Goldfield in Politics

From 1864 until about 1905, most outstanding Nevada political figures were identified with the Comstock Lode. All senators of the state and several representatives in Congress and governors had some association with the Comstock. When the Comstock declined, so did its domination of state politics; with the retirement of Senator Jones in 1903 and Senator Stewart in 1905, the era of the Comstock politicians ended. To a large extent, the towns of Tonopah and Goldfield supplied the political leaders of the next generation.

Tasker L. Oddie, a Republican, progressed from the little courthouse at Belmont to the State Senate, to the governor's chair, and to the U.S. Senate on the strength of his successes in the Tonopah

Tasker L. Oddie. Governor,
1911-1914; U.S. Senator, 1921-
1933

Key Pittman. U.S. Senator, 1913-1940

boom. He served as Nevada's chief executive from 1911 through 1914 and as senator from 1921 until 1933, during the years of Republican leadership in Washington.

George Nixon had already made his reputation in northern Nevada before he entered politics; he did not embark on his political career as a result of his Goldfield success. Nevertheless, during his tenure in the Senate from 1905 until his death in 1912, he was more closely associated with Goldfield than with any other town, because of his financial interests there.

Nixon's partner, George Wingfield, did not follow his older associate into senatorial politics, although he had an opportunity to do so. When Senator Nixon died, Wingfield was offered an appointment to his seat but declined. When Goldfield's prosperity ended, he moved to Reno and became a leading backstage politician, probably exerting more influence through a chain of banks and through his contacts with political officers than any other man in the state.

When Wingfield refused to go to the Senate, another man was eagerly waiting on the sidelines for a chance to win fame in Nevada politics. He was a Democrat, so he was not offered the appointment. (Since Governor Oddie was a Republican, he preferred to select a member of his own party for the honor.) This new figure, completely identified with Tonopah, was Key Pittman, an attorney.

Pittman was born in Mississippi. As a young man he decided that opportunity waited in the mining camps of Canada, Alaska, and the Far West. He was among the first to make the rush to the Klondike in 1897, and from there went to Nome, on the extreme western tip of Alaska. He had studied some law and found he could make a living by giving legal advice and representing his clients in court. When news of the Tonopah strike reached him, Pittman joined the swarm of adventurers who took the long expedition across the mountains and deserts to Nye County. He established a law office and within two years became wealthy. Like William Stewart, he was important to the mining community because of his talent in legal matters.

Pittman followed in Stewart's footsteps in another important respect; he eloquently pleaded the cause of silver money and the silver miner. Soon he was a leader of the Silverites, although he and

George Wingfield

George S. Nixon. U.S. Senator,
1905-1912

others decided it was wise to rejoin the Democratic party. His attitude toward silver made him popular in the state's mining towns, and in 1910 he was nominated as Democratic candidate for U.S. Senator. His opponent was the popular incumbent, Senator Nixon.

Nevada still elected its senators in the state legislature as of 1910, but there was a strong feeling that it would be more democratic to choose senators by popular vote. Sensing this feeling, Senator Nixon and Pittman agreed that their names could be put on the ballot on election day so that voters could express their preference, and the man who had the highest vote would be uncontested when the state legislature met for the election. This unusual arrangement gave the people of Nevada their first chance to choose a U.S. Senator by direct ballot.

In the unofficial election, Senator Nixon won by a vote of 9,779 to 8,624 for Pittman, but the Democrats won control of the state legislature. If Nixon and Pittman had not made their bargain to abide by the results of the ballot, Pittman would have been elected to the Senate by the Democrats in the 1911 legislative session. However, he instructed his fellow party members to vote for Nixon. He won much respect for his action, and when Nixon died in 1912, the Democrats were ready to support him again. In that election year, he won the largest number of votes in the regular election and also the election in the legislature.

Senator Pittman began a career in Congress which was to last for nearly twenty-eight years. He was elected six times and became one of the most important men in the Senate, serving as chairman of the powerful Foreign Relations Committee in the years just before World War II. No Nevadan ever had more influence in the national capital; later chapters will discuss his accomplishments which affected the state. Senator Pittman's policies and programs were largely developed from his interest in Tonopah and other Nevada mining communities. At times, people called him "the Senator from Tonopah."

Another man who ascended from the Tonopah boom into statewide and national political prominence was Patrick McCarran. A native of Reno and a graduate of the University of Nevada, McCar-

ran went to Tonopah during its most exciting period to practice
law, and he soon won election as district attorney. His years in the
famous camp made him well known, and he moved back to Reno
while he was still a young man. In 1912 he ran successfully for the
office of justice in Nevada's Supreme Court. In later years, McCarran made it clear that he wanted to go to the U.S. Senate, and
finally, in 1932, the voters elected him to that office. He defeated
his former Tonopah colleague, Senator Oddie.

During most of his life, Senator McCarran regarded Reno as his
home, and he became one of the city's most famous attorneys even
before his election to the Senate. But it was in Tonopah that he
gained his knowledge of the mining community and its needs, and
this endeared him to that part of the population when it was
politically powerful. Senator McCarran served in the Senate for
nearly twenty-two years, until his death in 1954. Like Senator Pittman, he became one of the most powerful and influential men in
Washington.

The Fringe Mining Rushes, 1905-1910

Although it was Tonopah and Goldfield which held the spotlight
and produced the future political leaders in the early years of the
twentieth century, many other parts of the state shared the new
enthusiasm.

Prospectors were still mainly interested in gold and silver; the
time had not yet come when the average mining company would
be content with copper, lead, or some other common metal. The
discovery of the great riches at Tonopah and Goldfield caused
thousands to believe that there must be many more treasures on the
desert, waiting to produce millionaires. As in the early days of the
Comstock Lode, men were reckless and willing to gamble on a new
bonanza.

Just as Goldfield was coming into prominence in 1904, another
discovery, seventy miles to the southeast, almost outshone it. On
the edge of Death Valley, near the pitiful Amargosa River, prospectors discovered a mine they called Bullfrog, and soon a roaring
town appeared. Given the name of Rhyolite, this town attracted

those who had not been satisfied in the earlier booms, as well as some who had seen the best. Among those who came to Rhyolite was William M. Stewart, who stepped down from the U.S. Senate in 1905. Rhyolite wanted a school, and the people elected former Senator Stewart to the first board of education.

Within three years, Rhyolite was served by three railroads (connecting it north and south), by three water companies, four newspapers, an electric light company, several expensive buildings, and more than three dozen saloons. Hundreds of people wanted to invest their money in the town. Its population may have been as large as 8,000 by 1908.

The ore of the Bullfrog district, however, did not justify the hopes of its builders. The mines, according to official reports, produced less than two million dollars between 1906 and 1912, while Tonopah and Goldfield were producing tens of millions. In a few years, most of Rhyolite crumbled or was hauled away. The town of Beatty, about four miles to the east, had been a kind of suburb of Rhyolite during the boom years, because it was situated on one of the railroads that brought supplies to Rhyolite. After Rhyolite died, Beatty survived because of its location on what is now U.S. Highway 95.

Another offspring of the Tonopah-Goldfield booms was Rawhide, situated in the isolated desert region northeast of Walker Lake. Prospectors often said that more money could be made by publicizing a mine and getting cash from the "suckers" than by finding a mine. Rhyolite proved this to many; Rawhide proved it to many more.

The dash to Rawhide came in 1908, partly because of the publicity given to it by promoters from Goldfield. Tex Rickard, who later became famous as one of America's greatest boxing promoters, owned a magnificent saloon and gambling house in Goldfield. When trouble came to Goldfield in 1907, he was looking for new money-making schemes, and he decided to capitalize on the news that a gold strike had occurred at Rawhide. Other speculators started stock companies, sent out "news" reports about the great wealth of the region, and soon thousands of dollars were pouring

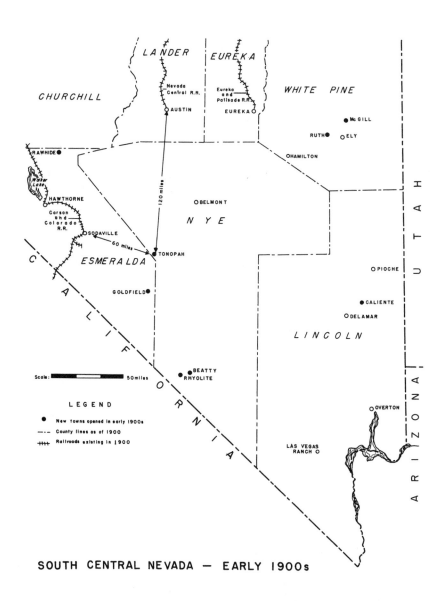

CHURCHILL

LANDER

EUREKA

WHITE PINE

Nevada
Central R.R.

Eureka
and
Palisade R.R.

○ AUSTIN

EUREKA ○

● McGILL

RUTH ● ○ ELY

○ HAMILTON

RAWHIDE ●

Walker
Lake

○ BELMONT

N Y E

HAWTHORNE

Carson
and
Colorado
R.R.

120 miles

UTAH

○ SODAVILLE

60 miles

ESMERALDA

↓ TONOPAH

○ PIOCHE

GOLDFIELD ●

● CALIENTE

○ DELAMAR

C A L I F O R N I A

LINCOLN

Scale: 50 miles

● BEATTY
RHYOLITE

LEGEND

● New towns opened in early 1900s

--- County lines as of 1900

++++ Railroads existing in 1900

A R I Z O N A

○ OVERTON

LAS VEGAS
RANCH ○

SOUTH CENTRAL NEVADA — EARLY 1900s

into Rawhide companies and over the bar of Rickard's saloon. Another luxurious city began to rise.

In September of the same year, Rawhide was almost entirely destroyed by fire, and the bubble of speculation burst. Its citizens pledged to rebuild, but they never did revive the town in its early grandeur. Its ore was not even as rich as that of Rhyolite, but a few men had become wealthy by tricking the innocent.

Nearly a hundred other Nevada towns appeared like Rhyolite and Rawhide in the early 1900's; nearly all of them failed. Although most of them eventually vanished, they gave new life to a dormant Nevada. Older towns, like Hawthorne, Winnemucca, Lovelock, Reno, Elko, and Pioche, prospered because of the new business which was generated. The despair and defeat of the 1890's was gone, and Nevada was progressing once more.

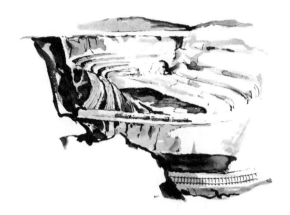

11. Latter-Day Mining

THE BOOMS AT Tonopah, Goldfield, Rhyolite, and the other towns of the early 1900's were merely the beginning of Nevada's twentieth-century mining story. Other minerals remained beneath the ground after most of the rich gold and silver had been discovered and developed. These resources included the nonprecious metals—copper, lead, zinc, tungsten, and iron—and some nonmetal industrial minerals such as gypsum, silica sand, and diatomite.

Until the present century there was no great demand for these minerals. America's participation in two world wars, however, and the growing industrial economy created new needs.

The mining communities of the modern era have been more peaceful and efficient than the gold and silver camps of a century ago. In the Ely area, a great copper industry grew up with only a few minor troubles. This district surpassed the Comstock Lode, Tonopah, and Goldfield in the dollar value of its ore, but it never received the reputation of some of the gold and silver camps. On the edge of Mason Valley near Yerington another great copper-producing region was opened in the 1950's. Copper became Nevada's most important metal.

Other mining operations have revealed that Nevada holds massive quantities and great varieties of valuable minerals. Nature was more generous in depositing wealth in the Great Basin than our ancestors realized. Mining is still a risky business; many camps have come and gone in modern times, but the excavation and processing of mineral resources remains one of the bread-and-butter industries of the state.

A MINING STORY THAT CONTINUED: ELY COPPER

The richest and most consistently prosperous mining region in Nevada between 1900 and 1964 was the Ely (or Robinson) District of White Pine County, the site of one of America's great copper deposits. Mining companies which developed this region also produced some gold, silver, molybdenum, and other metals, but these are by-products in the processing of copper.

Prospectors came into the Ely district as early as 1867, when miners and speculators from Virginia City and Austin were penetrating eastern Nevada. The pioneers discovered a small quantity of gold-bearing ore in the Egan Range. Excited developers formed a mining district, erected a small furnace and a stamp mill for crushing ore, and tried to mine the ore profitably. A new town —Mineral City—appeared in the district, but failed like many other Nevada communities. The tiny town of Ely, hardly more than a station on the stage line, replaced Mineral City and became a supply center for prospectors and stockmen in the area. In 1887, nearly two years after the courthouse at Hamilton burned, the legislature decided to move the seat of White Pine County to Ely, since Hamilton was nearly a dead town.

No important mining activity occurred near Ely in the 1880's or 1890's, but White Pine County was becoming an important ranching and cattle area during these years. Small-scale mining was attempted occasionally at Cherry Creek, Taylor, Ward and in other scattered locations, thus helping to keep Ely alive. No prosperity was possible, however, until the development of the copper resources.

The existence of copper in the Ely district had been known as early as the 1870's but in the nineteenth century it was unrealistic to consider mining the metal in such an isolated region. Gold and silver ore could be crushed and refined by a rather simple process. Small bars of these metals contained much wealth which could be transported easily; a single stagecoach was able to haul thousands of dollars worth of bullion bars. But this was not true of copper; it required much costly equipment to transform it from crude ore to refined metal, and it would have been very expensive to haul large tonnages of copper with teams and wagons. So the development of this resource had to await the arrival of a big investor and modern transportation.

In the last years of the nineteenth century, American industry needed increasing quantities of copper, and the long-neglected Ely district began to attract attention. In the late 1890's, prospectors were working in two areas west of Ely known as Pilot Knob and Copper Flat, near where the towns of Ruth and Kimberly later developed. They knew that low-grade copper ore existed in a wide area on the surface, but not until after 1900 was it proved that the ore body extended underground. The men responsible for this discovery were David Bartley and Edwin Gray, miners who arrived in Ely in the early fall of 1900. Although they had almost no money, they acquired an option to a few claims, found a grocer who would grubstake them, and sank a shaft to check the depth of the ore.

Their daring paid off. By the fall of 1902, they attracted the interest of Mark Requa, the son of a famous mine superintendent of Virginia City. Requa was also the operator of the Eureka and Palisade Railroad, which was having financial troubles, and he hoped to find some way of improving its business. If the mining property near Ely were to prosper, Requa thought, he might lay tracks from there to Eureka to connect with his unprofitable railroad. He persuaded some eastern investors to risk money in a new company which purchased the Bartley-Gray prospect.

Requa's men knew little about how to refine copper ore, but they began to test the rock and to explore the region thoroughly. Requa eventually became the general manager of a new firm, the Nevada Consolidated Copper Company, and his workers gradually learned how to process the ore effectively. As the exploration was expanded and milling and smelting experiments were enlarged, Ely began to prosper. Requa decided it would be wiser to build a railroad through the Steptoe Valley from the vicinity of Wells rather than to bring it eastward from Eureka. This allowed the rail line to run directly to the transcontinental railroad instead of being detoured through Eureka; it also passed through Ely on its way to the mines at Ruth and gave the county seat another important asset. Construction of the railroad was completed in 1906.

Ely had come of age. It had a major industry nearby and modern transportation. Also by 1906, the major technical problems had been solved. The wealthy Guggenheim interests—one of America's most powerful financial establishments—purchased a controlling interest in the Nevada Consolidated Copper Company. A site for a smelter was selected on William McGill's ranch, which held the rights to the extensive water in nearby Duck Creek Valley. The company built its smelter in 1908 and began to refine large quantities of ore. The new town of McGill, thirteen miles northeast of Ely, soon became the home of hundreds of smelter workers, many of them from foreign lands. McGill was entirely owned by the Nevada Consolidated Copper Company and remained a "company town" for a half century. Ely had the copper mines and the town of Ruth on one side—a few miles to the west—and the great smelter on the other side. A railroad between the two new places passed through the older community. Ely continued to be the crossroads of the county.

For a few months in 1906 and 1907, however, it appeared possible that Ely would be overshadowed and absorbed by a new company-owned town. The Nevada Northern Railroad selected a site one mile east of Ely for one of its main stations, and the Nevada Consolidated Copper Company decided to sell lots there, naming the place Ely City. Since the residents of old Ely feared the new community would steal not only its name but also its water supply and other important assets, a bitter feud erupted. Finally, the U.S. Post Office designated Ely City as East Ely, and the trouble subsided. East Ely continues to be a separate city and an important maintenance center for the Nevada Northern Railroad.

The mines west of Ely brought new methods and techniques to Nevada's most famous industry. Open-pit mining proved to be the most efficient way of handling the huge bodies of ore at Ruth, but some mining was also done by conventional underground shafts. As the years progressed, the Liberty Pit near Ruth became a massive hole, more than a mile long, three-quarters of a mile wide, and 700 feet deep. Such a huge excavation required the use of expensive modern machinery; giant mechanical shovels and whole trains raised the multicolored rock from the growing hole. In later years, the mining company used a giant skip, or elevator, to raise the ore. Nearby the towns of Ruth and Kimberly flourished, the latter town being supported by mining from underground workings.

Only a few years after this large-scale operation began, the Ruth-Ely-McGill-Kimberly area was the most important metal-producing area in Nevada. In 1909, the Ely district reported greater production in terms of money than the famous Tonopah area, although it remained second to Goldfield. By 1911, the mines and mills near Ely were producing more than those in Goldfield. Copper had become the most important mineral resource of Nevada, and it was to remain the number-one metal for more than a half century.

The growth of the industry was accompanied by social tension and labor troubles. Occasional trouble developed between the American-born and the immigrant workers. Many laborers who had come from eastern Europe and Asia were badly treated by the Americans, who feared that their jobs might be jeopardized if too many foreigners came to White Pine County. Besides, the mine and mill employers took advantage of the immigrants. Some could not speak English, and the companies paid them a lower wage than Americans. Hundreds of Greeks, Slavs, and Japanese workers and their families lived in separate sections of McGill and Ruth, without the same social standing as the native-born. This produced tension in the early 1900's, but as the years passed the families mingled, children of different nationalities shared the same schools and playgrounds, and the barriers between the various nationalities broke down in typical American fashion.

The Industrial Workers of the World and the Western Federation of Miners—the groups that had been involved in the trouble in Goldfield a few years earlier—sent representatives to the Ely district in 1911 and 1912. In October, 1912, a leader of the Western Federation of Miners named William Moyer urged mine workers at Ruth and Kimberly and mill workers at McGill to strike against the company to demonstrate their sympathy for other miners who were then striking in Utah. No serious controversies existed between the workers and the employers, but Moyer persuaded some workingmen—including a few of the dissatisfied foreign-born—to strike and to put an armed picket line around the smelter at McGill. The intention of the pickets was to prevent anyone from entering the smelter to work, but some men who were already on the job remained inside the fence surrounding the smelter.

On October 15, several rock fights broke out between the strikers and nonstrikers. The company hired thirty gunmen to protect its property from the strikers, and the local sheriff decided to call on Governor Oddie for help. The governor, remembering the bitter labor troubles at Goldfield, rushed to McGill and tried to establish peace. In spite of his efforts, fighting erupted again, and two Greek strikers were shot to death. Governor Oddie called Nevada State Police onto the scene. The police restored order, eventually enabling the company to resume its operations. Once more the IWW had failed in Nevada.

The operations at Ruth and McGill continued to prosper during the years 1914 to 1918, when World War I increased the world's demand for copper. During this period the famous Kennecott Copper Corporation began to purchase interests in the Ely area. During the next half century, it became the owner of nearly all copper-producing mines in White Pine County.

The copper industry of White Pine County had periods of prosperity and depression. After World War I—especially in 1921 and 1922, and again during the great depression of 1931-1935—the companies produced only a few million dollars worth of ore. During World War II, however, the need for copper rose sharply; the Ely area entered its most productive era, and output remained high in the twenty-year period following that war. Three more giant pits

The copper pit at Ruth

were begun near Ruth, and it even became necessary to move the town to make way for the massive earth-moving project.

As the Ruth-Kimberly-McGill operations became larger and more mechanized, the copper companies extracted and milled earth in volumes which would have amazed the early-day mining men. In 1960, for example, Kennecott Copper Corporation was moving 84,000 tons of rock every day and treating about one-fourth of that amount in its smelter at McGill—with fewer than 2,000 men. It was necessary to mine 500 tons of ore to get one ton of copper.

The vast production in the Ely area made it the richest mining region in Nevada in terms of the dollar value of the ore produced. Although the copper of White Pine County has been known as "lowgrade" ore (since it takes many tons of earth to produce a ton of copper) it has far surpassed the gold and silver camps in productiveness. By the mid-1960's the Ely area had produced about $1,000,000,000 worth of minerals—more than one-third of the total mineral production in all of Nevada's history.

The copper industry, however, did not guarantee permanent prosperity to the towns of White Pine County. As the pits became larger and deeper and as new machinery was required to mine the ore, fewer men were needed. The price of copper on the world market fell, and in the 1970's Kennecott reduced and then closed its mining operations. Like many other mining and milling towns of the past, Ely, McGill and their neighbors experienced depression times.

ANACONDA IN LYON COUNTY

On the edge of Mason Valley, near Yerington, a similar history of "boom and bust" mining was written in the period after World War II. Weed Heights is a recent example of the typical mining cycle.

Copper had been discovered in the Singatse Range west of Mason Valley in the 1860's and some of the ore had been shipped to Virginia City. Copper did not produce great fortunes in Nevada in those years, and the early investors lost money; only after 1900 did this district become prominent. In an effort to develop a paying operation, speculators built smelters and constructed a railroad to Yerington and from there into the copper-bearing mountains to the west. From 1912 to 1919, the district produced several million dollars worth of copper, but in the 1920's and 1930's it did not seem profitable to continue production on a large scale.

After World War II began, America needed new supplies of copper for her defense industry, and the Anaconda Copper Mining Company—one of the world's large mining firms—gained control of the mineral-bearing property. In 1942, the big company began to explore and develop the region, but it was decided that large-scale production could not begin in time to supply war industries. Nevertheless, Anaconda learned much about the resources of the Yerington district, and a few years later this knowledge became valuable to Nevada and the nation. When the Korean War erupted in 1950, the U.S. government and Anaconda entered into an agreement to begin production.

Huge power shovels started an open pit on the mountainside west of Mason Valley in 1952, and ore production began in 1954. For about twenty years, the annual copper-ore yield was measured in millions of tons, and the Anaconda operation resembled that of Kennecott in White Pine County. Weed Heights, like Ruth and McGill, was a "company town," but it was planned with more modern facilities. Its systematic rows of houses, swimming pool, tennis courts, and community center were much different in appearance from the residences and recreation places in the wild mining towns of early Nevada. Eventually, when the copper production ceased in the 1970's, the town was abandoned. At Weed Heights, the ore was essentially "mined out," and the chance of reopening the mines seemed very remote. Nevada has copper deposits elsewhwere, but prices in 1980 were too low to allow profitable, large-scale production.

The Wealth of Nonprecious Metals

The needs of modern industry which created a large new market for copper also stimulated greater demands for nonprecious metals such as lead, zinc, iron, manganese, tungsten, and mercury. Old diggings and claims which had once attracted interest because of gold and silver came into prominence in the 1940's and 1950's, because they had additional wealth which could be extracted with new techniques.

One of the old silver camps of the 1870's which experienced a revival of prosperity in the modern era was Pioche, where huge deposits of low-grade lead and zinc were discovered at deeper levels of the early-day mines. The pioneer companies had not worked on this ore because they could neither pump the underground water from the deep shafts nor profitably separate the lead from the zinc. In the 1930's however, cheap electrical power became available in Pioche (supplied by Hoover Dam on the Colorado River). This made it possible to pump the water economically. Also new methods of milling the ore were possible with electricity available.

In the fifteen years between 1938 and 1954, the Pioche district produced more than $70,000,000 worth of ore; for a brief period it was one of the ten largest lead-zinc mining districts in the United States. An important by-product of the mines during these years was silver. Pioche regularly led the state in the mining of the "white metal" in the 1940's and early 1950's, even though the amount was much smaller than it had been in the 1870's. The town, which had been almost a ghost camp in the early 1900's, bustled once more with activity.

In the early 1950's, the price of lead and zinc dropped drastically on the world market because mines around the world produced an abundance of these metals. When lead and zinc could be purchased more cheaply overseas than mined in this country, mines like those at Pioche began to curtail their operations. In 1958, the largest company in the district closed its mine and mill, putting the town into another severe decline. Millions of tons of valuable metals still existed deep underground, but it was unprofitable to mine these deposits with the prices and the governmental policies that have prevailed since the early 1960's.

The Eureka district, which won a reputation for its lead and silver deposits in the 1870's, also contributed to Nevada's production of these metals in the modern era. However, problems with underground water kept its production much smaller than that of Pioche.

As lead and zinc declined in importance, Nevadans learned that the state had another great mineral resource which could absorb some of the economic loss. Mining men had long known that tungsten-bearing ores existed in various parts of the Great Basin. Some had been mined in the 1940's and earlier, but it was not an important statewide industry. In 1950, when the Korean War began, America had a critical shortage of this metal and little was known about the domestic supply. The U.S. government urged mining companies to look for tungsten and promised them high prices for several years in the future.

Modern engineers who went into the mountains in search of tungsten had a remarkable new device to help them with their prospecting; science had developed an ultra-violet "black light" which, if shined on scheelite—the principal tungsten-bearing mineral —would cause it to glow in the dark. Tungsten often could not be recognized in its raw form—as gold, silver, lead, and copper can be recognized by a person with a trained eye. The "black light" prospectors found tungsten in several remote parts of Nevada, and soon this state was a leading producer in the United States.

By 1952 Nevada had sixty-four tungsten mines in operation, scattered throughout the state. Small communities grew up around the mines in many places, but unlike the "tent cities" of a hundred years ago, the residences of the modern miners were often trailer houses which had been carefully pulled across the desert roads by huge trucks.

Some of the most productive districts were in northern Nevada regions which had not previously yielded much mineral wealth. The Osgood Mountains northeast of Winnemucca, proved to be rich in tungsten. The most important deposit was found north of Mill City on the lower Humboldt River. Humboldt and Pershing counties emerged as important mining centers.

Even the old camp of Rawhide—which had been the scene of a false boom in 1907 and 1908—proved to have tungsten nearby; a plant known as Nevada Scheelite went into production. The Tempiute District in Lincoln County—in the vast desert between Pioche and Tonopah—became a busy little town within a few months.

Suddenly, during 1956, these new camps began to die, because the U.S. government stopped its tungsten-purchasing program when the critical shortage of the metal disappeared, thanks largely to the American mining industry which had so swiftly developed a domestic supply. One by one, Nevada's tungsten producers closed their plants and discharged the workers. Nevada had produced about $20,000,000 worth of tungsten each year in 1954, 1955, and

1956. In 1957, its mines yielded only $1,676,000 worth of the metal. Some tungsten towns disappeared as rapidly as the boom-and-bust camps of the 1870's. In the late 1970's tungsten brought high prices again, and the Tempiute district began to produce at a larger scale than ever before. Some tungsten-bearing ores were also being mined in other parts of the state.

Modern Nevada had a similar experience with manganese, a light-weight metal important in the making of steel. In the early 1950's, production of this metal in the United States was far below the country's needs. The federal goverment urged new mines to open and existing mines to expand. Once again the Silver State proved to have important deposits; the Three Kids Mine near Las Vegas became one of the major suppliers. In the late 1950's, Nevada produced more of this metal than any other state, but in 1962 the government stopped buying it and production ceased.

One other metal for which Nevada has gained a reputation in the modern era is mercury. This shiny, hard-to-hold substance is rare in most parts of the world, but Nevada's Cordero Mine near McDermitt, a few miles south of the Oregon border, became the major source in America.

As the history of the lead-zinc and tungsten mining proves, an area may still have large quantities of ore in the ground and yet suffer from economic depression because the price of the ore is too low to permit profitable mining. On the other hand, some minerals which have never been regarded as important in Nevada have proved to be very promising in recent years. Iron is an example.

It was not profitable to mine Nevada's iron deposits while the world's needs for the metal were smaller and while richer ore deposits existed elsewhere. After World War II, however, new conditions made Nevada's crude ore more valuable than it had been earlier. Japan needed to import large quanties of the ore to develop her industries, and Nevada's iron satisfied some of her needs. Small iron-producing mines opened in the Buena Vista Hills southeast of Lovelock, in the Paradise Range near Gabbs, in the Singatse Range southwest of Wabuska, in the Cortez Mountains of northern Eureka County, in the Jackson Mountains west of Winnemucca, and in the Battle Mountain area.

In the early 1970's, iron producers in Nevada had shared the experience of the lead-zinc and tungsten producers. The Japanese stopped buying their raw iron in this area, and most of the small operators closed their mines. Yet explorations had proven that Nevada's deposits could eventually be developed, probably when additional smelting plants are constructed in the West.

INDUSTRIAL MINERALS

Nevada's countryside has not only yielded some of the most needed industrial metals in recent decades, but also proved to be rich in other minerals which have many uses. The building of modern homes, for example, requires materials that were of little value only a couple of generations ago.

As millions of people moved westward in the twentieth century, and as new building techniques developed, the demand for gypsum in the construction industries increased. Several rich deposits of this mineral were found in Clark County. In addition, Nevada proved to have large quantities of gypsum, especially at the Blue Diamond Mine near Las Vegas and in northern Nevada near Empire. Gypsum is used in making the wallboard that goes into many homes. A number of Nevada hills and mountains have yielded diatomite, a mineral found useful for insulation and for filtering impurities from liquid products; the mines near Reno, Mina, and Lovelock are important producers of this commodity.

Nevada produces more barite and lithium than any other state. Barite is a heavy, dense mineral of great value in the drilling of oil and gas wells. There are more than sixty known deposits between Elko and Hawthorne. Lithium is a light alkali metal used in the manufacture of glass, air conditioning equipment, storage batteries, and aluminum. A mine near Silver Peak was one of the world's largest producers of this substance in the late 1970's.

The list of Nevada's nonmetal resources is long and includes talc and soapstone used in grinding machines, fluorspar used as a fluxing agent in iron-ore production, turquoise and opal used for jewelry, and silica sand which serves man in many ways.

The production of oil is not in the same category as the extraction of minerals, but since petroleum is a natural resource, it is often classed with the ores. Nevada's geology did not invite intensive exploration for oil until recent years, but it is now well known that the state does have reservoirs of "liquid gold" deep underground.

In 1954, the Shell Oil Company discovered oil in Railroad Valley near Currant, sixty miles southwest of Ely. This strike caused much excitement in eastern and central Nevada. Oil rights are not acquired in the same manner as a mining claim; one cannot simply go out and stake a claim and file it with the county recorder. To acquire an oil lease, an individual must first file an application with the U.S. Bureau of Land Management. Thousands of Nevadans did this early in 1954, after Shell had found oil. Eventually the Bureau processed these applications and granted many leases.

No one became wealthy because of Nevada oil development in the first decade and a half after the discovery; as late as 1970 there were only about fifteen producing wells, and their output was small. Nevertheless, several companies continued exploration and testing in the valleys of eastern and central Nevada, and the prospects for major production in the future seemed good.

In 1976, a new oil-producing field was discovered in another part of Railroad Valley, not far from the site of the 1954 discovery. By mid-1977 it was producing 1,200 barrels each day, not large by Texas standards, but important to Nevada's economy.

The earth resources that have created excitement in the middle years of the twentieth century give new testimony to the generosity with which nature endowed Nevada millions of years ago. The alternating ranges and valleys of the state apparently still hold secrets that the wandering prospectors and the trained geological engineers have not discovered. In recent years, sites near Carlin and Battle Mountain that were thought to be virtually barren of gold were found to have commercial quantities of the precious metal. Several other gold mines have gone into production, and in 1976 Nevada was the second-largest producer of this metal. The discovery of new mercury deposits in Humboldt County and the reopening of the old tungsten mine at Tempiute seemed to promise that Nevada would maintain the lead it formerly had in the production of these metals.

At the close of the 1970's—almost exactly 100 years after the end of the first boom period on the Comstock Lode—a new gold-silver mining boom began in Gold Canyon. High world prices for the precious metals made it profitable for a large company to excavate a huge pit at Gold Hill, and in the process several historic sites were destroyed. Similar large earth-moving projects were being planned for other old mining regions in the 1980's.

12. Transportation and Tourism

JUST AS THE TWENTIETH CENTURY brought great changes in Nevada's mining industry, so it changed the transportation picture. Railroads were serving a number of Nevada communities in 1900, and the laying of tracks was renewed in scattered parts of the state after that year, but the most impressive additions to Nevada's transportation system came with the building of highways and—more recently—of modern airports.

Railroading, like mining, had fallen on hard times in the 1880's and 1890's. Once the early mining camps began to decline in the late 1870's and 1880's, the railroaders were no longer eager to build new lines. After the new century began, however, investors revived their construction schemes. We have already seen that the Tonopah-Goldfield boom accounted for some railroad construction.

One group of businessmen financed a line between Salt Lake City and Los Angeles, which passed through the neglected southeastern corner of the state and created a new town at Las Vegas. In a short time, this became Nevada's second most important community—eventually to become the state's largest city. In addition, the old Central Pacific across northern Nevada was acquired by new owners, the Southern Pacific Company, which rerouted the tracks and established the community of Sparks.

The coming of the automobile brought a demand for improved roads, and by the 1920's, Nevada had entered into a program of highway construction. Each year brought more automobiles into the state, constantly increasing the need for better highways and for roadside establishments like hotels, cafes, and service stations. Almost without noticing it, Nevada became an important tourist state, serving recreation seekers and temporary residents. The state legislature began to pass laws to attract more visitors to Nevada. The lenient divorce and marriage laws are, in part, a product of the mobility of modern America.

Finally, the air age added another chapter to the transportation evolution in Nevada. The changes in transportation—and the opportunities they provided—altered the state's personality in a dramatic way.

RAILROADING IN SOUTHERN NEVADA, 1900-1905

Although only a few thousand persons lived in Lincoln County —which included virtually all of the southeastern corner of the state in 1900—they had long dreamed of a railroad which would bring cheap transportation to the area and allow the mines of Pioche and the nearby rich valleys to produce for the outside world. In 1890, despite the economic slump, a railroad line was actually surveyed from Utah into the northern part of the county, but construction did not begin for another decade.

The Union Pacific Railroad Company, a rival of the Central Pacific, planned a railroad line in Lincoln County because it wanted to connect Salt Lake City with Los Angeles. This was a difficult region through which to build a railroad; it either had to follow the narrow, flood-threatened Meadow Valley Wash or go out across the parched desert toward Death Valley, where water is scarce and working conditions severe. The most logical place to build a road-bed into Nevada from southern Utah was at Clover Valley, which lies east of the present city of Caliente. The Union Pacific had claimed this route in the 1890's, but then work stopped.

Suddenly, in 1900, two rival companies wanted the old Union Pacific grade. U.S. Senator W. A. Clark from Montana formed the San Pedro, Los Angeles, and Salt Lake Railroad Company and announced construction plans. Also, a company known as the Oregon Short Line claimed it had obtained title to the Clover Valley route. After several months of arguments, each company moved men into the valley in the spring of 1901 to hold the ground and destroy the work of the other. In the encounters, rival teams of workers battled with shovels and axes, but the county sheriff managed to prevent serious injuries. After a few weeks, a federal-court order instructed Clark's men to withdraw. Eventually, an agreement and a partnership was arranged between Clark and the owners of the Oregon Short Line, and after 1903 no more conflicts delayed the construction.

As the line was extended to the point where Clover Valley joins the Meadow Valley Wash, a new town appeared. Since some natural hot springs exist in the valley, the founders used the Spanish word *caliente* (hot) as the name for their town. Stores, saloons, and boarding houses were serving the construction crews by mid-year of 1901. For two years, it was a dusty or muddy little hamlet where free-spending railroad builders came to pass their leisure hours. In 1904, as the line was being laid down the Meadow Valley Wash, Caliente was made a "division point" on the railroad; this meant that repair shops, a round house, and offices would be built there. For more than forty years, it continued to be one of the major points on the Salt Lake City-Los Angeles railroad, but after the diesel locomotives replaced steam engines, in the 1940's, it became less important as a railroad center.

As the crews extended the line south through the twisting Meadow Valley Wash in 1904, speculation arose about where the next important town would be built. In 1902, Senator Clark had purchased the old Las Vegas Ranch—the location of the Mormon mission of 1855—and in 1904 he announced that this would be the site of another "division point."

The old ranch had been little affected by the changes in Nevada life in the previous forty years. O. D. Gass, the Arizona rancher who had obtained the property when the Mormons left, had sold it to Archibald Stewart, a man who had come West for the 1849 gold rush and who had seen many of the camps of Nevada. The Las Vegas Ranch thus became the "Stewart Ranch" until purchased by Senator Clark.

THE BIRTH OF LAS VEGAS

Even before the town was born, many people sensed that Las Vegas was destined for importance. The first train arrived there in January, 1905, and shortly thereafter the first through train went from Salt Lake City to Los Angeles via the Las Vegas Valley. The railroad company announced that it would establish a community in the valley and sell lots at auction. The date of the sale was set for May 15, and hundreds of men rode into the valley for the occasion.

The auction was a hectic affair. The railroad's representative made ambitious promises; Las Vegas would have paved streets, an attractive depot, and water piped to every lot. Railroad maintenance shops would be built, giving employment to hundreds of men. Many listened attentively and then bought. The railroad collected more than a quarter million dollars in two days of selling, and within hours tents and shacks were being thrown up on newly purchased lots. About 1,200 lots were sold, most of them only patches of greasewood.

Although Las Vegas began with a flourish, its early years were marred by bad luck. A fire destroyed many buildings, and a severe wind in 1907 caused serious damage. Floods in Meadow Valley Wash wrecked the railroad line in the same year, and for six weeks no trains arrived from Salt Lake City. But these early misfortunes meant only a temporary setback. By 1909 the residents had erected stronger and more permanent buildings and the railroad company had started the construction of its maintenance shops.

In 1909 Las Vegas passed beyond the stage of infancy. As a result of the population growth and the demands for governmental service, the legislature created the new county of Clark—named for the railroad financier—and designated Las Vegas as the county seat. Soon after the legislature acted, a group of citizens met to form the Las Vegas Promotion Society. This forerunner of the Chamber of Commerce voted to publicize the advantages of the town to attract industry and business. The ambitious promotion program was the first step in making Las Vegas one of the most famous of America's small cities, but it took more than a third of a century for the change to occur.

Another factor which benefited Las Vegas in the early years after its settlement was the prosperity of Goldfield and Tonopah. At first, most of the freight for these mining camps had come from the direction of Reno, improving the business climate in that end of the state. But Senator Clark felt there was no reason why Las Vegas could not profit from the mining boom, so he decided to build a railroad from that city to Rhyolite, Goldfield, and Tonopah. Locomotives began to haul passengers to and from Goldfield just at the time when that camp was entering its greatest period of prosperity, and for a few years picture postcards boasted that Las Vegas was the "gateway to Goldfield."

In addition to the benefits it received from the mining towns to the northwest, Las Vegas profited from smaller rushes in Clark County. Prospectors combed the mountains in the southernmost corner of the state during the early 1900's, and this meant dollars in the pockets of Las Vegas merchants. The most important of the towns to grow up in the area was Searchlight, seventy-five miles south of Las Vegas—near the extreme tip of the state. This district produced a few million dollars worth of gold during the period of Las Vegas' youth.

Another asset that helped Las Vegas to prosper—and this was far more important than any mineral wealth in the region—was a large supply of underground water from artesian wells. This gave the community a potential which many other older Nevada towns did not have.

The coming of the automobile age gave special advantages to Las Vegas. Placed conveniently between Salt Lake City and Los Angeles, the town became a favorite stopping point for some of the earliest long-distance motorists in the West. Las Vegas recognized early that automobile traffic could be an important source of income, and laid the first portion of a highway toward Salt Lake City in about 1915. In later years, volunteer crews of workers constructed improved roads to serve visiting motorists.

Even though geographical advantages served Las Vegas well, the town did not grow rapidly during its first few years. Although it was prosperous, it continued to be a small city. As late as 1930, Las Vegas's population was no more than 5,165—much smaller than several of Nevada's present cities. The construction of Hoover (Boulder) Dam on the nearby Colorado River in the 1930's and the impetus of legalized gambling on the tourist industry began to transform the city, and the developments of the 1940's and 1950's made it one of the fastest growing communities in America. It is difficult to realize, in view of the cosmopolitan reputation of Las Vegas today, that it was a small railroad city only forty years ago.

REROUTING THE SOUTHERN PACIFIC: CITY OF SPARKS

Another new railroad project in western Nevada accounted for the founding of Sparks a short time before the birth of Las Vegas. In 1902 the Southern Pacific, new owners of the main line across northern Nevada, began to rebuild part of their railroad along the Truckee River and across the Forty-Mile Desert, and in doing so they bypassed the old town of Wadsworth. The railroad's managers felt it was more efficient to move their maintenance shops and round house nearer to Reno and to establish a new railroad town.

This was bitter news for the people of Wadsworth, some of whom had lived there since the early days. The Southern Pacific tried to ease the hardship by offering to move the homes of the Wadsworth residents to the new town. Most of them accepted the offer.

In 1902 only ranches and swampland existed four miles east of Reno where the future town was to be built. The railroad hauled in thousands of carloads of dirt and rock to provide a more solid base for the townsite. By July of 1904, the railroad company had shifted hundreds of persons from Wadsworth to the new location. For several weeks, there was a question about the naming of the new community; some persons called it New Wadsworth and for a brief time its post office was called Harriman. Some residents wanted it to be known as East Reno and others preferred Glendale. The name Sparks was finally selected in honor of the popular cattle man and mine owner who was then serving as governor.

Although Sparks appeared on the maps at about the same time as Las Vegas, it did not achieve the fame of the railroad city in the south. Whereas Las Vegas quickly became the most important community of southern Nevada, Sparks grew up in the shadow of Reno and did not become famous beyond the borders of the state. After World War II, however, Sparks shared the general prosperity of Reno and increased in population from 7,000 to 27,000 in fewer than twenty years. This growth occurred in spite of the fact that the Southern Pacific company shifted to diesel locomotives and curtailed its railroad operation. The growth of the tourist business more than compensated for the partial loss of railroad employment.

As Reno and Sparks expanded, the two cities covered more of the Truckee Meadows and eventually blended into a single metropolitan area. On a few occasions businessmen or civic groups proposed that a single municipal government be established for the whole area. Residents of Sparks, however, generally opposed any plan to merge with Reno or to change its name to East Reno. Sparks continued to be a community with a separate identity, eager to build economic prosperity on a basis different from that of Reno.

In 1907-1909, when Sparks was in its infancy and the Southern Pacific was being rerouted, a new railroad company crossed Nevada with an interstate line. The Western Pacific Railway was constructed from Salt Lake City to Oakland, using part of the route which the Southern Pacific followed. Along the Humboldt River between Wells and Winnemucca, the two lines ran close together, but west of Winnemucca their paths parted. The Western Pacific did not run southward to Lovelock and Sparks, but instead went westward through the Black Rock Desert and Beckwourth Pass north of Reno and on to Oakland. A branch line later connected Reno with the Western Pacific.

The Western Pacific opened a region of northwestern Nevada to modern transportation for the first time, establishing the town of

Downtown Las Vegas

Las Vegas Strip

Gerlach and making handy transportation available for mining and agricultural interests. The building of the Western Pacific was one more step in enlarging Nevada's transportation facilities.

A NETWORK OF HIGHWAYS

The development of highways and roads was just as important as the expansion of the railroads—perhaps more important. In the days when horses or oxen were necessary to cover long distances in most parts of the state, no official road system existed. Usually the paths that had been worn in the desert by early prospectors or boom-town followers became unofficial "roads" linking Nevada's communities together. Usually the election officials of the state and counties did little to keep them in good condition. In the earliest days of Nevada history, the legislature authorized individuals to operate toll roads. A person obtained a franchise for a toll road and would be expected to build at least a crude thoroughfare between specified points. He then was entitled to collect cash from everyone who used it. But tradition and the attractiveness of toll roads declined in the depression years of the late nineteenth century.

We have already mentioned that Tonopah and Goldfield became lively camps just as the earliest automobiles were becoming available on the American market; Tasker L. Oddie's achievement in driving a car from Sodaville to Tonopah in 1903 was regarded as a historic event. Within a few years, automobiles could be seen in mining camps and in remote places on the desert, even though there was nothing except trails and wagon ruts to follow. More and more "gas buggies" appeared, and as increasing numbers of them ruined their tires on rocks, bogged down in mud or sand, and scraped their undersides on the "high centers" of the old trails, a public demand for road improvement arose.

The man who started the campaign for better roads in Nevada was Oddie himself, who recognized how important easy automobile transportation could be to the future development of Nevada. On becoming governor in 1911, he asked Nevada's legislators to put money into a "general road fund" and to pass a law making it possible to use convicts from the state prison for road-building. The

Early highway construction

legislature did as Governor Oddie asked, and this permitted a small beginning toward road improvement in the state. The use of prisoners did not prove to be successful, however, because they did not work diligently and often managed to escape.

Nevada did not get far in the construction of good roads until the federal government became interested in developing a nation-wide network of highways for automobile traffic. Congress passed a law in 1916 which provided for federal-state cooperation in building and financing highways. Nevada could not have built the necessary roads on its own. Its area was so large and its population so small that the people of this state could not have borne the financial burden of thousands of miles of highways.

World War I diverted America's main construction resources to military ends in 1917 and 1918, so the U.S. government did not invest much in roads during those years. It was 1919 and 1920 before Nevada's modern road program actually began. In those years, there was no huge earth-moving equipment to cut hills or to fill gullies. Some of the earliest highways were made with horse-drawn scrapers, and they followed the contours of the land. Anyone who has been on one of the "back roads" in the Nevada mountains, where no bulldozers or graders have cleared the way, can appreciate what the first highway construction crews encountered and conquered by hand or animal power.

At first only a few roads were paved with concrete; most of the so-called "improved roads" were merely leveled and sometimes covered with gravel. But the 1920's have been described as "the decade of road-building" because of the progress that was made in eliminating the worst hazards. Eventually oiled roads—which were found to be better than concrete ones—connected Nevada's major towns.

Although Nevada's Department of Highways built roads at a fast pace, it never managed to get ahead of the needs and demands of the motorists. Automobiles became more common every year, and thousands of them crossed Nevada annually after 1919. Two of the nation's main east-west highways crossed the state, carrying an ever-increasing volume of traffic between California and the East. In 1923, the state began to levy a tax on gasoline to help pay for the highways it was building and maintaining. As automobiles became faster and more elaborate, more and better roads were necessary; additional safety precautions had to be built into the thoroughfares and the costs of construction constantly grew.

It is easy to see why the Department of Highways has become the largest single agency of the state government and why highway construction is one of the most expensive responsibilities of Nevada's taxpayers. Especially in the 1950's and 1960's, when the volume and speed of modern traffic required the construction of multiple-laned freeways, highway-building became big business. U.S. Highway 40 (also known as Interstate Highway 80) was designated as the route for one of America's new super traffic arterials. Curiously, it almost follows the Humboldt-Truckee route used by many emigrants, passing through or near Wendover, Wells, Elko, Carlin, Battle Mountain, Winnemucca, Lovelock, Sparks, Reno, and Verdi. In southern Nevada, U.S. Highway 91 (also known as Interstate Highway 15) crosses the same region once traversed by the Old Spanish Trail or the Mormon Trail, serving the Las Vegas valley. Tens of millions of dollars are committed to the construction of these highways.

The most remarkable symbols of the transportation progress in Nevada in the 1970's are the modern airports which serve Las Vegas and Reno. McCarran Field on the outskirts of Las Vegas and the Cannon International Airport in the southeastern Truckee Meadows have sparkling new terminal buildings, costly runways, and modern equipment to increase the safety of large airliners. Built with the aid of the U.S. government, these airports have helped to make Nevada rapidly accessible to millions of persons around the world. Ely and Elko also began to be served by commercial airlines in the 1950's; the time distance between the most important Nevada communities gradually decreased.

NEVADA'S TEMPORARY RESIDENTS

The improved transportation facilities of the twentieth century—first in railroads, then in highways, and more recently in airports—have given Nevada its most important new industry: the serving of visitors to the state. Since Americans have developed a willingness to travel long distances on special occasions, Nevada has found that a thriving business can be operated on the needs and wants of the transients.

Nevada first became known for its temporary residents in the early 1900's when Reno began to develop a reputation for relatively quick divorces; before that few divorces were granted in the state. In 1899, an English earl, a member of the House of Lords, came to Genoa to live briefly and obtained a divorce from his wife after he had become a legal resident in Nevada. A few years later, the wife of a millionaire, William Corey, president of the United States Steel Corporation, came to Reno for a few months and then sued her husband for divorce. The newspapers carried many reports of this divorce, and it became evident throughout the United States that it was easier to get a divorce in Nevada than in most eastern states, because the laws were less strict. By 1910, hundreds of persons were traveling to Reno by train every year to establish residence for divorce.

Most states adopted laws making it difficult to dissolve a marriage. In most parts of the United States, divorce could be granted by the law courts only after a waiting period of a year or more. Many American courts also expected the person seeking the divorce to prove clearly that his or her partner had committed a shameful or improper act. In Nevada, the legal waiting period for a divorce was only six months in the early years of the century and the courts did not usually demand extensive evidence of wrong-doing if both partners were willing to agree to the divorce. This made it possible for persons from New York, for example, to end their marriages in Nevada more quickly and more simply than in their home state.

Nearly all divorce seekers came to Reno, since it was Nevada's largest city during most of the early years of the century and because it was served by the transcontinental railroad. Reno was already Nevada's financial and business center and the supply point for mining men and stockmen in northwestern Nevada. The mining activities in communities like Tonopah, Goldfield, and elsewhere benefited Reno because some of the money made in those camps was invested in the older community. The new "divorce

McCarran International Airport, Las Vegas

A modern freeway through Truckee Canyon

business" only supplemented Reno's other activities, but it made the little city famous throughout America and Europe.

Some persons regarded it as sinful that judges in a Nevada court would dissolve a marriage so easily, and Reno developed a bad reputation in some parts of the country. Other persons argued that Reno was performing a needed service for unhappy married couples and that the divorce laws of other states were cruel and unrealistic. The debate goes on today on a small scale.

The businessmen of Reno soon learned that serving and selling to the divorcees was profitable business. Eastern divorcees gave the city a cosmopolitan flavor; Reno heard much of the gossip of New York City, Washington, London, and other social centers. Well known authors, theater and movie personalities, and heiresses came, lived for the required length of time for legal residence, and departed after being divorced. When famous persons received their divorces, newspaper publicity followed and Reno became still more prominent. In the 1920's, it was often called the "divorce capital of the world." It had become as well known as any small city in America. Improved railroad and highway facilities made Reno even more accessible to the East in the 1920's and 1930's.

In 1927, Reno's lawyers and merchants heard rumors that easy divorces in Paris and Mexico City might soon draw prospective divorcees away from Nevada, and a group of them persuaded the state legislature to reduce the legal residence requirement from six months to three months. The change was made swiftly by the legislature, without any debate and without an opportunity for public consideration. It brought Nevada new criticism, but it also increased the number of persons who came for legal services. In 1931, the legislature went a step further, reducing the residence requirement for divorce to only six weeks. This introduced Reno—and to a lesser extent Las Vegas—to a new era of prosperity based on divorce clients. The law remains in effect today and accounts for thousands of temporary residents in the state every year.

Since the age of the automobile began, Nevada has also become a favorite place for marriages, although the state has never received as much recognition for this as for its divorce business. In some neighboring states, laws have existed for many years which require a waiting period between the time of applying for a license and the time of the wedding. Most states have also enacted laws requiring examination for diseases before a marriage license is issued. Nevada requires neither a physical examination nor a waiting period before issuing a license and permitting a marriage, and thousands of couples come from other states each month to marry in order to avoid the requirements of their home states. Nevada has been criticized for its liberal marriage law as it has for its liberal divorce law. Nevada's political leaders have generally ignored this criticism because the visitors from outside the state help local business when they come here to be married and spend a few days.

Nevada's divorce and marriage business would not be possible without the rapid transportation facilities of the modern age. First, the railroads brought Nevada most of the temporary residents who, in the twentieth century, began to build the state's tourist industry. By the 1920's the automobile was bringing a large number of visitors, and by the 1940's air service had become important in shuttling visitors in and out of the state by the thousands. By 1964, nearly 20 million persons from outside Nevada visited the state in a single year.

Most of the tourists who have arrived in recent years have been attracted by Nevada's resorts. Legalized gambling—which we shall discuss in more detail in Chapter 14—and highly publicized entertainment spectacles have made Las Vegas, Reno, and Lake Tahoe some of the most popular tourist centers in America. The elaborate stage shows and the identification of Nevada with "high rolling" bets have often captured the attention of national television networks.

Just as in the era when mining was the state's most important business, the most dramatic national attention came at a time of disaster. The Yellow Jacket mine fire in Gold Hill in 1869 took 37 lives when men were trapped underground in the kind of accident that mining men dreaded most. In more recent times, the fear of a fire in a high-rise hotel has been widespread, and in November, 1980, flames and smoke killed 84 people in the Las Vegas MGM Grand Hotel; in 1981, another hotel fire in Las Vegas killed 8 people and injured many others.

Nevada's strategic location in the Far West is also an important fact in the transportation revolution of the twentieth century. As massive quantities of supplies and equipment are shipped east and west across the United States, much of it must go through or over Nevada, and more and more companies are storing some of their goods in the Reno and Las Vegas areas. Nevada's voters in 1960 amended the state constitution to approve a free-port law, which

13. Federal Government Projects

WE HAVE SEEN that Nevada was revitalized in the early years of the twentieth century by the discovery and development of new minerals and by the construction of new transportation facilities. We must also give credit to several projects of the U.S. government which have transformed the resources of the desert.

One of the first and most important federal achievements in Nevada in this century was the Newlands Reclamation Project which diverted waters of the Truckee and Carson rivers out onto a parched valley for irrigation. This permitted the growth of the city of Fallon and brought under cultivation tens of thousands of acres of land. Later, a smaller irrigation project was sponsored by the federal government in the lower Humboldt Valley. Known as the Rye Patch Dam, this facility impounded water for the region around Lovelock.

Much larger reclamation projects changed the face of southern Nevada. The construction of Hoover and Davis dams on the Colorado River gave Clark County a thrust forward which made that region one of the most important in the state. The erection of these massive dams required thousands of men, many skilled engineers, and millions of dollars, but their benefits to Nevada and nearby states have been enormous.

Another type of federal-government program of importance to Nevada has been associated with national defense. In 1930, a U.S. Navy ammunition depot was established near Hawthorne, and thirteen years later a Naval air station went into operation near Fallon. During World War II, the government established military air bases near Reno and Las Vegas. Nevada has been playing an ever larger role in military defense, and agencies of the federal government have been playing an ever greater part in the state's economy.

IRRIGATION: THE TRUCKEE-CARSON PROJECT

We have seen that most of Nevada's arid valleys were not inviting to small farmers; large ranchers predominated on most of the state's cultivated land, and homesteaders were not generally encouraged to claim land because most areas could not be irrigated cheaply and easily.

Government officials had long recognized that some parts of the desert might become productive if water could be channeled to them. Nevada's Congressional representatives, in the same years when they were waging the fight for free silver coinage, were seeking money for irrigation. A group of senators, including Senator Stewart, conducted a hearing on the state's water needs in 1889, and several of Nevada's governors in their official messages mentioned the need for government irrigation projects. It was Congressman Newlands, the Silverite representative in Congress of the 1890's, who provided the decisive leadership.

In 1902 Congress passed a law proposed by Congressman Newlands which provided that irrigation systems would be constructed by the federal government with money obtained from the sale of public lands. Because of the Nevada congressman's important role in the program, the first reclamation project was started on the Truckee and Carson rivers. People in many parts of the United States—and especially in Nevada—became interested in this new venture, which included the building of a dam on the Truckee River and the diverting of some of its water by canal to the valley of the Carson Sink. The waters of both the Carson and the Truckee rivers were to be stored in a reservoir, for use during the dry, rainless season.

The Truckee Canal—more than thirty miles long—was excavated, and water from this source irrigated crops in the reclamation area as early as 1906. The canal served not only the lands near the sink but also some of the fertile bench lands east of Wadsworth. Here the town of Fernley grew, later to be served by a railroad and two transcontinental highways. The canal was designed to carry most of the water to the basin of the Carson River and eventually into Carson Sink Valley.

Lahontan Dam, one of the most important parts of the project, was begun in 1911 and completed in 1915. Situated on the Carson River, this facility stores the waters from the Truckee Canal and the Carson River for use in the Carson Sink Valley during dry periods. The Lahontan Reservoir is twenty-five miles long and about four miles wide in places; it is the largest man-made lake in western Nevada. A power plant at the dam generates electricity for homes and industries in the project area.

The benefits derived from the Truckee-Carson Project—later named the Newlands Project—appeared most rapidly in the Carson Sink Valley, where farm land was taken up and several hundred miles of small canals were built to distribute the water. Before the announcement of the project, there was only the tiny town of Stillwater and a few ranches in the Carson Sink Valley. Stillwater was the seat of Churchill County, which for years had been one of the poorest, least populated counties in the state. With the advent of the Truckee-Carson Project, a town was carefully planned on the site of a ranch formerly owned by Michael Fallon. The planners provided wide streets—some of the roomiest in Nevada— and made arrangements for city-owned water and power plants. Fallon became the seat of Churchill County and an attractive, wellordered community with frugal, industrious citizens.

The city of Fallon and the surrounding farm lands soon testified to the success and wisdom of this project. Nearly a thousand farms and small ranches were developed as a result of the Truckee-Carson Project. The U.S. government invested less than $10,000,000 to construct the main installations, which produced more than $90,000,000 worth of crops between 1903 and 1963. In addition to the crops, millions of dollars worth of livestock have been raised or fattened on project lands.

Farmers had to overcome several problems to make Fallon and the project prosper. At first the desert land was so barren that organic matter had to be added. Besides, after a few years of irrigation, the alkaline content of some land became troublesome and special chemical treatments were required. In other places, the ground would not drain properly, and farmers needed special pumping equipment to remove excess water. But the science and technology of the twentieth century came to their aid, and the major problems were solved. Fallon farmers had assistance, knowledge, and equipment at their disposal which were unknown to the Nevada pioneers of the 1860's.

The most difficult challenge faced by the Truckee-Carson Project farmers arose because the system at first did not furnish as much water as was needed. The original water supply would not provide for the wants of all project farmers in dry years without taking more than the normal flow of water from upstream sources— mainly from Lake Tahoe. The users of the Truckee-Carson Project demanded the right to use Lake Tahoe as a reservoir, to store large quantities of water there during the wet season, and to pump or drain a large flow from the lake during the dry periods. Persons who owned property along the shore of Lake Tahoe objected, and for many years a legal fight was waged. At one point, farmers threatened to dynamite the rim of the lake to allow more water to flow. Finally, the federal government established the maximum and minimum levels of Lake Tahoe.

The agricultural products of Fallon became famous. Melons of high quality came from this valley, and Fallon turkeys went into homes in many parts of the United States. Alfalfa hay was raised extensively for local livestock and for export to other states and overseas. In addition, Fallon gardens responded to the food needs of a growing population in western Nevada.

The farmers of the Fernley-Fallon region have not solved all their problems, and the Newlands Project has occasionally been called wasteful because it diverts so much water onto marginal land. Pyramid Lake Indians assert that their rights have been violated by the Project. But it serves as an example of what imaginative engineering can accomplish on the desert.

IRRIGATION IN THE LOVELOCK VALLEY

The earliest immigrants to cross Nevada had learned that the Humboldt River could be disappointing. If the previous winter had brought little snow or if the summer had been hot and dry, there was a shortage of grass and good water in the lower Humboldt Valley. In the 1860's, the first ranchers and farmers to settle the Big Meadows—just north of the Humboldt Sink—relearned this fact. Much land was claimed by farmers and cattlemen during the era of territorial government, but the water supply was not always dependable.

As the Humboldt Valley became more thoroughly settled in the 1870's, the problem of the Big Meadows settlers became more serious. More water was being used upstream for irrigation and cattle, and less came down to the Big Meadows. Nevertheless, hundreds of families managed to raise crops, hay, grain, and cattle in the vicinity of Lovelock, which became an important town after the Central Pacific was built in 1869. It became the seat of newly created Pershing County in 1919.

In 1933 Lovelock Valley ranchers took steps to overcome their most serious water problem. They borrowed money from an agency of the U.S. government, purchased some of the water rights of ranchers who lived further up the river, and prepared to store the additional water in a reservoir at the northern edge of their valley. With government aid, the Rye Patch Dam was built in 1937; when the artificial lake behind it was filled to capacity, it stretched for about twenty miles. Thus waters could be stored during wet years for use during the drier seasons. Tens of thousands of acres could be cultivated in the Big Meadows with more confidence.

The Rye Patch Dam project was much smaller and less expensive than the Newlands Project, but it had a similar objective. The water users are repaying the federal government for the money invested, and meanwhile Nevada is benefiting from the new wealth and stability which the project provides.

RECLAMATION OF THE COLORADO RIVER

The Newlands and Rye Patch projects, while important to western Nevada, are small operations by comparison with some of the federal government's enterprises on the Colorado River at the state's southern border. Two of America's greatest dams—Hoover and Davis—span the river to generate electricity and provide water supplies for part of Nevada, California, Arizona, and Utah.

The wild and muddy waters of the Colorado were of little benefit to man until the U.S. government decided to control them. In 1928, President Calvin Coolidge approved a plan for the highest dam in the world, and two years later, during the administration of President Herbert Hoover, Congress provided money for construction. The actual work of building the dam required more than two years, during the administration of President Franklin D. Roosevelt. Thousands of workmen poured a massive wedge of concrete—726 feet high and 660 feet wide at the bottom—into a steep, narrow canyon of the river channel. Within this monumental block of concrete they placed seventeen giant electrical turbines which are turned by a stream of water to create power for millions of homes and thousands of industries.

One must see the magnificent dam to appreciate its size and the amount of human labor and skill which were required to build it. Men had to fight a long battle with the surly river in a narrow canyon which had walls nearly a thousand feet high. In the summers of 1933 and 1934, when the main construction was underway, temperatures reached 130 degrees during the daytime shift. The construction companies had to use some of the largest equipment the world had yet devised to prepare the site and to pour nearly seven millions tons of concrete.

The top of the dam is so wide that four lanes of highway traffic can cross it between Arizona and Nevada. It creates a reservoir—known as Lake Mead—which extends for 115 miles up the channel of the Colorado River. It is one of the largest man-made bodies of water in the world, and most of it lies in Nevada. As the lake filled with water after the completion of the dam, it covered the old site of Pueblo Grande, where prehistoric men lived a thousand years ago, and it also covered the Mormon town of St. Thomas. The U.S. government bought the property of people whose homes and lands were flooded by the new lake.

Although a few persons were inconvenienced by the Hoover Dam project, millions of others benefited when the wild and dangerous river had been tamed. For many years before the dam was built, farmers in the lower river basin—in California and Arizona—suffered from devastating floods. In 1934 alone, about $10,000,000 worth of damage was done to property and crops by the rampaging river. Such damage did not recur after 1935. Flood water can now be stored for use during periods of drought. Also, because no more big floods seemed likely on the lower Colorado, the cities of southern California were able to build another dam—the smaller Parker Dam—155 miles below Hoover Dam. From behind this dam, the communities of the Los Angeles area could divert part of the river to the west. One of the world's largest aqueducts carries this water 242 miles from the Colorado River to the cities, and the project would not be possible without Hoover Dam.

The Los Angeles region also gets most of its electrical power from the Nevada side of Hoover Dam. Countless homes and factories are served by the whirling generators beneath the dam. Southern Nevada's communities, of course, also use this inexpensive source of electrical power. In Nevada, the electricity from Hoover Dam reaches into the valleys north of Pioche—more than 200 miles away. Majestic steel towers carry power lines in all directions from the dam.

When the idea of Hoover Dam was first conceived, few people foresaw that the great structure would also have recreational benefits. Every year since completion of the dam, hundreds of thousands of sightseers have come to marvel at its size and beauty, and thousands of fishermen, boaters, water skiers, and vacationers have enjoyed the lake. The U.S. government created a great reserve of land above and below the dam, known as the Lake Mead Recreational Area, which is a favorite playground of the American South-west.

The building of the dam and the creation of Lake Mead changed the destiny of Las Vegas, twenty-five miles away, and another important Nevada community—Boulder City—was born because of the project. Las Vegas had remained a small railroad city with only about 5,000 residents until the dam construction began in 1933. It soon became evident that the millions of dollars which Uncle Sam was spending on the river would do more for Las Vegas than any gold or silver mine had ever done for a Nevada town. Hundreds of workers traveled from the dam site to Las Vegas during their idle hours to buy supplies or to be entertained. Most tourists who came to see the dam and enjoy the desert air also went to Las Vegas, which responded to this opportunity by creating a lively entertainment industry based on gambling and floor shows.

Boulder City developed as a different kind of community. Situated twenty-three miles from Las Vegas and twelve miles from the dam, it was built entirely by the U.S. government. Experts in the field of city planning were employed to design a model city, noted for its beauty and efficient streets and facilities. It became one of Nevada's cleanest, greenest, and most charming communities. The federal government owned the entire town for nearly thirty years after it was founded, but eventually it began to sell the property to persons who had leased the land for many years.

The U.S. government did not stop its work on the Colorado River after it had built Hoover Dam and Boulder City. These projects had only been in operation a few years when construction began on another large facility about fifty miles to the south—almost at the extreme southern point of Nevada. Here, in 1942, construction of Davis Dam was begun. The plan was to create another large reservoir which would provide still more electrical power, irrigation, flood control, and recreational possibilities.

Davis Dam did not rise as rapidly as Hoover Dam, nor was it as large. During World War II, work was stopped for several years so that necessary manpower and material could be used for military purposes. Most of the work on the dam was done between 1946 and 1953. This dam is 200 feet high—less than one-third of Hoover

Dam—and Lake Mohave, which formed behind it, is much smaller than Lake Mead. Davis Dam does, however, give southern Nevada another great potential source of power, water, and recreation.

It was a long step from the diversion of the Truckee River in the Newlands Project to the harnessing of the Colorado River with Hoover and Davis dams, but the big southern Nevada reclamation projects are logical outgrowths of the public-works idea which Senator Newlands proposed two-thirds of a century ago. It is appropriate that Nevada, which was the site of the first reclamation project, should be one of the states to benefit greatly from the modern programs for utilizing water resources.

The work of controlling rivers and streams for the benefit of man is a continuing process. In the 1950's and 1960's, construction of reservoirs in the Truckee and Carson basins continued. The Prosser Creek dam on a tributary of the Truckee made it possible to store additional snow water for beneficial uses and to reduce floods. Although this dam is in California, its major benefits are felt in Reno and western Nevada. The Bureau of Reclamation plans another dam on the upper Carson River, also for flood control and irrigation. Both of these dams are part of the so-called Washoe Project for western Nevada. It is small by comparison with the developments on the Colorado River, but it is important to Reno, Carson Valley, and Fallon.

With federal aid, Las Vegas built an advanced water distribution system from 1969 to 1983. The Las Vegas Valley Water Project, which cost over $200 million, pumps most of Nevada's share of Colorado River water through a four-mile tunnel into the valley, allowing the metropolitan area to continue its growth.

The U.S. government's increased interest in Nevada since 1900 has not been confined to reclamation. The problems related to national defense in the twentieth century have also accounted for new communities and for the rejuvenation of old ones.

War Potential in Magnesium—Gabbs and Henderson

The great Hoover Dam project had only been operating for a few years when it made possible an important new industry for

United States military defense. The community of Henderson—one of Nevada's youngest and largest cities—grew as a result.

When World War II began in 1939, little was known about how to process or use magnesium. It is a metal that can be used as an alloy in the construction of light-weight machines and instruments; it has been found especially valuable for airplanes and rockets. Magnesium can also be used in explosives because it burns with great heat when properly ignited, but this potential was not well understood when the war began. The Germans, however, learned to make deadly magnesium bombs and in 1940 spread much destruction over England with them. When a few German planes were shot down, the Allies discovered that some of the instruments had light-weight magnesium parts. The British and Americans quickly began to look for supplies of the metal and intensified their study of its properties.

The U.S. government eventually discovered that large amounts of magnesite and brucite—the ores from which magnesium can be extracted—existed in Gabbs Valley, about fifty miles northeast of Hawthorne. Although this was a remote area, the United States needed magnesium for its defense and—as in pioneer days—the problem of distance had to be overcome. To produce magnesium from raw ore, however, requires great sources of electrical power. The government calculated that it would take enough electrical energy for a city of more than a million people to process the amount of magnesium needed. No such source of power existed in the desert-mountain region between Hawthorne and Austin.

Thanks to Hoover Dam, the power was available within Nevada. In the early years of the war, plans were drawn for a massive magnesium plant—known as Basic Magnesium—in the desert between the dam and Las Vegas.

Nevada and the West had witnessed hundreds of "boom camps," but this one was extraordinary. The government was so eager to stimulate rapid production that it engaged contractors who hired 12,000 men to erect the factory and a town to house its workers. Work began late in 1941, and, within a few weeks, a four-square-mile area of desert had been transformed into a bustling city. The main units of the magnesium factory soon loomed on the landscape

Hoover Dam

like giant railroad boxcars. Power lines, water systems, and community facilities rose almost in the twinkling of an eye. The men who worked at "Basic" (soon its name was changed to Henderson) at times suffered from severe heat and some were sickened by chlorine fumes; their difficulties bore some resemblance to those of the early miners on the Comstock Lode. But in spite of the problems, a full-scale city and a roaring industry mushroomed into existence.

The Basic Magnesium plant did its work so well that it filled America's needs for magnesium by 1943 and provided a surplus; only about 2,400 tons of the metal had been produced in the United States in 1938, but, thanks largely to the Nevada operation, more than a hundred times this amount was available in 1943. In fact, output was so great that by 1944 the U.S. government did not need any more magnesium; in November it stopped production and the massive plant became idle. It seemed that the old Nevada story of boom-and-bust mining and milling had been repeated and that a multi-million dollar investment and a city of more than a thousand homes were destined to decay.

But cooperation between federal and state governments avoided this decline. In 1947, the Nevada legislature passed laws making it possible for the state to purchase Basic Magnesium from the federal government and to make it available to private industry. During the late 1940's and 1950's, the plant passed to the state government, and eventually its facilities were sold to private companies for industrial operations. By the middle 1950's, old equipment had been converted and new machines had been installed by companies which were making such varied products as chlorine, caustic soda, DDT insect spray, weed killer for gardens, fuel for guided missiles, lime, and titanium metal. The Three Kids mine nearby became one of the country's largest producers of manganese ore, and this rock was hauled to Henderson for processing. All this industrial growth came about because southern Nevada had a large, unneeded wartime plant which could be converted to peacetime uses and a large source of electric power which could be made available to industry.

During the war years when magnesium was being produced in

The industrial plant at Henderson

great quantity and in the postwar period when several smaller industries flourished, Henderson provided jobs for thousands of men and valuable supplies for modern society. Nearby Las Vegas, which had already begun to grow rapidly because of the Hoover Dam project and the expanding tourist economy, shared the benefits of the Henderson prosperity, because many persons went there for necessities, luxuries, and entertainment.

But what of Gabbs Valley in west-central Nevada, where the mountain of magnesite and brucite existed? Although the operation here was smaller and less spectacular than that at Henderson, it became an important industry for modern Nevada.

During World War II, when large quantities of ore were being extracted for the first time in this region, there were serious transportation problems. The deposits at Gabbs were about 330 miles from Henderson, and at first it seemed undesirable to haul ore all the way to southern Nevada by truck because of wartime restrictions on gasoline and rubber. So the ore, after receiving preliminary processing at Gabbs, was transported to the railroad at Luning (twenty-five miles east of Hawthorne) and then through northern Nevada to Salt Lake City and southward to Henderson—an eleven hundred mile roundabout journey. After a few months, arrangements were finally made to haul the ore by trucks on the more direct highway route.

The little town of Gabbs was developed near the ore deposit and became the home of several hundred persons—mine and mill workers and their families. After the war, Basic Refractories, Inc., an Ohio company which first developed the property, maintained the production of the much-needed metals and kept the town alive. In more recent years, magnesite has been used not for the production of metal but for the manufacture of refractory bricks, which line the furnaces of steel mills in many parts of the world. The Gabbs brucite-magnesite deposit is the largest being mined in the world today.

The magnesium industry is only one of several industries created by military requirements. Henderson and Gabbs are only two of the communities which have grown because of the nation's defense program.

HAWTHORNE: A GIANT ARSENAL

In the middle years of the twentieth century, the U.S. government had growing need for large open areas of land for military uses. Nevada could offer such expanses, and the federal government made use of them.

The first important defense installation in Nevada was near Hawthorne. After the town's establishment by the builders of the Carson and Colorado Railroad in 1881, it became the seat of Esmeralda County and a freighting center for mountain mining towns. During the early 1900's, the county seat was moved to Goldfield, and for a while Hawthorne seemed destined to become another ghost town. In 1911, however, the legislature created Mineral County from the western part of Esmeralda, and Hawthorne once again became a seat of local government. It did not prosper, however, until the U.S. Navy established an ammunition depot there.

It may seem odd that the Navy should seek the parched desert for storing its ammunition. But in 1926, an arsenal of highly explosive ammunition near the Atlantic Ocean, in a populated region of New Jersey, was struck by lightning which ignited thousands of tons of explosives. Several Navy men were killed and wounded; fire damaged many homes in nearby areas. The military leaders decided that the ammunition depot should be rebuilt in a less populated area in the Far West. So it was that the Hawthorne region was chosen. The new Naval Ammunition Depot opened in 1930.

The Navy sent ammunition experts to the depot to prepare underground huts where explosives could be stored safely and facilities where dangerous shells could be handled. As ammunition gets older, it must be reprocessed or destroyed because it becomes undependable. This became a major operation of the Hawthorne Naval Ammunition Depot. Several thousand persons worked there during World War II, but fewer than one thousand were assigned to the operation in the early 1960's because of reduced activity.

The Naval Ammunition Depot completely surrounds Hawthorne, and motorists driving through the countryside near the town notice scores of concrete mounds or earthen lumps—the cellars where the ammuntion is stored. Since Hawthorne was not large enough to serve all the people who came to work at the depot, the Navy established a community called Babbitt, with several hundred family units.

Inside the huge depot are more than 200 miles of railroad tracks and 550 miles of oiled roads, an extensive transportation system for hauling the dangerous cargo. An intricate system of electrical lines and water lines, plus hundreds of vehicles, are needed to service the sprawling base and its massive collection of bombs, naval depth charges, rifle bullets, missiles, and other devices. It is one of the greatest concentrations of ammunition in the world.

After 1930, Hawthorne's economy was based primarily on the Ammunition Depot. In 1977, the U.S. Army assumed control of the facility, and it continued to be a major source of revenue for citizens of the area. In 1980, a civilian company took over the management of the Depot.

MILITARY AIR BASES: RENO, LAS VEGAS, FALLON, TONOPAH

During the war in 1940, it became evident that the government needed many new military bases to train men and to prepare for emergencies. Four Nevada communities became centers for various types of instruction for combat pilots.

The Nellis Air Force Base north of Las Vegas was originally an Army Air Corps Gunnery School, founded in 1941 to prepare men to use the weapons on World War II planes. Excellent flying weather and the availability of large desert areas for gunnery practice convinced military leaders that this would be a good site for a base. Thousands of fliers received their training there during the war years of 1942-1945. When the conflict ended, the base was inactivated (in 1947).

The beginning of the Korean War in 1950 led to a re-activation of Nellis, and its primary mission became the training of fighter pilots for that war. The Las Vegas base trained most of the men who flew the Air Force's fighters in Korea during the months of combat.

Men stationed at the base called it "the home of the fighter pilot." They were frequently seen soaring over Nevada communities in their Thunderbirds, Thunderchiefs, Super Sabres, and Sabrejets.

Another important base which served the nation's defense needs during World War II and the Korean War was Stead Air Force Base north of Reno. It was established to train signal companies in 1942 and later became a center for radio and navigation schools. It was closed after World War II, serving only as a training station for the Air National Guard Units. During the Korean War, the Air Force once again put Stead on an active basis to give men special training on how to survive in harsh climates if their planes were forced down in remote areas. The Sierra Nevada mountains and the Nevada desert provided ideal situations for teaching men how to live in extreme climates and rugged country. A helicopter school later operated there.

Fallon and Tonopah also shared the impact of the military expansion which came during World War II. Thousands of men received part of their preparation at the Naval Air Station at Fallon and at the Army Air Base at Tonopah. The Tonopah base was closed after the war, but its huge runway and hangars remain for the use of fliers in the area. At the Fallon Naval Air Station pilots receive gunnery practice over the northern Nevada desert.

In each of these instances, the military bases contributed to the prosperity of the towns and cities near which they were situated. Reno and Las Vegas owed much of their postwar growth to Stead and Nellis Air Force Bases. Yet many Nevadans realized that economic prosperity which relies upon military bases can be unreliable. Ranching, mining, transportation, commerce, education, or other occupations which contribute to the improvement of our normal living are preferable to occupations which prepare for war. Stead Air Force Base was closed in 1965 because the government no longer needed its facilities, and at first this appeared to be an economic setback for the Reno area. The property at the base, however, passed under the control of the University of Nevada, local school authorities and local governments, and private business firms. This made it possible to offer new educational and industrial opportunities to the region. William P. Lear, one of America's best known figures in the field of aircraft development, acquired some of the facilities for new industries.

In the 1950's, the federal government located one of its largest defense and research projects—the atomic testing site and the nuclear rocket center—in Southern Nevada. We shall discuss the history of these activities in Chapter 16.

In June, 1979, President Jimmy Carter made a proposal which, if implemented, would dramatically change the landscape and social life of most of eastern and southern Nevada during the 1980's. He endorsed an Air Force plan to locate 4,600 launching sites for 200 gigantic nuclear warhead missiles in Nevada and Utah. The plan, widely known as the MX (missile experimental) system, would require a vast network of roads, huge vehicles to move the missiles, and thousands of construction workers. It was widely described as the largest project ever conceived by humans; the estimates of cost varied between 30 billion and 60 billion dollars.

The proposal provoked one of the most spirited public debates in the state's history. The Air Force spokesmen and some Nevadans argued that MX was needed for national defense and that it would be good for the economy of the state. Many others both within and outside Nevada objected to the system on the ground that it would do severe damage to the environment, disrupt the lives of small communities, and make Nevada especially vulnerable to nuclear attack. In 1980, extensive environmental studies were made, and Nevadans in eight counties voted 41,000 to 19,000 against MX in a preferential ballot.

14. Political Problems
in the New Era

WE HAVE SEEN how much Nevada has changed in the twentieth
century, and how diversified her industries have become because
of the economic trends of modern times. The expansion of the
railroad and highway systems, the need for new types of minerals,
and the establishment of national defense operations have created
a more complex society in every decade. In this respect, Nevada is
typical of most other states in the Union.

In her internal politics, however, Nevada has retained a large
measure of independence, and some of the pioneer attitudes about
laws and government have lived well into the latter years of this
century. During most of the modern era, Nevada has elected Senators and Representatives in Congress who spoke for the mining
industry and voted in the tradition of John P. Jones and William M.
Stewart. It often has chosen small-town men as governors, and men
from the Comstock continued to have political appeal well into the
modern era.

Nevada gained world attention because of its legalized gambling
and quick divorces. Many people did not realize that these institutions were rooted in a live-and-let-live philosophy inherited from

early bonanza days. Many times, Nevada has been criticized by citizens of other states for practices not tolerated elsewhere, and Nevadans themselves have not always agreed on the wisdom of allowing them to exist. They have given the state a unique personality.

The modern age has brought Nevada hundreds of new political problems, which have not always been met rapidly and decisively. Still operating on the original constitutional framework and with an old tax system, Nevada found itself outgrowing its governmental agencies, its educational facilities, and its revenue sources in the 1950's and 1960's. A new era of politics, government, and education was unfolding.

NEVADANS IN CONGRESS: THE NEW ERA

We have seen that some of Nevada's most successful politicians after 1900 began their careers in Tonopah. Key Pittman, Tasker L. Oddie, and Patrick McCarran were the most notable men from that camp to win voter approval, and each of them served for many years in the U.S. Senate.

No Nevadan ever became more influential in national government than Senator Pittman. He was able to exert much political power on behalf of the silver-producing industry and thus helped the Nevada mining towns. More important, he became chairman of the Senate's Foreign Relations Committee with an important voice in the international affairs of the United States.

Twice during his career Senator Pittman was able to obtain benefits for the silver-mining industry. The price of silver was low during his early years in the Senate (his first term began in 1913), but during World War I the demand for silver increased because of monetary and industrial needs. The price of silver was 59 cents an ounce in 1916, but Senator Pittman sponsored legislation in 1918 to guarantee that the federal government would purchase millions of ounces for one dollar an ounce. A period of financial confusion plus Senator Pittman's legislative skill made possible the enactment of his bill, and the law came to be known as the Pittman Act. The high price remained in effect until 1923, when the act expired.

Senators Pittman and Oddie tried unsuccessfully to get it extended. For the next several years, Senator Pittman tried to get the federal government to buy more silver at a higher price. In a sense, he was carrying on the fight which Senators Jones and Stewart had waged thirty years before. He won a reputation as an expert on monetary affairs, and this served him well in the early 1930's, when a severe depression gripped the nation. Hundreds of Nevadans were out of work, and, like their predecessors in the 1890's, many felt that a government silver policy more favorable to them could be their salvation.

In 1933 a worldwide financial conference was called in London, with experts from the most important countries of the world. President Franklin D. Roosevelt appointed Senator Pittman among the men who represented the United States, and the one-time Tonopah lawyer helped to write an international agreement raising the price of silver. In the following year, Senator Pittman contributed to still another victory for the silver producers when Congress passed a new silver-purchase act. Once again, the price rose with government support, and the impact of the depression was lessened in Nevada and other mining regions of the West. The Silver Purchase Act of 1934 was a controversial piece of legislation, which some industrial and financial firms in the East regarded as an unfair subsidy to the mining population of the West. Most Nevadans, of course, did not agree with this view, and showed it by giving large majorities to Senator Pittman in the elections of 1934 and 1940.

Even though Senator Pittman waged a fight for the miners for a quarter-century, this was not the sole reason for his stature. He supported progressive legislation during the early part of his career, and in 1924 he was asked to become the candidate for vice president on the Democratic ticket. He declined the offer. From 1933 to 1940—a dangerous time when war was approaching in Asia and breaking out in Europe—he served as chairman of the Foreign Relations Committee. His long career ended with his sudden death in 1940, just after he had been elected to his sixth term.

Senator Pittman's political success rested not only on his achievements in Washington but also on his wide acquaintance with the people of Nevada. He personally knew a large percentage of the citizens in the state. At the time of his first election, there were only 20,000 votes cast in Nevada, and even in the year of his death only about 53,000. Nevada had a much smaller voting population than any other state in the Union. A senatorial candidate could shake hands with most of the voters in those years. Furthermore, Nevada's citizens usually expected him to do so.

For twelve years, Senator Pittman worked in the Upper House with another resident of Tonopah, Tasker L. Oddie. Senator Oddie's role in Nevada politics was more notable during his term as governor (1911-1914) than during his service in the U.S. Senate (1921-1932). As the state's chief executive, Oddie was one of the early advocates of a good highway system. A systematic program of road-building was begun under his leadership in 1911. While serving in the Senate, Oddie worked with Senator Pittman on legislation that would aid the mining industry and on behalf of the bill that authorized the construction of Hoover Dam. He also used his influence to have the Naval Ammunition Depot built at Hawthorne. Senator Oddie, a Republican, lost his seat to Senator McCarran in the election of 1932.

Senator McCarran was a politician who made good use of Nevada's handshaking tradition and her small population. Winning election to the Senate in 1932, he became one of Nevada's master campaigners. He soon established a reputation for doing favors for his constituents, and a number of young men from Nevada obtained jobs in Washington, D.C., with the Senator's help. Some of these young men managed to go to law school in off-hours because of these jobs and later returned to their home state to become prominent attorneys. In Nevada Democratic circles, they were often referred to as "Pat's boys." One of them, Alan Bible, served as attorney general (1943-1950) and eventually won election to Senator McCarran's office after the Senator's death in 1954.

Although Senator McCarran served in the Senate with Pittman for about seven years, they were not friends. Nevertheless, the junior Senator worked as hard in Washington for the mining interests of Nevada. Senator McCarran's main legislative accomplishments, however, were in different areas. Having been a prominent

Patrick A. McCarran
U.S. Senator
1933-1954

Alan Bible
U.S. Senator
1954-1974

George W. Malone
U.S. Senator
1947-1958

Walter S. Baring
Congressman
1949-1952, 1957-1972

lawyer and a state supreme court justice, he became a respected spokesman on judicial matters. When President Roosevelt sought to enlarge the U.S. Supreme Court in 1937, Senator McCarran fought against the plan, and his reputation advanced when the President lost his battle to change the court. In later years, he became chairman of the Senate's Judiciary Committee and sponsored controversial conservative legislation on internal security and immigration. He also won fame in the field of airport development. As a tribute, the large airport in Las Vegas was named for him.

Although Senator McCarran had started his political career in Tonopah, he regarded Reno as his home during most of his life. His political appeal was statewide, and only once after his initial victory in 1932 was he seriously threatened in a close election. That was in 1944, when he fought for his political life against Vail Pittman, the brother of his old foe, Key Pittman. Senator McCarran's personal contacts gained him victory in this and every other political campaign in the latter years of his life.

Since 1905 the Republicans of Nevada have not been able to keep a member of their party in the Senate for long periods of time, as the Democrats did with Senators Pittman and McCarran. Only two Republicans served as long as twelve years: Senator Oddie and Senator George W. Malone of Reno.

Although Senator Malone did not become as influential as some Nevadans who preceded him, he embodied the interests of Nevada in the transitional middle years of the twentieth century. He had been trained as an engineer at the University of Nevada and had taken an active interest in the mining problems and mining resources in the state; he was a staunch representative of the old miner-oriented tradition of Nevada politics, like Stewart, Jones, and Pittman. In addition, he had served as official engineer for the state government from 1927 to 1935, when Hoover Dam was conceived and constructed and had therefore participated actively in the transformation of southern Nevada which that project accomplished. He was identified with a number of other engineering projects, including highway development, which helped to shape modern Nevada. Because of these accomplishments, Nevadans twice elected him to the U.S. Senate.

Senator Malone won his first victory in 1946 and his second in 1952; each time a bitter split among the Democrats helped him to power, but his own personal appeal was an asset. In the Senate, he was a consistent conservative, opposing the large federal budgets and foreign-aid programs of the 1940's and 1950's. By 1958, when he sought a third term, Nevada's political climate had changed and the voters turned Senator Malone out of office for the younger, more liberal Howard Cannon of Las Vegas. The political pendulum was moving away in the 1950's from the kind of politics which Senators McCarran and Malone represented. Later, political attitudes became more conservative once again, and in 1980 Senator Paul Laxalt, a Republican, was one of the closest political advisors of President Ronald Reagan as his administration took office in 1981.

Since members of the House of Representatives are elected for only two years, it has been more difficult for a Nevadan to accumulate a long period of service in that body. Before the 1980's, only four men had served for as long as ten years in the House, and before 1983 Nevada had only one Representative because of its small population. The four men who did have extended service in the House were Francis G. Newlands (1893-1903), Samuel S. Arentz (1921-1923; 1925-1932), James G. Scrugham (1933-1942). amd Walter S. Baring (1949-1952; 1957-1972). Nevada voters found in each of these men qualities that seemed to reflect their own aspirations.

In the 1920's, when mining was still Nevada's primary industry, Arentz was a logical person for Congressional service. He was a mining engineer who had come to the state in 1906. He tried to develop the copper resources near Yerington before World War I. He also helped with the building of railroads in Lyon County and owned a ranch in Smith Valley, near Yerington. He had interests in mining properties in several parts of the state. Thus he was associated with several aspects of Nevada's economy—mining, transportation, ranching, and irrigation

When Congressman Arentz, who was a Republican, lost his seat in the House, it was to another engineer who also had a wide range of interests. Congressman Scrugham went to Washington in 1933 after having served as professor of engineering at the University of Nevada, as official engineer for the state government, and as Governor of Nevada (1923-1926). After ten years in the House of Representatives, he won election as U.S. Senator (1942). He died about two years later.

Congressman Baring was not an engineer, like Arentz and Scrugham, but his roots were in a Nevada mining town and he was identified in his politics as a friend of the miners. He was born in Goldfield and won the support of labor organizations in the mining communities and in Clark County early in his career. As a political conservative and a constant spokesman for Nevada interests, he continued the tradition of Pittman, McCarran, and Malone. This was the basis for his political support.

GOVERNORS OF NEVADA

Nevada's governors before 1908 had usually been associated with mining (Governors Blasdel, Kinkead, Stevenson, and Colcord) or with ranching (Governors Bradley and Sparks). After 1908, men who had a background in mining or engineering continued to do well in elections for governor, but Nevada voters also favored newspapermen and attorneys in high political office.

Governor John Sparks, who died suddenly in 1908, was the last governor representing the old generation of mining and ranching men who guided Nevada in its earliest years of statehood. All governors before 1908 had been born in the East or in foreign countries; all had been born before Nevada had been settled— they belonged to the pioneering generation. The governors who served after 1908 were younger men, most of whom had been born in the West and had grown up with it. For example, Governor Denver Dickerson (1908-1910), who assumed office on the death of Governor Sparks, was a native of California. He did not know Nevada in the boom days of the 1870's but had come to Ely in the early 1900's when the copper industry was becoming big business. He edited newspapers there before his service as governor.

Governor Dickerson was followed by Tasker L. Oddie (1911-1914), whose reputation as an attorney and mining man launched his career. Following Oddie was Governor Emmet Boyle, a native

James G. Scrugham
Governor, 1923-1926
Congressman, 1933-1942
U.S. Senator, 1943-1945

Charles H. Russell
Congressman, 1947-1948
Governor, 1951-1958

Grant Sawyer
Governor
1959-1966

Mike O'Callaghan
Governor
1971-1978

Paul Laxalt
Governor, 1967-1970
U.S. Senator, 1975-1986

Howard W. Cannon
U.S. senator
1959-1982

of the Comstock Lode who had grown up in Virginia City in the years when that camp was declining. Trained as a mining engineer, he had worked in British Columbia and Mexico as well as in Nevada mines. He served as Nevada state engineer before his election as governor in 1914. After two terms (1915-1922) in the governor's mansion, he was followed by another engineer, Governor Scrugham (1923-1926).

Nevada's next chief executive, Governor Fred Balzar (1927-1934), was also a native of Virginia City and interested in mining. He had been a mining man, a cowboy, a railroader on the Carson and Colorado, and a small-town businessman before he entered politics in Mina and Hawthorne. He served as state assemblyman, state senator, sheriff, and assessor before he became governor in 1927; he died after having been elected a second time and after nearly eight years in office.

Governor Balzar's term was completed in 1934 by Morley Griswold, a native of Elko who had become a lawyer and had followed his profession in Elko and Reno. After Griswold's brief term, Nevada's voters once again chose a native of Virginia City, Richard Kirman, to head their government in Carson City. Governor Kirman (1935-1938) had gone to school on the Comstock and had become prosperous in the banking and hardware business in Reno. He, like so many political favorites of his era, represented a link with the past in the state's history.

After Kirman, Nevadans turned to another attorney, E. P. Carville. He had been raised in Elko and, after attending law school, had returned to that community to follow his profession. He became a district judge in his middle years; his legal career eventually took him to Reno and into the governor's office (1939-1945). Governor Carville resigned to take a seat in the Senate. For about a year (1945-1946) he served in the Senate, but he was not able to win election to a full term in Washington.

When Governor Carville resigned, his executive office went to Lieutenant Governor Vail Pittman, the brother of Nevada's famous senator. Governor Pittman arrived in Nevada in 1904 and, like his elder brother, went to Tonopah. After brief experiences as an undersheriff in that booming town, he entered the newspaper business and moved later to Ely. From there he engaged in the political activities which carried him into the offices of lieutenant governor (1943-1945) and governor (1945-1950).

The next governor, Charles Russell (1951-1958) had also entered politics in Ely. He had been a newspaperman and a state legislator from White Pine County as a young man, and in 1946 he won election to the House of Representatives. The voters put him in the governor's office twice, but they denied him a third term in 1958. His successor, Grant Sawyer (1959-1966), an Elko lawyer, also had two terms and failed in his efforts to win a third time. He was defeated by Paul Laxalt (1967-1970), a Carson City attorney and the son of an immigrant Basque sheepherder. Then came Mike O'Callaghan (1971-1978), a former teacher and welfare director, and Robert List (1979-), an attorney.

Nevada politics, then, developed some patterns and preferences in the twentieth century. It was a political asset for a politician to have some connection with mining or a mining town. Before 1900, voters were willing to select "newcomers" and even persons of foreign birth for their highest offices; in the twentieth century, there has often been a preference for "native sons." Most senators of the modern era have come from Tonopah or Reno. Several governors have come from Ely, Elko, or Carson City.

The political history of Nevada before the 1950's does not include much reference to Las Vegas or to southern Nevada. Although Las Vegas was the second largest city in the state (after Reno) during most of the twentieth century and the largest city after about 1953, none of its residents were elected to the U.S. Senate until 1958, when Senator Cannon won the office. No governor had come from Las Vegas, and only once had a resident of that city been elected Representative in Congress. In the 1950's and 1960's, Las Vegans began to argue that the old voting habits and political traditions of northern and western Nevada were working against their region. It became clear that the political balance of power was shifting southward in the elections of the 1960's, as Clark County became the fastest growing section of the state in terms of industry and population.

Some of the growth of southern Nevada can be explained by railroad developments, by such federal-government projects as Hoover Dam and Basic Magnesium, and by a huge atomic testing program (described in the next chapter). But much of the growth was also due to the liberal policies of the Nevada government, especially regarding gambling. No one can begin to understand modern Nevada or its politics without knowing something about its most famous and most controversial industry.

GAMBLING IN NEVADA

Nevada has historically been a place for people with a sense of adventure and a desire to experiment; its people have often sought the exciting or the unusual, rather than the quiet and predictable. The state's experiment with legalized gambling is an offspring of this attitude.

The gambling industry matured in Nevada without plan or specific design; games of chance prospered because the residents of the early mining camps liked to bet and speculate. Modern Nevada inherited the gambling spirit of the bonanza days. Not all Nevadans approved of wide-open betting; twice the state's leaders tried to make table games illegal. For a time, government officials were successful in outlawing the business, but it came back, healthier than ever.

Nearly half the states in the nation permit some kinds of gambling—usually betting on horse races. Nevada is the only state which permits most table games, like roulette, blackjack, and craps. Because gambling is regarded as morally questionable by many people and because gangsters have been known to infiltrate some casinos for a share of the profits, the state government in recent years has created an elaborate licensing and policing system to keep the gamblers operating in a proper manner. The management of the multi-million dollar gambling business is one of the biggest single jobs of state government.

Gambling is as old as civilization in Nevada. Early records indicate that one of the earliest residents of Carson Valley operated games of chance for pioneers who passed through the region in the 1850's. The first prospectors in Gold Canyon—before the discovery of the Comstock Lode—gambled with Chinese residents of the region during the same period. When the mining rush came, "card sharks" were in the first groups of miners, and their games were well patronized.

When Nevada Territory was organized in 1861, the legislature declared games of chance illegal, but the residents of the turbulent silver camps ignored the law and the sheriffs were not willing or able to enforce it. After Nevada became a state, another antigambling law went into effect (1865) but it did not fare better. The Nevada legislature decided to repeal the restrictions in 1867, but Governor Blasdel—a man of strong Christian principles—vetoed the bill. Two years later, the legislature again passed a bill legalizing gambling. Again the governor vetoed it. This time, the legislature passed the law over his veto. For the next forty years, gamblers were able to operate without hiding from the law and without penalty or punishment.

The gambling of the bonanza days was not the same colorful, lively kind of operation which one sees now on the main streets of Nevada towns. Before the 1930's, there were no casinos, with their doors opening onto the streets and neon lights flashing throughout the night. Early-day gambling was usually conducted quietly in the back rooms of saloons, and the social codes of the day discouraged respectable women from entering such places. No proper Nevada lady would be seen in a saloon or near a gambling table.

After 1900, some women's groups and religious organizations decided that even this kind of betting should be prohibited and began a campaign to outlaw the games once more. In 1910, they succeeded in having the gambling rooms closed by state law, and for the next twenty-one years games of chance were officially forbidden. However, hundreds of Nevada men in the mining and railroad towns regarded betting as a proper sport, and games of chance continued to operate in back rooms of many saloons. Although it was illegal, sheriffs and police did not prevent it, and Nevada governors also felt powerless.

During this era, Nevada was like most other states in the Union.

Much unlawful, secret gambling occurs in most cities, and law-enforcement officials either cannot or will not stop it. Illegal gambling is one of the major problems of many states today; it pays no taxes and causes much expense in law enforcement. The Nevada legislature decided in 1931 that it would be wiser to let the gambling operations come out in the open, so they could be licensed, taxed, and policed. Accordingly, games of chance were permitted once more and county governments were authorized to collect a tax from their operators.

During the 1930's and 1940's, Nevada's gambling industy rapidly began to change its personality. It moved from a back-room operation to a main-street business. On Virginia Street in Reno and Fremont Street in Las Vegas, neon lights appeared, advertising the games and inviting visitors to play. Slot machines appeared in large numbers, not only in the bright casinos but also in drug stores, grocery stores, and cafes. Gambling swiftly became an obvious part of the state's business life, and it spread rapidly.

Although the growth of Nevada gambling was impressive in the fourteen years after 1931, the most spectacular change came after 1945. In that year, World War II came to an end and the wartime restrictions on travel were removed. In the next few years, tourists flocked to Nevada, and the gambling industry grew to accommodate the new customers. Reno's downtown casino area flourished as new businesses opened and as older gambling establishments expanded. Las Vegas boomed even more wildly than Reno. Multi-million dollar casinos grew and multiplied on Fremont Street, and a whole row of lavish, extravagant hotels opened on the federal highway south of Las Vegas, popularly known as "the Strip." Glittering resort areas appeared on the north and south shores of Lake Tahoe—with gambling as the main feature.

Nothing in the history of America resembled the uniquely spectacular growth of the gambling business in Nevada. Within a single ten-year period after 1945, gambling in Las Vegas became one of the nation's greatest tourist attractions. Because the casinos were eager to bring customers, they hired famous entertainers and movie stars who received thousands of dollars for a single performance on the casino showroom stages. Entire stage-show casts

Reno skyline

were imported from New York and Paris. Reno and Lake Tahoe did the same on a smaller scale. The gambling-club owners could afford to build some of the most elegant hotels and present some of the most expensive shows in America, because their winnings on the gaming tables were so great. By the 1960's, Nevada gambling casinos were winning about a quarter of a billion dollars a year. Gambling was one of the most lucrative businesses in the world.

The Nevadans of the earlier generation who legalized gambling did not anticipate such a turn of events. In the 1930's, as we have seen, gambling was a rather quiet, little-noticed business, and the legislators of 1931 had no reason to expect it to change. But the widespread advertising of the casino owners caused the dramatic transition. And with this transformation, the character of Nevada changed.

Since 1945 Nevada can no longer be called simply a mining, ranching, and railroading state; these industries are still important, but their impact does not equal the tourist business which gambling has created. Nevada is no longer a state where the small cities and towns predominate. In 1942 one writer observed that Reno and Las Vegas—the largest cities—were hardly more than villages. This was a slight overstatement, because Reno had about 25,000 residents and Las Vegas had about 10,000 at the time. But by the middle of the 1970's, the Reno area had more than 150,000 residents and the Las Vegas area exceeded 400,000. Nevada was the fastest-growing state in the nation, and the tourist-gambling industry was winning one billion dollars annually.

Most of Nevada's modern governmental problems have arisen from this expansion of the tourist business and population. Thousands of new residents came to Nevada between 1945 and 1981 because of additional jobs created by the tourist industry. They generated a demand for more schools, more housing, and more governmental services (police, fire protection, highways, and so on). The old Nevada governmental and political system, conceived in 1864 and little changed, began to feel the burden of the new responsibilities.

One of the greatest problems which the Nevada government had to face in the post-1945 period was the supervision of gambling.

When the great expansion began in 1945, the state had no police force or agency to assure that the gamblers would operate fairly or that they would pay their fair share of taxes; the county sheriffs held full responsibility. In that year, the legislature passed a law which imposed a small state tax on the gamblers and placed them under the supervision of the Nevada Tax Commission. As the gambling industry continued to expand, more regulations were imposed and higher taxes were assessed because state and local governments needed more money. By 1957, under the leadership of Governor Charles Russell, the state had developed an elaborate system of taxation and a highly trained bureau of investigators and accountants to check on the gambling operation. During the administrations of Governors Sawyer, Laxalt, O'Callaghan, and List, this work of the state government has been expanded.

Most of those who are licensed to operate casinos have been careful to maintain honorable operations. Most professional gamblers recognize that tourists will be willing to gamble in Nevada only as long as the games are believed to be honest. Casino owners have also tried to avoid any suspicion of affiliation with criminal elements.

Nevada officials have expressed worry about the danger that a crime syndicate might try to gain control or get an interest in Nevada gambling, and thereby channel winnings into the coffers of gangsters. Some persons have been denied gambling licenses because of their underworld reputations, and others have been ordered to stay away from Nevada casinos. The gamblers can operate their businesses only as long as they have a state license and the state police agency has the power to revoke any license for just cause. The state's Gaming Commission must be kept informed of the inner operations of all casinos. It has the right to inspect a casino's record book at any time.

One reason for the close check on the casino owners, in addition to watching for hoodlums, is to be certain that the state gets its fair share of tax money, because taxes are based in part on the gamblers' winnings. About one dollar of every five which went into the state's general fund in the late 1950's and early 1960's came from gambling taxes. This was an important source of income in a time of rapidly increasing population.

Many Nevadans recognized the dangers in tolerating the gamblers and relying on gambling taxes to help support education, welfare, and other governmental functions. Suppose the casino owners were to try to dominate the state's elected officials, as the mining companies and the railroad firms tried to do for many years in the 1800's. Could the residents of the state tolerate such a situation? Were they running the risk of having gangsters in positions of power within the borders of Nevada? Governors Russell, Sawyer, and Laxalt all warned that this must not be allowed to happen.

Several developments in the 1960's seemed to promise a better image for Nevada's unusual gambling industry. Prominent businessmen from other fields began to acquire interests in the local casinos. By 1968 it was possible to acquire an interest in Nevada gambling through a stock exchange in much the same way that investors buy stocks in other companies. The wealthy industrialist Howard Hughes, who won fame as a wartime aircraft producer and movie maker, purchased several casinos and other property in the Las Vegas area and helped to make it appear that investment in gaming establishments was more nearly like other kinds of business ventures.

Growing Pains of Nevada's Government

Sometimes government procedures, laws, and political habits change more slowly than the society around them. We have seen an example of this when, after mining had ceased to be the predominant industry in the state, Nevadans often continued to give their highest political offices to men with mining connections and mining-camp backgrounds. We have also seen that the gambling industry, based on an old Nevada tradition, suddenly became bigger and more challenging, and new laws to regulate it had to be developed gradually.

Thus governmental and political change is always slower than social change, and Nevada government—which was designed in a pioneer age—is trying to cope with the problems of a jet-age civilization.

Nevada's political problem might be compared with that of an old-fashioned, rambling house. When the house was designed and constructed a hundred years ago, it was modern and well equipped; it met the needs of its occupants well. As the years passed and the original occupants left, the new owners had different tastes, different jobs, and different needs, so it became necessary to remodel. The neighborhood changed and society became more crowded and complex. Every few years, the house seemed to need a few repairs, or a new roof, or a new story. When the number of residents increased, new wings were added.

In short, after a hundred years, the house was a rambling old monstrosity—still the same building with the same foundation, but altered in many ways and still not quite adequate for modern needs. So the Nevada government, still operating on the Constitution of 1864 (although much amended), has been groaning and creaking under the responsibilities of the 1960's and 1970's.

The problems caused by modern developments become most evident when the state legislature is trying to deal with them. The legislature itself is an instrument created in 1864 and bound by principles of past generations. An amendment in the Nevada Constitution provided that each county would have one state senator; this meant that in 1964, for instance, a county like Storey, with fewer than 1,000 citizens, had equal representation in the state senate with Clark County, which had a population of more than 235,000. The intention of the Constitution was to have this situation balanced in the other house of the state legislature, the assembly, where representation depended on population. Each county could have at least one assemblyman, and the heavily populated counties elected larger delegations. If Clark County had had a 235-to-1 majority over Storey County in the assembly, the residents of each county would have been about equally represented, but this was prevented by other provisions in the Constitution which put a ceiling on the number of members in the assembly. In the early 1960's, Clark County had only twelve assemblymen. As a result, the average voter in Clark County had much less voice in the selection of the legislature than the average voter in Storey County or the other thinly populated counties.

The following table shows how the legislature of 1963-1965 "under-represented" Clark County and Washoe County:

	Estimated population 1963	Number of senators	Number of assemblymen
Clark County	235,000	1	12
Washoe County	116,000	1	9
Other 15 counties	89,000	15	16

Under this arrangement, many residents of Clark and Washoe counties complained that they did not have their fair share of legislators, while most residents of the thinly-populated counties insisted that the system should not be drastically changed. This kind of problem existed in many states, and in 1964 the question of legislative representation became the subject of a major decision by the United States Supreme Court. The court had been asked whether a state has the right to maintain a system of legislative apportionment that put the residents of larger cities at a disadvantage in the lawmaking bodies. The Supreme Court answered no, and ordered that state legislatures redistribute their seats to give all people approximately the same representation in both houses.

The Nevada reapportionment finally came in 1966, and it provided the following formula for the 1967 and 1969 sessions of the legislature:

	Number of senators	Number of assemblymen
Clark County	8	16
Washoe and Storey counties	6	12
Other 14 counties	6	12

The new arrangement reflected for the first time the population changes that had occurred in Nevada in the 1950's and 1960's. Furthermore, the Nevada Constitution provided that the legislature must be reapportioned after each official ten-year census by the United States government. Since the 1970 census revealed that more than half of Nevada's people live in Clark County, that area now elects more than half the members of the senate and assembly.

Legislative Building in Carson City

In the 1981 reapportionment, the legislature distributed seats in this manner:

	Number of senators	Number of assemblymen
Clark County	12	24
Reno, Sparks, Verdi, Incline	5	10
Other 15 counties; part of Washoe	4	8
Totals	21	42

GROWING COST OF GOVERNMENT

Another example of how Nevada's modern growth has created problems for state government can be seen in the expansion of bureaus and offices to serve the public. When the first legislature met in 1864, it had to consider a budget for seven state officers and one state agency. The pioneers expected little of their state government and were unwilling to pay much money for it. One hundred years later, however, Nevadans had radically changed their expectations about government and were willing to pay much higher taxes than their ancestors.

This transition occurred gradually and resulted from the growing complexity of society. We have already seen that the coming of the automobile forced both the state and federal governments to spend large sums of money building ever better roads, and thus the Department of Highways became an essential and costly bureau after 1920. We have also noted that the rapid growth of the gambling industry after 1931 created the necessity for special commissions to supervise its operation. These are only two examples; by 1964, Nevada had nearly a hundred commissions or bureaus or agencies, formed by the legislatures over the years for specific jobs.

Lawmakers have added new bureaus to the original handful of offices to supervise banks and insurance companies, to care for needy persons, to give homes to orphans and special training to young people with disciplinary problems, to aid the unemployed and those injured in industrial work, to promote industry and tourism in Nevada, to conserve and develop our natural resources, to provide recreational facilities, libraries, museums, and a historical society, and to offer a modern education to Nevada's young people and adults. Each of these responsibilities which the state has assumed since 1864 requires substantial expenditures and the hiring of many people, and this represents only a small part of the work which has been directed from Carson City in recent years. To complicate the problem, the state's bureaus have not been formed and enlarged according to a logical and systematic plan. Some legislatures created new bureaus to meet a specific problem when an already existing bureau might have handled the situation just as well, and at times there was confusion about which agency should handle certain responsibilities. In 1925, a special survey commission studied the growing governmental structure and said the state organization was becoming inefficient. In 1948, another survey team recommended a streamlining of government, the removal of some duplication and confusion. Little was done to improve the situation, however, and Nevada's government could have been compared to a tangled mass of weeds in an uncultivated field. Governor Sawyer persuaded the Nevada legislature to enact a partial reorganization in 1963, but much remained still to be done to remove the complications which history had created since 1864.

This does not mean that all government agencies are inefficient or careless with the taxpayers' money. Much of the enlargement of state government occurred because the people wanted better service—such as better schools, better insurance protection, and better care for the mentally ill, for example—and in most cases the bureaus concerned have provided it.

Nevada's tax program has had to adapt to the enlarged role of the government. During most of the state's history, the property tax was a primary source of income, and the Constitution provided that no property owner could be taxed more than 5 per cent of the assessed valuation of his property in any one year. This money had to support many of the functions of the state, county, and city governments and the school operations for many years, but as the demand for services increased, this amount was not enough to do the work which the people of the state were expecting.

In the 1950's, the state government needed much more money than the old sources of revenue were producing, and the state legislature placed heavier taxes on gambling and enacted a sales tax. Nevadans had traditionally been proud that they could operate their governments and schools without a sales tax, but in 1955 their representatives found it necessary to begin this taxation. These new sources of revenue made it possible to have some new and improved governmental services, but the rapid growth of the state's population made it questionable whether even these taxes would prove adequate.

EDUCATION: A BIGGER RESPONSIBILITY

Throughout the history of the state, political leaders have considered the education of young people to be among their greatest responsibilities. The 1864 Constitution required the state legislature to encourage public education, to assure that a school would operate in each district for at least half of every year, and to provide for a university. Since that time Nevadans have spent a large part of their tax money for educational needs.

Like other responsibilities of government, the operation of schools has become more costly in modern times. A century ago, a few years of elementary school was thought to be adequate training for a young man or woman; as long as he could read and write, he was thought fit for most jobs and responsibilities available in a frontier state like Nevada. In the pioneer era, most Nevadans had no opportunity to attend high school, unless they could afford to leave the state. The high school did not become a common feature in Nevada education until after 1900. The typical Nevada school before that time was a small building, usually with fewer than five teachers (often only one or two), and with a minimum of furniture and equipment.

Early records contain many reports of the crude conditions in some Nevada schools. The state Superintendent of Public Instruction told of visiting rickety little buildings where the pupils sat on boxes, where almost no textbooks were available, and where teachers could be paid very little. It was often difficult to hire and keep good teachers, partly because qualified persons often did not want to come to a frontier land and partly because until the 1880's Nevada had no adequate teacher-training program of its own. Only after the University of Nevada took on the task in 1887 did the state begin to fill some of its own teacher requirements.

As the years advanced and as Nevada's society became more diversified, it was evident that the successful adult would need more than a knowledge of reading, writing, and arithmetic to become a successful member of the community. This led to the demand for the establishment of high schools in the various counties, training

The campuses in Reno (top) and Las Vegas

in industrial fields, and increased supervision by the state Department of Education over local school districts to assure good instruction. Today's modern school facilities are the product of a slow but continuous improvement which has continued for nearly a century.

The transition of the University of Nevada has been typical of this change. It is the only institution of higher learning in the state and the one to which most Nevada students have turned for a college education in the last three generations. The framers of the Nevada Constitution in 1864 wanted the state to have a university, but it was just as difficult to put this institution into operation as it was to create an efficient public school system. To open a university, Nevada needed trained faculty members and a place for them to teach and carry on their studies. For the first ten years of statehood, Nevada could provide no such facilities.

Finally, in 1874, an effort was made to open the University of Nevada in Elko, and it functioned for a few years. However, many of Nevada's young people were not yet ready for university work and most lived too far from Elko to take advantage of the opportunities it offered. In 1886, the University was moved to Reno, and for the next sixty years it grew slowly, serving fewer than a thousand students during much of this period and never exceeding an enrollment of 1,300 full-time students. During those years, the state government had to spend relatively little money for classroom buildings, and the legislature provided only modest sums for professors' salaries and library books. Fortunately, the University received a number of important gifts from persons who had much affection for Nevada. Mrs. John Mackay, the widow of the famous Virginia City mine owner, and her son Clarence gave the University more than a million dollars to build a school of mines, a science building, a stadium and field house, and to provide additional land for the campus. William A. Clark, Jr., whose wife was a native of Virginia City, granted money for a library building. Without these gifts, the University would have made little progress in the years between 1920 and 1940, because the state government provided very little to improve the campus.

After World War II ended in 1945, it was evident that the Uni-

versity plant would have to be expanded to serve the large number of veterans returning from the war. This situation became aggravated as the population of the state rapidly increased. It became apparent that the University facilities were inadequate; the buildings were often too old and too small, and the cost of hiring professors and buying equipment was increasing. Millions of dollars were spent for new classrooms, library facilities, and instructors. In the 1950's, the state belatedly responded to the need for higher education in southern Nevada and created a University branch just outside Las Vegas. The first classes were taught in 1951 and a regular program began in 1954. Ten years later the college—initially called Nevada Southern—offered its first bachelors' degrees, and in 1968 it became independent of the parent campus in Reno. The Reno operation of the University grew rapidly, too, and by 1972 more than 14,000 students were engaged in higher education in Nevada.

The expanding University System took on ever increasing responsibilities. The 1960's brought a phenomenal growth in research, inspired in part by the Desert Research Institute—a unit that sought funds from outside the University to conduct highly specialized studies. And the early 1970's were marked by the creation of a Community College system, devoted primarily to technical and occupational training between the high school and University levels. Elko pioneered this experiment in the late 1960's—as it had done for a University preparatory school in the 1870's—and in 1971 both Clark County and Western Nevada had fledgling colleges in operation. In 1977, there were more than 30,000 students enrolled in the universities and the community colleges.

The University expansion has been accelerated by a series of gifts. The Max C. Fleischmann Foundation of Nevada provided millions of dollars for agriculture and home economics buildings, for a unique atmospherium-planetarium, for library books, and for research. The industrialist Howard Hughes aided the Community College program and helped finance a medical school in Reno. A Southern Nevada Land Foundation gave invaluable assistance to the University in Las Vegas, and scores of other gifts supplemented the state appropriations as never before.

15. Human Rights in Nevada

THE HISTORY OF AMERICA is closely related to the story of the struggle for human rights. The Revolutionary War resulted from the efforts of English colonist in North America to assert the rights and privileges that were being denied them by the British government. The Civil War arose, in large part, from a struggle over the question of whether any human being could be kept in slavery—in violation of the principles of freedom set down in the Declaration of Independence and the Constitution of the United States.

Nevada entered the Union as the Civil War was reaching its climax. One of the main reasons that President Lincoln proposed statehood for Nevada in 1864 was that he expected its senators to vote for the proposed Thirteenth Amendment to the Constitution, which called for the abolition of slavery. Thus Nevada became the thirty-sixth state in the struggle to give freedom to millions of people who had previously been denied it. The state constitution contains many sections and clauses that bear witness to the victories won for human rights a hundred years ago and earlier. Section 1 of Article I of the Nevada Constitution says: "All men are, by nature, free and equal, and have certain inalienable rights, among which are those of enjoying and defending life and liberty; acquiring, possessing and protecting property, and pursuing and obtaining safety and happiness." This is a clear echo of early passages of the Declaration of Independence.

Yet even such a strong statement, standing at the beginning of the basic governmental document, is not an absolute guarantee that society will honor the ideals that it has proclaimed. Nor can any constitutional convention anticipate all the changes that future citizens may want to make in their laws to enforce their rights. The Nevada Constitution, in spite of the opening proclamation, contained some shortcomings that later generations decided to correct. The struggle for greater freedom and equality has continued in Nevada as well as in America as a whole, and steps are still being taken to make a reality of the principles that are the basis of our governmental system.

VOTING RIGHTS

One of the fundamental rights of a citizen is that of voting in free elections for those who will make his laws and direct the administration of his government. For many years, however, this right was not extended to all groups in the society. When Nevada became a state, not only were most Negroes excluded from the political process, but also most Indians and Orientals lacked basic rights. Women could not vote nor could they exercise many of the legal privileges that men regarded as fundamental. Little by little the legislature and the people of Nevada altered their political procedures to change these conditions and to bring practice and principle nearer together.

During the constitutional debates of 1864, the state's founding fathers discussed the possibility of imposing a poll tax on male citizens, with a provision that only those who paid the tax could vote. In some of the older states—particularly in the South—it was common to assess such a tax as a means of keeping poor people from casting ballots, and later it was normal to use such a tax to discourage Negroes from going to the voting booths. Some men in Nevada wanted to adopt this system, and in the 1864 convention did approve a poll tax for all males. It left to future legislatures, however, the question of whether payment of the tax should be a requirement for voting. For more than a century, Nevada men paid the tax, but it had no connection with their voting rights, and in 1910 they adopted a constitutional amendment to eliminate the possibility of making voting rights subject to taxation. Thus one potentially undemocratic provision of the Constitution was removed. The U.S. Constitution was not amended to make this principle nationwide until 1964. The Nevada poll tax was eliminated completely in 1966.

Late in the nineteenth century and early in this century there were many reform movements that tried to assure that the people's rights and interests would be well protected, or even improved, in ways not anticipated by the early constitution-makers. The Populist movement and later the Progressive movement represented some of the most imaginative of these groups. By gradual steps, they amended most state constitutions so that the people could make or repeal laws or amend their constitutions, without resorting to the legislatures, by means of petitions and voting at the polls; the initiative and referendum procedures made this possible. Nevadans adopted a referendum clause in their constitution in 1904 and an initiative provision in 1912. They also worked out a procedure by which voters could petition for the removal of an elected official who was not performing his duties well; the "recall" section of the Nevada Constitution won final approval in 1912. All of these measures enlarged the voting rights of the citizens of the state.

The denial of voting rights to women and to members of nonwhite races presented a much more serious challenge to the American political ideals than the questions involved in the initiative, referendum, and recall. Even the U.S. Constitution failed to guarantee voting rights to all adults in the beginning, and the work to change this condition had to be undertaken on a state-by-state basis. The U.S. Constitution was amended in 1870 to extend voting rights to all male citizens regardless of race, and Nevadans adopted the same provision in their own constitution ten years later. One important barrier to full political rights for Negro, Oriental, and Indian men had fallen, but many of them still found the society not very responsive to their interests. For women, the barriers to voting rights were even slower to fall—at least at first.

In the agitation for equal political privileges for both sexes, Nevada women played an important role. An outstanding organizer of the woman suffrage campaign was Anne Martin, a University of Nevada professor who gained national prominence for her work in politics. When Miss Martin and her feminine companions began trying to convince the men that they had as much intelligence and talent for politics as their husbands and brothers, they were regarded as radicals and troublemakers. Gradually, their arguments made headway, even though men outnumbered women by more than two to one in Nevada. The Nevada Equal Franchise Society, which Miss Martin headed, organized branches in every county of the state, issued pamphlets, engaged speakers, and contacted political leaders to press their arguments. They visited remote ranches and towns with their message and even went underground into the mines—a practice that was uncommon for women in that era—to press the case. After a few years they won approval of an amendment to the Nevada Constitution (finally ratified by the people in 1914) providing that there could be no denial of the right to vote on the basis of sex. Nevada acted on woman suffrage six years earlier than the nation as a whole; the United States Constitution was not amended in the same manner until 1920.

Woman suffrage came during an era when America was attempting reform in many fields. We have already mentioned the initiative, referendum, and recall, and we have previously indicated that direct election of U.S. Senators by popular vote—instead of by legislative action—began in Nevada as early as 1910. In this era effective regulation of railroads, restrictions on child labor, regulations to assure pure food and drugs, and other comparable measures to protect citizens were written into the law books. The same era saw the addition of the primary elections to the American political scene; Nevada held its first primary election in 1910, thus ending the practice of having political conventions select party nominees for state and local offices. The primary was another attempt to give the people a more direct and more effective control over their political instruments.

One thing that the crusaders for reform and for new political rights proved was that well-organized and dedicated groups of citizens, even though few in number, can have an important effect on the laws and institutions of society. They and their allies across the country brought about peaceful changes in many places. Their lesson was to be repeated and relearned by other groups in more recent years. Racial minorities have been among those who have seen their disadvantages and handicaps slowly reduced in the last hundred years.

INDIAN PROBLEMS

Since pioneer days when Indians were regarded as a threat to emigrants and prospectors, the public attitude toward these original Nevadans has gradually changed. We have seen that the white men often treated Indians with contempt and abuse a century ago, and it has not been until recently that the Paiutes, Shoshones, Washos, and other tribes have begun to approach equality of opportunity and rights.

After the Pyramid Lake battles of 1860, a number of other skirmishes and incidents caused tension across the state, and the pioneer generations remained suspicious of all Indians. Nevada Indians were primarily peaceful, however, and no trouble as serious as that of the 1860's ever recurred. The United States government adopted a policy of trying to place the Indians on reservations, both to keep them from trouble with the white men and to assure them limited lands of their own. The government only slowly responded to the fact that miners and ranchers had seized some of the Indians' choice lands, had cut thousands of the pine trees that supplied them with nuts for winter food, and had otherwise made their traditional existence impossible. As late as the 1960's, the federal government was still trying to find ways to compensate several thousand Indians for the seizure of lands from their ancestors a century ago.

The federal government established the two most important Indian reservations near the large desert lakes of western Nevada —Pyramid Lake and Walker Lake. Subsequently, lands were set aside for Paiutes and Shoshones at such scattered locations as Duck Valley on the Nevada-Idaho border north of Elko, at Old Fort McDermitt near the Oregon border, at Summit Lake northwest of Winnemucca, on the Goshute lands northeast of Ely, in the Moapa Valley northeast of Las Vegas, and in small colonies on the outskirts of several cities and towns. In nearly all cases the land parcels were too small and too poor for the number of people they were intended to serve. Indians found it difficult to carry on their traditional ways of life and, on the other hand, to become functioning members of the larger society. Fewer than half of Nevada's Indians could make a living on the lands of the reservations.

Indians often had to work at menial jobs for low pay to maintain even a bare existence. By 1918, only about 10 per cent of the Indian residents of the state were regarded as citizens, and fewer than 1 per cent of them were voters. The federal government provided a few schools, but they were inadequate to prepare young people for successful roles in society. Only in the 1930's did Indian children begin to attend public schools of Nevada in substantial numbers. By the 1960's, some Indians had made successful records in government, business, education, and industry, and they had largely assumed responsibility for their own affairs. Groups like the Inter-Tribal Council of Nevada, the Western Shoshone Nation, and the United Paiutes became active political organizations and seemed to be achieving a balance between maintaining their traditions and rights as Indians and becoming active participants in the larger community. Coincidental with the improvement of the social position of the original Nevadans has come increased interest in native languages and customs. Scholars and scientists from the University of Nevada and the Nevada State Museum took the lead in new studies that cast light upon the achievements and the culture of people long neglected by the majority of Americans.

PROGRESS AMONG NEVADA'S BLACKS

American Black people have had problems at least as serious as those of the Indians. Their ancestors were first captured and enslaved in a distant land, transported under brutal conditions across the Atlantic Ocean, and finally "emancipated" during the Civil War without being given adequate opportunity to share the benefits or rights of the society in that part of the country where most of them lived—the Deep South. Their struggle for rights and opportunities did not affect Nevada directly in the early years of statehood, because few of them lived in the West.

Some Blacks did join the earliest pioneers, and they had an impact on the frontier even though their numbers were small. In Carson County in 1860—the year before Nevada became a territory—there were about forty-five Blacks in a population of 6,800. They were soon recognized as skillful cowboys and ranch hands, but most of them had little opportunity to try their luck at mining. As the mining camps grew, they provided few openings for Blacks to work at the skilled trades. Virginia City had nearly a hundred black citizens in 1870 and Hamilton counted fifty-five in that boom year, but most of them had to work at the less profitable jobs. So it was to be for most of the next century. They most often worked in service positions—as janitors, porters, servants, or laundry women—because other employment was usually not available to them.

For the first ninety years of Nevada's history, government census takers never counted more than a few hundred Blacks in the state. The picture began to change in the 1940's with the introduction of large governmental programs resulting from the wartime economy. Nevada, like other states in the North and West, became more attractive to southern Blacks.

Nevada, again like other states, found that it had problems meeting its responsibilities to the black citizens. Since most of them had received their education in inferior schools in the South, they were poorly prepared for jobs requiring special skills. Nevada's growing entertainment industry, one of the important sources of employment for white people in the 1950's and 1960's, was slow to make job opportunities available to Blacks, except in the lowest paying service categories. Labor unions did little to help their cause. Resort hotels were quick to recognize the talents of outstanding black musicians and vocalists; in the era of lavish entertainment that has come to Las Vegas, Reno, and Lake Tahoe, Blacks have often commanded high fees and prominent billing. But prior to 1965 they were sometimes welcomed as artists in the same establishment that would not hire Blacks as cooks and waiters, and in the same hotel that would not rent rooms to other black people. Nevada, of course, was not alone in this strange situation; all across America, similar patterns of discrimination existed. Although the problem was most serious in the South, citizens of the North and West recognized that they too must seek new ways to break down the barriers of discrimination.

In the 1950's, Blacks and their white allies—many of them young people—began to call for new legislation in many states to put into practice the ideals of the constitution. The barriers that had kept Blacks out of the better jobs and away from some educational institutions gradually began to fall as the pressure increased. The courts of the federal and state governments ruled that many discriminatory practices were unconstitutional. In Nevada, the crusade for equal rights came later than in most states because of the relatively small Black population. By the late 1950's, however, each session of the legislature found itself confronted with demands for laws guaranteeing fair employment practices, equality of treatment in places like restaurants and hotels, and open housing.

Unlike the southern states, Nevada did not discriminate against Blacks in voting rights and in state-supported educational systems. But its lawmakers were not eager to pass the kinds of laws that Blacks felt were necessary to overcome disadvantages in getting jobs or buying homes. Finally, in 1961, after Congress had taken the lead, Nevada's legislature created a Commission on Equal Rights of Citizens to investigate accusations of discrimination. In 1965 it passed a law making it illegal to discriminate on the basis of race or religion in most fields of employment and in most places of public accommodation. Between 1961 and 1968, Blacks made more progress toward social equality than in all the previous years of the state's history, and hundreds had jobs and homes in places that were previously segregated.

Many problems remained in the late 1970's, however, particularly in areas such as the west side of Las Vegas where thousands of blacks made their homes and where the unemployment rate was high. But there was more effective leadership from professional and political spokesmen in the black communities than ever before. The first black to be elected to the legislature, Woodrow Wilson, took his seat in 1967. Charles Kellar of Las Vegas and Eddie Scott of Reno, officers of the National Association for the Advancement of Colored People, worked successfully for progressive legislation; Nevada passed its first fair housing law in 1971. Dr. Charles West and Dr. James B. McMillan, in the Las Vegas medical community, were significant contributors to the cause of racial equality in the state.

Woodrow Wilson. Assemblyman, 1966-1970; first Black legislator

Anne Martin. Woman suffrage leader

Sarah Winnemucca Hopkins, author of *Life Among the Piutes*

RECORD OF THE CHINESE

The third important racial minority that had a role in Nevada history was the Orientals—primarily the Chinese. Because thousands of them had come to California during the years of the gold rush, many were on the scene for the earliest rush to the Washoe region. Dayton, one of the oldest towns in the state, was once called Chinatown, and men of Oriental descent were often seen operating placers in Gold Canyon in the 1850's. Even in the earliest years, Chinese workers were unwelcome; when the Gold Hill mining district regulations were written in 1859, they provided that Chinese would not be allowed to own mining claims in the region.

Many of the first Chinese in Nevada operated small businesses or worked as servants. When construction of the Central Pacific Railroad got underway in the 1860's, thousands joined the labor crews and many more came from China at the urging of the railroad company. When construction work ended in 1869, hundreds tried to find employment in the mining towns of the West, usually with little success. Because white miners were afraid the Chinese would take their jobs, they often banded together to keep Orientals away from the towns, or in their own districts.

When William Sharon hired some Chinese workers to help build the Virginia and Truckee Railroad, laborers from Virginia City tried to drive them away. When a few Orientals went to work as woodchoppers near the mining community of Tybo in Nye County, armed posses ordered them to get out of the district and threatened to kill any who remained. When the number of Chinese seemed to be getting too large in Carson City—at one time nearly one-fifth of the population was Oriental—riots broke out between the races.

Nearly every significant community had a "Chinatown," and in most cases the Chinese residents managed to live peacefully if they did not threaten the jobs of the white men. At Tuscarora in northeastern Nevada, for example, hundreds of Chinese made homes in the 1870's after most of the original settlers had left. They proved to be excellent placer miners, extracting gold dust from gulleys that white men had previously abandoned. Here, as in several other Nevada towns, they had a temple for worship, gambling rooms, and exotic huts where some smoked opium.

The Chinese worked at many trades. They became best known as cooks and laundrymen, but some of them hauled borax on the edge of Death Valley and others engaged in logging on the slopes of the Sierra Nevada. They became well-known as cutters and marketers of firewood during the winter months. All too often, however, they encountered hostility from the majority of whites and in some cases they provoked trouble by their sharp dealings. Several riots marred the historical record; because of its large Chinese population, Carson City was the most prominent community involved. In the 1870's and 1880's the legislature passed a number of measures aimed at removing the Orientals from the state.

As the years passed, the problem eased because the Chinese population became smaller. In 1880, there were more than 5,000 Orientals living in Nevada when the total population was about 62,000. In 1900 there were only about 1,300, and in 1920 fewer than 700. The Chinese pioneers had either died or left the state, and the problem no longer seemed so acute. Restrictions on Chinese immigration prevented large numbers of younger people from coming to America, and white Nevadans gradually learned to live on cordial terms with those few who remained. They were widely admired for their diligence and energy, and in the twentieth century gained equality with their white fellow citizens.

There were similar periods of hostility toward the Japanese, who formed a much smaller group. Japanese men, who helped build the railroad between Caliente and Las Vegas in the period just before 1905, encountered severe hostility. As late as World War II, when the United States and Japan were at war, American citizens of Japanese ancestry were harshly treated. But Orientals as a whole have steadily moved toward full equality. In the early 1960's, the Nevada Commission on Equal Rights of Citizens did not find any pattern of discrimination against people whose ancestors had come from the Far East. In 1964, during the celebration of the centennial of Nevada statehood, the state government erected a monument in Sparks in honor of Chinese pioneers. Such a change offered hope that continued progress against discrimination can be expected in other areas.

The Indians, Blacks, and Chinese are not the only groups that have experienced animosity from the majority community in Nevada and elsewhere in America. Other immigrants, notably from southern and eastern Europe and from Mexico, have occasionally had trouble winning the rights and social opportunities offered by the American system. Italians, Slavs, and Greeks occasionally found social barriers standing against them in early railroad and mining towns. More recently, with the influx of thousands of Spanish-speaking migrants from Mexico, the government has adopted policies to assure more equitable treatment. Leadership qualities of individuals from minority groups are more frequently being demonstrated. In 1981, there were two women from minority groups serving as members of the University's Board of Regents—Lilly Fong, whose heritage is Chinese, and June Whitley, a black lady— both from Las Vegas.

The most controversial political issue in Nevada in the middle years of the 1970's was the question of whether to ratify the Equal Rights Amendment (ERA) to the U.S. Constitution. The ERA was proposed by women's groups who said that it was essential to give women their full rights. Opponents of the amendment, many of whom were women, argued that they might be forced into undesirable social and economic situations if the amendment were adopted. Most states had ratified the proposed amendment by 1978, but an amendment to the Constitution requires a favorable vote in two-thirds of the state legislatures. Nevada's legislature, like those in many other states, has thus far refused to ratify, although the vote has been close at times.

16. New Frontiers: Atomic Testing, Recreation, Ecology

IN THE LAST HALF of the twentieth century, Nevada's open spaces have been recognized as one of the state's most important assets. For both scientific research and recreation, Nevada has been "rediscovered" since 1950 because it has more unoccupied and undisturbed acreage than nearly any other state.

In 1950, a new kind of pioneering venture began with the U.S. government's selection of a southern Nevada site for atomic energy testing. Like Jedediah Smith and John Fremont more than a century earlier, the engineers and scientists who experimented with atomic explosions and nuclear rockets were exploring the unknown. Nevada provided a vast laboratory for discoveries that are of potential importance to all of mankind.

Almost simultaneously, Nevada became known more widely as a good place for outdoor recreation. As neighboring states grew more crowded and as population pressures on Nevada's two largest cities increased, more people looked to Nevada's mountains, valleys, and lakes for their leisure activities. There is belated recognition that the so-called wastelands of the previous era now have possibilities for those who want to enjoy nature as it manifests itself in the desert. And in a period of increased emphasis on the preservation of the environment, Nevadans realized that they were more fortunate than most Americans in the amount of the natural heritage that remained.

ATOMIC TESTING, 1951-1955

When American scientists successfully tested the first atomic bomb in July, 1945, the world had entered a frightening new era.

The first bomb was tested at a small site in New Mexico. Later, U.S. tests were held in the South Pacific, but American scientists and military experts felt that atomic science could be developed much faster if tests could be conducted at a large, permanent site on American soil.

Southern Nevada was best suited for this operation. Large open spaces were available in the Las Vegas Bombing and Gunnery Range, operated in World War II. Not many people lived in the vicinity of the range, and weather conditions allowed testing without extreme danger. The Nevada Proving Grounds were designated for atomic testing in December, 1950, and about a month later the first bomb was exploded there.

Forty-five atomic experimental devices were fired at the test site between January 27, 1951 and May 15, 1955. Some of these blasts were large enough to be felt in far-distant towns, and Nevadans became witnesses to one of history's most dramatic episodes. The explosions were often detonated before dawn, causing a flash a hundred times brighter than the sun, and often the light of a blast could be seen 400 to 500 miles away. People in all parts of Nevada and in some neighboring states could watch the brightened sky of the early morning tests.

There were dangers, also, but most of them were slight. Some minor damage to buildings and a few broken windows were reported in Henderson and Las Vegas in the earliest tests. When such damage occurred, the Atomic Energy Commission compensated the owners of property for their losses. Considering the number of tests conducted and the power of the mighty bombs, the physical damage was minor.

Radioactive fallout also presented a hazard. Since the earliest bombs were exploded above the ground, they sucked up great quantities of dust and threw it into the atmosphere, creating a mushroom cloud. This dust could be harmful if too much of it happened to fall on a populated area soon after the explosion. For this reason, the Atomic Energy Commission conducted its early tests only when weather was favorable and when winds would not carry the "hot" dust over towns.

On a few occasions, the Atomic Energy Commission demonstrated to the public how terrible atomic power could be. One of the most important of these demonstrations was called "Operation Doom Town." Two typical frame houses were constructed in the vicinity of "ground zero"—where the nuclear bomb was to be exploded. One was less than a mile away and the other about a mile and a half from the explosion. The massive force of the blast completely destroyed the closer house; parts of the second remained standing, but it suffered severe damage. About 600 persons witnessed the blast at the test site, and an estimated 15,000,000 saw it on television.

After May, 1955, testing was halted in Nevada for two years, while scientists experimented with larger explosive devices in the Pacific Ocean testing area. There came a lull in operations at the Nevada Test Site.

CAMP MERCURY

The "camp" at the south end of the test site from which most workers operate is called Mercury. It is Nevada's newest town—if one may call it a town—and one of the strangest in the world, situated 65 miles northwest of Las Vegas, on a bleak part of the desert.

Mercury has only the faintest resemblance to those pioneer towns of the last century. It is a type of frontier town and it is basically a man's town, like the mining communities of old, but this is a camp of highly trained engineers and scientists, carefully selected for their responsible jobs. Nothing could be further from the chaotic stampedes of prospectors of a hundred years ago.

These new pioneers have the finest in equipment and work in specially constructed buildings to protect them from the intense heat and cold. They have access to instruments ranging from the most delicate devices for measuring radiation, weather conditions, soil conditions, and human well-being, to massive earth-moving machines and huge balloons. A generation ago, many of the implements now in use were unknown. Instruments which used to be only science-fiction are scientific fact at Mercury.

In addition to its technical equipment, Mercury has mess halls, dormitories, warehouses, and recreation facilities for its workers. The population of the camp fluctuated greatly during the first twelve years of operation, from a few hundred men during periods of no testing to about 10,000 in 1962.

In terms of investment, Mercury is one of the most expensive small towns ever built, but, of course, it is much more than a town. The U.S. government spent about half a billion dollars in the first decade of operations on Mercury and the test-site operations, and the program was being expanded greatly in the 1960's. Not all is spent on equipment and housing, however. A good share of this money is paid to employees at the test site. A great amount has been spent also on equipment and materials purposely destroyed by nuclear detonation.

THE SECOND PHASE OF TESTING

When testing resumed in the spring of 1957, new techniques and new equipment had been devised. Most of the earlier explosive devices had been dropped from airplanes or detonated from a tower 300 to 500 feet high. In the post-1957 series, the Atomic Energy Commission began to place its bombs on balloons, which could then be allowed to soar as high as a quarter of a mile above the earth at the time of the explosion. The scientists also attached a nuclear device to a missile and fired it from an aircraft to explode high above the ground. And during 1957, the AEC began to detonate bombs in long underground tunnels to avoid the danger of radiation fallout in the atmosphere.

During these tests, thousands of Nevadans became active participants in the experiment. The AEC asked many residents of the state to wear "film badges" on their clothing to determine how much radiation exposure from fallout their bodies were receiving. Government representatives would collect the badges from time to time and give new ones to the people who had agreed to wear them, and they would conduct tests with the used badges to check the amount of fallout. In Alamo and the surrounding Pahranagat Valley—about fifty-five miles northeast of the test site—the entire population wore badges for several months.

In the latter part of 1963, the American, Russian, and British governments signed a treaty which provided for a suspension of atmospheric tests. This history-making treaty meant that the Nevada Test Site would conduct all its experiments underground in future years. The fireballs and mushroom clouds which had become so familiar in the 1950's seemed to be a relic of history by 1964. A major part of the operation at the Nevada Test Site in the 1960's was the preparation of underground tunnels and vertical, drilled holes where instruments could be installed and where devices could be exploded. In the digging of the tunnels, contractors working for the AEC obtained some of their most useful personnel from the mining camps of eastern and southern Nevada; miners from Pioche, Tonopah, and other Nevada towns who no longer had jobs in the conventional types of mines were among the men hired to prepare caverns deep in the earth for the dangerous experiments with the atom.

America has learned much about the force of the atom since 1950, but in order to use it successfully in peace or war, other experiments are being conducted. The testing of related equipment has also been big business at or near the Nevada Test Site in recent years.

BOMBS, ROCKETS, AND "PLOWSHARE"

One part of the Las Vegas Bombing and Gunnery Range east

of Tonopah was set aside as the AEC's Tonopah Test Range for experiment with some of the materials that would have to be placed around or with atomic matter. An AEC contractor began in 1957 to experiment with fuses, firing systems, bomb cases, and other parts necessary to guide an atomic weapon to its target and explode it there. This required modern experiments with bomb-dropping. Rockets have been fired there also for upper atmospheric research. The operation is separate from that at the Nevada Test Site and complements work done at laboratories in Albuquerque, New Mexico, and Livermore, California.

Another, much larger development program for nuclear rocket-propulsion systems was started in 1957 between Mercury and Beatty, adjacent to the area where atomic explosive devices had been tested. Here, the AEC and the National Aeronautics and Space Administration have been working on rocket engines for space travel. This project provided some of the technology for the flights to the moon, and future space travel is likely to depend on the discoveries made at the Nevada Nuclear Rocket Development Site. This site, like the adjacent atomic-testing ground, may become a historic site in another generation because of its contributions to man's exploration of outer space.

Slightly more than a century ago, Governor Henry G. Blasdel wandered through the southern Nevada deserts in the hope that he could establish a new county in eastern Nevada. His party suffered from lack of water and one man died of thirst before help came. This pioneer party traversed the treeless valleys and hills by the most ancient transportation—on horses and on foot. To compare Governor Blasdel's weary trek with the space-age transportation which is being developed in southern Nevada is to summarize the changes that have occurred in Nevada in the past century.

The Book of Isaiah includes the prophecy that men will someday "beat their swords into plowshares"—turning away from the practice of war to the works of peace. Taking this quotation as its symbol, the U.S. government began a new type of project at the Nevada Test Site in 1962, involving experiments to find peaceful uses for atomic energy. The AEC called this the "Plowshare Program."

Scientists and engineers have conducted tests to learn whether nuclear power can be used to dig massive new harbors along the seacoasts or big canals. Perhaps in a few years, experts will be able to use the information they have gathered in Nevada to develop a new and bigger Panama Canal—which is now needed. The AEC also believes that it may be possible to harness small underground explosions for the mining of ore, the development of underground water supplies for agriculture and industry, and the opening of new reserves of oil which cannot be tapped by present drilling and pumping methods.

Perhaps massive chemical transformations can be made underground with atomic power—far more spectacular than anything we see represented in our familiar high-school and college chemistry laboratories—and these changes may produce new industries for the benefit of man. Some scientists believe it will be possible, through the Plowshare Program, to create great underground sources of heat to generate electricity or perhaps to remove salt from sea water on a large scale. Beyond this, we can only dream of the benefits that might come to future generations. It may be that ways will be found to irrigate the vast and uninhabited Nevada desert and to provide the resources which will sustain additional hundreds of thousands of people.

The Plowshare Program and the Nuclear Rocket Development program are not only two of the most important projects in recent American history, they are also part of the age-old effort of man to understand himself, the planet on which he lives, and the vast universe. Nevadans of the present and the future, like those of the past, seem destined to share in the continuing process of search and discovery.

CONSERVATION AND RECREATION

In earlier chapters, we saw that Nevadans were primarily interested in conquering the desert and exploiting its resources. Miners extracted the ore, stockmen utilized the rangelands, the government harnassed the streams, built highways, and experimented with the atom. But in the last few years, there has been emphasis on protecting the resources and on preserving as much of the state as possible in a semi-primitive condition for the pleasure and benefit of future generations.

Nevada has more than five million acres of forest land, much of it managed by the National Forest Service of the U.S. Department of Agriculture. The Bureau of Land Management, under the Department of Interior, supervises tens of millions of acres— more than half the total area of Nevada. The use of this land must now be carefully controlled if wanton destruction of remaining resources is to be prevented. We now recognize that too much of America has been spoiled by needless fires, by careless disposal of waste, and by commercial exploitation. The Forest Service and the Bureau of Land Management have developed programs designed to preserve the basic resources of the land while encouraging more people to enjoy it. There are now hundreds of campsites in Nevada—many of them new or improved in the last few years. The government has also designated scenic wilderness areas in the Snake Range and the Ruby Mountains, and near Jarbidge.

The Nevada State Department of Conservation and Natural Resources has assumed an important role in preserving the natural attractions of Nevada while simultaneously making them available to residents and visitors. A network of state parks—begun nearly a half-century ago in a modest way—has become an important contribution to the state's ecological-recreational program. The most spectacular of these areas—the Lake Tahoe–Nevada Park and the Valley of Fire Park near Overton—have large acreages of scenic wilderness. Most smaller parks are designed to preserve and emphasize either natural curiosities or historical sites—such as the ichthyosaur fossils near Berlin, the cathedral-like canyon near Pioche, the reconstruction of Mormon Station at Genoa, or the old charcoal ovens near Ely. In the early 1970's, a million people were visiting the state parks each year, and the voters approved $5,000,000 for the acquisition and preservation of additional land.

Modern environment planning demands much more than the preservation of the most interesting or attractive places. For years scientists and naturalists have worried about the possible destruction of Lake Tahoe by the overpopulation of its shoreline and the adjacent forests. One of the most beautiful lakes in America seemed

Lake Tahoe State Park (above) and Red Rock Canyon

threatened by commercial and residential building. During the administration of Governor Laxalt, Nevada and California arranged a compact, which created a planning agency to control developments near the lake and to reduce pollution of the waters and destruction of the wildlife. The compact also provided for the careful use of the waters of the Truckee, Carson, and Walker Rivers. It was an important experiment in interstate cooperation.

Pollution of the Colorado River and Lake Mead has increased recently because more sewage effluents, industrial and agricultural wastes, and silts have gone into the waters upstream. Since the tributaries originate in neighboring states to the east and north, Nevada alone cannot control the pollution. More federal or interstate control of water use is inevitable if this river system is to be made cleaner.

Nevada's interior streams and its air were relatively clear in the early 1970's, but there were warning signs. Las Vegas and Reno both noticed an increase in the amount of pollution from automobile exhaust, and a Governor's Council reported that citizens of four smaller communities—Gabbs, Henderson, Fernley, and McGill—had complained about the amount of dust and gas created by local industries. The council found that the number of mule deer and golden eagles had declined in the 1960's, that the number of fish in Lake Mead had dropped in the same decade, and that serious soil erosion had occurred in several places. University specialists in Reno expressed alarm about the deterioration of the rangelands, and scientists from the Las Vegas campus worked to save endangered species such as the pupfish. The legislature provided the first comprehensive program to assure clean air in 1971.

It was obvious that the battle to save the environment must be fought on many fronts; government cannot do the job alone. Young people appeared to be one of the first lines of defense against the enemy—pollution and the destruction of wildlife. Often students persuaded their parents to adopt better habits in disposing of litter, and in many schools they showed their political influence by writing enough letter to Congress to bring about laws for the protection of wild horses on the western rangelands. Young people's organizations collected cans for recycling and cleaned up trash that had been carelessly strewn by those less respectful of nature than themselves.

At the beginning of the 1980's the governments of the United States and of Nevada were engaged in a controversy over who should own and manage the vast acreages of unappropriated public land. This dispute, commonly known as the "Sagebrush Rebellion," began in the Nevada legislature and spread to other Western states where the federal government also controls millions of acres. The Nevada legislature was not disputing the right of the federal government to own and manage such areas as military bases, test sites, national forests, and Indian reservations, but it was objecting to a recently announced plan to hold most of the rest of the "public domain"—unclaimed land not presently used for any specific federal purpose—on a permanent basis. Nevada's lawyers were planning legal action in the courts to force the federal government to sell some of the unappropriated land or to turn it over to the state. It was argued that the state government had as much right and ability to plan future uses and conservation as the federal government.

17. The Dynamic 1980's

DURING THE 1980's, Nevada experienced more change than at any earlier time in its history. When the state celebrated the 125th anniversary of its statehood in 1989, its population was growing more rapidly than that of any other state in the Union. The number of residents approached 1,100,000 — about 300,000 more than had been counted in the 1980 census. New challenges in matters of national defense, nuclear industry, environmental concern, human services, and city planning had appeared on Nevada's agenda. Here are a few of the important historical developments of the 1980's:

1) The Las Vegas Valley continued to be a region of phenomenal growth and diversity — one of the most dynamic and most interesting metropolitan areas in America.

2) The Nevada Test Site and the proposed Yucca Mountain nuclear waste repository site became centers of national controversy.

3) The so-called Silver State experienced the most remarkable gold rush of the twentieth century, with wealth that promised to put the Comstock Lode and the Tonopah-Goldfield bonanzas in the shadows.

4) A vigorous debate was under way over what portions of the land and water should be preserved for ecological reasons and what prices should be paid by those who exploit the land for profit.

5) Because of the state's remarkable growth, Nevada's government and its public institutions were struggling to find the means to provide decent schools, universities, and human services for all its citizens within a historically small tax base.

LAS VEGAS VALLEY—THE EXPANDING METROPOLIS

The most obvious development for Nevada in the 1980's was the continuing expansion and prosperity of Las Vegas. In less than twenty-five years, it had become one of the principal metropolitan regions of the nation and one of the best known cities in the world. The population of Clark County in 1990 exceeded 600,000 people; only fifty years earlier it had been less than 20,000.

The reasons for this may be summarized in a single paragraph: Nevada's citizens found a formula for combining three elements into a successful business policy that defied conventional economics. First, the hot, sunny, desert climate appealed to a new generation of homemakers and recreation seekers. Second, the national defense and nuclear industries needed the Mojave spaces. And third, worldwide tourist publications regularly listed Las Vegas as one of the most appealing entertainment meccas in the world. Hollywood, New York, and Paris had to share the travel industry headlines with a new challenger—Las Vegas.

Much of the economy of Nevada relied upon the magnetism of Las Vegas. More than fifteen million tourists arrived in this valley every year during the mid-1980's, primarily to visit the famous showrooms and casinos. But as its tourist-oriented business grew, so did the arts and humanities. It built one of the most attractive city halls and one of the most garish airport terminals in the nation, and it won respect for the athletic and academic achievements of the University of Nevada, Las Vegas, for its newly established museums and orchestras, and for its ambitious efforts in municipal planning.

Las Vegas was never a community to plan its future in modest terms. It built one of the largest convention centers in the world, and it offered its tourists nearly 60,000 hotel and motel rooms by the late 1980's. Since 1985, its leaders have committed themselves to a rejuvenation of the decaying downtown sections near Fremont and Fifth streets with a "Festival Marketplace," and they are promoting a high-speed train that will carry passengers from southern California to Casino Center at the rate of 200 miles per hour. And its success story expanded to other nearby regions; a thriving new resort area emerged at Laughlin, below Davis on the Colorado River at the extreme southern

The Las Vegas Strip

tip of the state. Tourist promoters were also trying to develop Las Vegas-style resort areas in several other places in southern Nevada.

The parched valley through which John Frémont traveled in 1844 and where Archibald and Helen Stewart maintained their small oasis ranch in the late 1880's and 1890's became, a hundred years later, a sprawling crazy quilt of human activity with impressive fountains and large patches of verdant greenery. This became possible largely because of the Southern Nevada Water Project, constructed between the 1960's and 1980's to divert nearly 300,000 acre feet of water per year from the Colorado River, through a tunnel in the mountains, into the center of Las Vegas Valley. It was an engineering feat that made the famed Sutro Tunnel on the Comstock Lode seem puny by comparison.

Beyond the immediate boundaries of Las Vegas, the U.S. government defense projects continued to flourish. At the Nevada Test Site, the Department of Energy and its contractors employed 8,000 people in research and testing of nuclear devices. The Nellis Air Force Base near North Las Vegas provided payrolls for another 12,000 workers. Among the expanding private industries, food processing, printing and publishing, and chemical and electrical manufacturing became important. The neighboring communities and suburbs, especially Henderson and North Las Vegas, shared the growth of the central city.

Las Vegas received an abundance of publicity, both good and bad. Millions of American and foreign tourists obviously liked the city and were attracted to it because of its famous shows and entertainment, and no city in America did a better job of advertising its attractions. On the other hand, the national press and television often carried reports about elements of organized crime that preyed upon the city's main business. In addition, a federal district judge, Harry Claiborne, faced criminal charges and went to prison on the ground that he had not properly reported his income tax. He underwent the first impeachment trial in the U.S. Senate in more than fifty years, in spite of his defense that he had been singled out for unfair treatment by government agents.

Nevada also found itself in a bitter struggle to resist the federal government and congressmen from more populous states, who wanted to establish a nuclear waste dump deep underground at Yucca Mountain in Nye County, about 100 miles northwest of Las Vegas. The U.S. Department of Energy had major responsibility for selecting the site where the most dangerous nuclear wastes—some of which will be deadly for 10,000 years—will be stored. Early in the 1980's, several sites across the nation were under consideration for the disposal site, but due to congressional pressure all sites except that at Yucca Mountain were eliminated. There was also much resentment over the fact that various military branches were taking increasing amounts of "air space" for their exercises and making the land surface below unusable or unsafe for traditional mining and ranching operations.

NORTHERN NEVADA

The growth of Reno/Sparks, Carson City, and other parts of northern Nevada continued during the dynamic 1980's, but they were modest by comparison with the changes in Clark County. Reno's civic leaders gradually became accustomed to the idea that "The Biggest Little City in the World" (a slogan that had been adopted for a Virginia Street sign in the 1920's) had become a distant second to Las Vegas in population, as an entertainment center, and as the business center of the state.

Like Las Vegas, both Reno and Sparks began downtown rejuvenation programs in the 1980's, and they struggled to find policies that would allow orderly expansion of their populations. The Truckee Meadows is much smaller than the Las Vegas Valley, its water resources much more limited, and thus its possibilities for commercial and industrial development much more restricted. Yet even as the population of Reno/Sparks and the adjacent area passed the quarter-million point, optimism for future expansion ran high, and it too ranked high on America's list of favorite tourist attractions.

Carson City shared the commercial energy of Las Vegas and Reno, but in more modest measure; its population approached 50,000 as the decade came to an end. Its future development was questionable because of the lack of a dependable supply of water during drought periods. More than any other community, Carson City was the custodian of Nevada's early architectural and social heritage. The state museum system, including newly acquired railroad memorabilia, provided tangible ties with Nevada's pioneer past. With the help of the Division of Archeology and Historic Preservation, the community established a historic district, embracing the restored state capitol building and a hundred other governmental, commercial, and residential buildings dating from the nineteenth century.

The Lake Tahoe Basin is another area that felt the expanding population pressures. At Stateline near the southern end and at Incline Village near the northern shore, major residential and commercial zones emerged. The permanent year-round population on both sides of the state line exceeded 60,000 in 1980, and during the summer tourist season nearly a quarter of a million residents and visitors crowded onto its scenic shoreline. The quality of the lake's water and the ecological balance of the forests both suffered from this onslaught. In the meantime, the California-Nevada Interstate Compact (see pp. 286-287), adopted by the legislatures of both states to share their joint streams and to try to preserve the beauty of Lake Tahoe, failed to win ratification by Congress.

The state government in cooperation with conservationists proposed a $20 million bond issue in 1984 to provide money to purchase some of the most environmentally sensitive land and to preserve it from further exploitation. The recommended bond issue was defeated by the voters in that instance, but two years later, a larger, $31 million bond issue won approval.

THE GOLD RUSH OF THE 1980's

All across the Humboldt Basin from Elko to Lovelock and southward through the central region as far as Tonopah, Nevada experienced a gold rush of major importance. The ores were unlike those on which the early miners had worked; they did not occur in distinct veins and pockets that could be extracted in small quantities. Rather, the gold was widely distributed in microscopic form—the workers playfully describe it as "no-see-um-gold"—which was extracted from huge pits by massive earth moving equipment, in the manner of the copper mining at Ruth.

Through the mid-1980's Elko and adjacent regions of Eureka, Lander, and Humboldt counties were the center of the largest gold-

Virginia Street, Reno

Round Mountain pit, Nye County

producing region in the United States. Nevada was producing more than half of the nation's "yellow metal"—with an estimated value of nearly $1.5 billion dollars in 1987. There were frequent predictions that the reserves of gold were extensive enough to last for 20 or 25 years, if prices remained high. People with long mining experience knew, however, that the prices of raw materials—and especially of the precious metals—are impossible to predict. In the meantime, however, the old Humboldt River communities of Elko, Carlin, Battle Mountain, Winnemucca, and Lovelock were thriving as never before at the end of the 1980's.

More than 3,000 people were working in the mining business in the Elko-Carlin-northern Eureka region in the fall of 1988—greatly outnumbering those employed in agriculture. Local schools were crowded, and housing costs soared. Nearly 300,000 active mining claims had been staked in the state in the late 1980's, according to the Bureau of Land Management, and new ones were being filed by the thousands in the courthouses along the Humboldt River. The Nevada mining business had not witnessed anything like this since the bonanza days of Tonopah and Goldfield, and the new bonanza produced volumes of ore undreamed of in the earlier period. In the meantime, a controversy arose over whether the mining industry, which had some important tax advantages under the Constitution of 1864 (see pp. 103-104), were paying their fair share of the tax burden.

POLITICAL TRANSITIONS OF THE 1980's

The decade of the eighties brought several important adjustments within the political leadership of the state. The rapid population growth enabled Nevada to send a second member to the House of Representatives for the first time in history, and a new generation of officeholders came to the front in the top offices.

Two influential senators—Howard Cannon and Paul Laxalt—closed their careers in the nation's capitol, and two of Nevada's younger politicians—Harry Reid and Richard Bryan—filled those seats following long apprenticeships in lower political positions. Two other powerful politicians of the late 1970's—James Santini and Robert List—terminated their political careers in the early 1980's.

Senator Cannon, who first won his seat in 1958, gained reelection three times and became powerful on the Commerce and Armed Services committees. In 1982, however, when he sought his fifth term, he suffered much damage to his reputation because of a bitter primary fight and because some of his political associates were accused of criminal activity and were placed on trial just before the election. He lost to the little-known Las Vegas businessman Chic Hecht, a Republican who mounted a highly successful media campaign with the support of President Reagan and Senator Laxalt.

As we saw in chapter 14, Senator Laxalt held an unusually powerful place in the Senate during the early 1980's because of his friendship with the president. He was campaign manager for Mr. Reagan in both 1980 and 1984 and became national chairman of the Republican party. He retired from the Senate in 1986 to make a race for the presidency himself, but this attempt received little support. He tried to assure the election of a hand-picked successor, James Santini, to the Senate, but that effort failed.

Congressman Santini, who was one of the most popular politicians in the state in the late 1970's and won four successive terms in the House of Representatives, complicated his career by challenging Senator Cannon in 1982 and then by switching from the Democratic to the Republican party to seek the seat being vacated by Senator Laxalt four years later. After his defeat, he continued to have a voice in state politics and wrote a weekly column from Washington.

Governor List was another personality whose star rose in the 1970's but set in the 1980's. List lost his bid for a second term in the executive mansion in 1982 partly because he had advocated a complicated "tax shift," which proved damaging to state and local governments and to schools during a recession in 1982-83. The "tax shift" was intended to reduce property taxes and shift the burdens to tourists through increased sales taxes, but during a nationwide downturn in the economy, it resulted in a serious shortfall in government revenues.

The replacement for Governor List was Richard Bryan, a Las Vegas attorney with strong ties in the north. A graduate of the University of Nevada, Reno, a former assemblyman and state senator from Clark County, he had succeeded List in the attorney general's office before running against him for governor. A highly popular, gregarious

Richard Bryan
Governor, 1983-1988
U.S. Senator, 1989-

Harry Reid
Congressman, 1983-1986
U.S. Senator, 1987-

governor, Bryan moved up to the Senate in 1988 by successfully challenging Senator Hecht, who developed a reputation for unfortunate misstatements.

The other political leader whose rise accelerated during the 1980's was Harry Reid, former lieutenant governor and chairman of the Nevada Gaming Commission in the 1970's. He had sought a seat in the Senate in 1974, narrowly losing to Senator Laxalt. When, in 1982, Nevada became entitled to elect two representatives in Congress, Reid won the Las Vegas seat easily. In 1986, his reputation for hard work and integrity enabled him to move up to the U.S. Senate.

The population distribution of the 1980's made it possible for Las Vegas people to win nearly all the major offices in the state during the decade. The most successful northern Nevadan in the political arena was Barbara Vucanovich, a Reno Republican who had been closely associated with Senator Laxalt. She won the second Nevada congressional seat, which included all sixteen northern counties and part of North Las Vegas, on four successive occasions in the 1980's.

Obviously the earlier pattern of Nevada politics, in which the northern mining, ranching, and Reno-based personalities had dominated the higher offices, was reversed. Virtually all the newer leaders in statewide and national offices had their roots in the Las Vegas area. This was true of Nevada's newest congressman from the first (southern) congressional district, James Bilbray, and of Lieutenant Governor Robert Miller, who replaced Bryan as chief executive in 1989.

THE 1988 FISCAL STUDY

In 1989, the state government received a study dealing with the manner in which state and local governments financed public services. This 900-page document, which had been commissioned by the 1987 legislature, was the most thorough analysis of state and local fiscal matters in the history of the state, and it was widely regarded as a guideline for future decision making on taxation and spending.

The legislature had arranged for two nationally known research groups to make the study.[1] Although it was not meant as a document to suggest policy for the legislature, it nevertheless drew some important conclusions and made thoughtful projections and suggestions about financial policies.

The study predicted that Nevada's population would continue to increase rapidly in the 1990's and in the twenty-first century. Its authors predicted that Nevada's schools and public service agencies would need more revenue by the mid-1990's simply to offer the same kind of education and government that existed in 1988, even if economic conditions remained favorable for the next few years. (If there were to be a recession, the study warned, either services would have to be reduced or taxes would have to be raised earlier.) The growth of population—especially the increasing number of children, of the elderly, of those in need of welfare assistance, and of those sentenced to prison—would require more tax dollars for the same services.

The study showed that Nevada's taxes in the 1980's were quite low by comparison with those fifteen other western states or states whose economic prosperity, like Nevada's, relied heavily on tourism. "When compared with other states in terms of the relationship between its potential fiscal capacity and its actual tax effort, Nevada has fiscal room to maneuver. When ranked with other states, Nevada is next to last in tax effort." The report made several criticisms of the state's existing tax policy, including the statement that the retail sales tax was "regressive"—i.e., it put an unfair burden on the poorest section of society. It argued that Nevada voters would be unwise to close the door on the possibility of a state personal income tax—as they voted to do in a proposed constitutional amendment in the 1988 election.

It had long been evident from other studies that Nevada's government was spending substantially less money for education and welfare on a per capita basis than the national average. The Urban Institute/Price Waterhouse data confirmed that this was still the case. Across the nation, Americans spent an average of more than $600 per person each year for primary and secondary education; in Nevada the figure was $550. In higher education the average expenditure was $235 per person nationally, $198 in Nevada. In public welfare, Nevada's per capita departure from the national norm was even more marked: the national average was $318, but Nevada's was only $155. Obviously Nevada's government gave a lower priority to education and welfare aid than most other states.

The Urban Institute/Price Waterhouse report did not win much praise when it was first released, and there was criticism of it from both official and unofficial sources. But it did prompt the citizens of the state to begin a serious dialogue on social priorities and public finances for the first time in thirty years.

ENVIRONMENTAL CONCERNS

Worries about the environment moved nearer to the top of Nevada's agenda in the 1980's as both the general public and state government took keener interest in what was happening to the air, land, and water around them. We have already seen, earlier in this chapter, that much controversy has been aroused over the question of whether to make Yucca Mountain a site for the storing of nuclear waste that will be dangerous for thousands of years. This was only the latest dispute about environmental matters. The Nevada Test Site became a center of increasing controversy as peace-movement activists and environmentalists regularly protested the continuation of nuclear experimentation there.

In Chapter 13, we observed that in 1979-1981, the U.S. Air Force created much controversy when it proposed locating thousands of underground M-X nuclear missile launching sites on the Nevada and Utah deserts. This was the most hotly debated subject in the region as the decade of the 1980's opened, and opposition within Nevada grew as the details of the proposal became known. The vocal majority of citizens asserted that their traditional Nevada life-styles and the natural environment would be jeopardized by such a massive project. When President Reagan announced his decision late in 1981 against the Air Force scheme, most Nevadans hailed it as a major victory.

At the same time, both the Las Vegas Valley and the Truckee Meadows continued to struggle with frequent air pollution problems, with little relief in sight because of the growing numbers of people who resided and visited in these areas. Another disturbing sign of environmental trouble was the death of tens of thousands of birds and thousands of fish at the Stillwater Wildlife Refuge near Fallon. Apparently the accumulation of toxic wastes, compounded by a series of dry years, had caused the ecological damage and threatened one of the major water resources for migratory birds.

THE MAGNIFICENCE OF WHEELER PEAK

One of the natural cornucopias of the Nevada landscape was finally added to the national park system in 1987 with the creation of the Great Basin National Park. Located in White Pine County near the Utah border, this park includes Wheeler Peak, the 13,063-foot jewel of the Snake Range. It has several nearby neighbors which reach above the 11,000-foot level—Mt. Baker, Mt. Washington, Mt. Lincoln, Mt. Moriah—each of which is a majestic example of the natural beauty of the Basin and Range province of the West. Not all of these sites are within the new park—which was limited by Congress to 76,800 acres—but all are witnesses to the abundant natural variety of Nevada's eastern borderland.

Within the park is Nevada's most remarkable cavern—the Lehman Caves—the largest limestone opening still being formed by nature in the Far West. In the same region is Nevada's only permanent ice field. The world's oldest known bristlecone pine tree survived on Wheeler Peak until a few years ago, when an overzealous curiosity seeker cut it down.

For decades before the 1980's, the wonders of the Wheeler Peak area had been known to a fortunate few, and it had been proposed as a national park several times. The actions of a lone Nevada congressman in the 1960's managed to block the addition of this landscape to the protection of the National Park Service for many years. This attitude had come to be regarded as shortsighted by the majority of the Nevadans of the 1980's.

Early in 1988, the National Parks and Conservation Association, an important private conservation group, called for a major expansion of the national park system. It proposed 86 new national historical and natural parks across the country, including four in Nevada. Those regions identified as especially appropriate for such special designation were Lake Tahoe, the Black Rock Desert in northern Washoe County, and the Owyhee Canyonlands and Ruby Mountains, both in Elko County. Ordinarily, it has required many years for such ideas to win political approval.

The Question of Wilderness

While Nevada has been a favorite site for expansive military and technical experiments, it has received little attention for its wilderness heritage.

Nevadans have been generally slower than their western neighbors in the recognition of the natural wonders of their state and in the effort to preserve them. Not until the middle 1980's was there a strong and successful drive to establish the Great Basin National Park and to set aside a significant number of unspoiled "wilderness areas" for permanent preservation. Even then, much debate developed between the proponents of the wilderness designation and some miners, cattlemen, and sportsmen who had long regarded the wild lands as their privileged domain.

A wilderness area is different from a national park. It is a region that is basically in its natural state, largely unaffected by human activities, which has been set aside by Congress as a permanent natural preserve. The purpose of a wilderness designation is to select some regions as permanent natural enclaves for wildlife and for future human generations, and to reduce damage by vehicles and commercial exploitation. Nevada had only one small, remote region in this category—a 64,000-acre preserve near Jarbidge in northern Elko County.

On the other hand, the state had more than 5.1 million acres of national forest, and about 3.6 million acres of that was roadless. At least 1.5 million acres of this—located in 21 different areas of the state—was deemed to be worthy of consideration as wilderness. The majority of Nevada's congressional delegation responded to local pressures and tried, in the mid-1980's, to limit the wilderness protection to 136,000 acres, leaving Nevada with the smallest proportion of wilderness land among all the western states. Some local groups, however, pressed for at least a million acres for preservation as wilderness.

In the summer of 1989, Senator Reid prepared a compromise bill that selected fourteen areas of unspoiled scenic highlands—a total of 733,400 acres—for wilderness designation. With the assistance of Senator Bryan and Congressman Bilbray, this measure won approval in both houses of Congress and was signed into law by President George Bush. One area is in the vicinity of Mt. Charleston near Las Vegas, another is on Mt. Rose near Reno, and most of the others are in the mountains of central and eastern Nevada.

Nevada is a jurisdiction that embraces some of the most pristine wild country in North America, and at the same time it is the location of sensitive research in nuclear testing and the potential site for the deposit of nuclear waste. History was being made all around us as we observed the 125th anniversary of the creation of the State of Nevada.

NOTE

1. The Urban Institute and Price Waterhouse, "Final Report. A Study of the Fiscal Affairs of the State and Local Governments in Nevada" (Carson City: November 18, 1988).

Senators, Representatives, Governors

UNITED STATES SENATORS

James W. Nye, Republican, 1864-1873

John P. Jones, Republican and Silver, 1873-1903

Francis G. Newlands, Democrat, 1903-1917

Charles B. Henderson, Democrat, 1918-1921

Tasker L. Oddie, Republican, 1921-1933

Patrick A. McCarran, Democrat, 1933-1954

Ernest S. Brown, Republican, 1954

Alan Bible, Democrat, 1954-1975

Paul Laxalt, Republican, 1975-1986

Harry Reid, Democrat, 1987-

William M. Stewart, Republican, 1864-1875

William Sharon, Republican, 1875-1881

James G. Fair, Democrat, 1881-1887

William M. Stewart, Republican and Silver, 1887-1905

George S. Nixon, Republican, 1905-1912

W. A. Massey, Republican, 1912-1913

Key Pittman, Democrat, 1913-1940

Berkeley L. Bunker, Democrat, 1940-1942

James G. Scrugham, Democrat, 1943-1945

E. P. Carville, Democrat, 1945-1946

George W. Malone, Republican, 1947-1958

Howard W. Cannon, Democrat, 1959-1982

Chic Hecht, Republican, 1983-1988

Richard Bryan, Democrat, 1989-

REPRESENTATIVES IN CONGRESS

H. G. Worthington, Republican, 1864-1865

Delos R. Ashley, Republican, 1865-1869

Thomas Fitch, Republican, 1869-1871

Charles W. Kendall, Democrat, 1871-1875

William Woodburn, Republican, 1875-1877

Thomas Wren, Republican, 1877-1879

Rollin Daggett, Republican, 1879-1881

George W. Cassidy, Democrat, 1881-1885

William Woodburn, Republican, 1885-1889

Horace F. Bartine, Republican, 1889-1893

Francis G. Newlands, Silver and Silver-Democrat, 1893-1903

Clarence Van Duzer, Silver-Democrat, 1903-1907

George A. Bartlett, Silver-Democrat and Democrat, 1907-1911

E. E. Roberts, Republican, 1911-1919

Charles R. Evans, Democrat, 1919-1921

Samuel S. Arentz, Republican, 1921-1923

Charles L. Richards, Democrat, 1923-1925

Samuel S. Arentz, Republican, 1925-1933

James G. Scrugham, Democrat, 1933-1942

Maurice J. Sullivan, Democrat, 1943-1944

Berkeley L. Bunker, Democrat, 1945-1946

Charles H. Russell, Republican, 1947-1948

Walter S. Baring, Democrat, 1949-1952

Clifton Young, Republican, 1953-1956

Walter S. Baring, Democrat, 1957-1972

David Towell, Republican, 1973-1974

James Santini, Democrat, 1975-1982

DISTRICT ONE

Harry Reid, Democrat, 1983-1986

James Bilbray, Democrat, 1987-

DISTRICT TWO

Barbara Vucanovich, Republican, 1983-

GOVERNORS

H. G. Blasdel, Republican, 1864-1870

L. R. Bradley, Democrat, 1871-1878

John H. Kinkead, Republican, 1879-1882

Jewett W. Adams, Democrat, 1883-1886

C. C. Stevenson, Republican, 1887-1890

Frank Bell, Republican, 1890

R. K. Colcord, Republican, 1891-1894

John E. Jones, Silver, 1895-1896

Reinhold Sadler, Silver, 1896-1902

John Sparks, Silver-Democrat, 1903-1908

Denver S. Dickerson, Silver-Democrat, 1908-1910

Tasker L. Oddie, Republican, 1911-1914

Emmet D. Boyle, Democrat, 1915-1922

James G. Scrugham, Democrat, 1923-1926

Fred B. Balzar, Republican, 1927-1934

Morley Griswold, Republican, 1934

Richard Kirman, Sr., Democrat, 1935-1938

E. P. Carville, Democrat, 1939-1945

Vail M. Pittman, Democrat, 1946-1950

Charles H. Russell, Republican, 1951-1958

Grant Sawyer, Democrat, 1959-1966

Paul Laxalt, Republican, 1967-1970

Mike O'Callaghan, Democrat, 1971-1978

Robert List, Republican, 1979-1982

Richard Bryan, Democrat, 1983-1988

Robert Miller, Democrat, 1989-

Index